Killer Colt

Killer Colt

MURDER, DISGRACE, AND THE MAKING OF AN AMERICAN LEGEND

HAROLD SCHECHTER

BALLANTINE BOOKS · NEW YORK

Published in the United States by Ballantine Books,
an imprint of The Random House Publishing Group,
a division of Random House, Inc., New York.

BALLANTINE and colophon are registered
trademarks of Random House, Inc.

Library of Congress Cataloging-in-Publication Data
Schechter, Harold.
Killer Colt : murder, disgrace, and the making of an
American legend / Harold Schechter.
p.   cm.
Includes bibliographical references and index.
ISBN 978-0-345-47681-4 (hardcover : alk. paper)
eBook ISBN 978-0-345-52274-0
1. Colt, John Caldwell, 1810–1842. 2. Murder—New York
(State)—New York. 3. Colt, Samuel, 1814–1862.
4. Inventors—United States. I. Title.
HV6248.C646S34 2010
364.152'3092—dc22
2010016777

Printed in the United States of America on acid-free paper.

www.ballantinebooks.com

2 4 6 8 9 7 5 3 1

First Edition

Book design by Julie Schroeder

For Richard Vangermeersch

Good people all, I pray give ear;
My words concern ye much;
I will repeat a Tragedy:
You never heard of such!

—"The New-York Tragedy,"
broadside ballad (1842)

CONTENTS

Killer Colt

Prologue

NEW YORK CITY, FRIDAY AFTERNOON, SEPTEMBER 17, 1841

Franklin's umbrella shop, featuring "parasols, sun shades, and walking canes of all descriptions." John Wilson's saddle, harness, and trunk manufactory. The warehouse of Brown & Decker, dealers in whale oil, lampblack, and sperm candles. Ball & Tompkin's tinware and cutlery establishment. And more: druggists and drapers, cobblers and corset makers, stationers and snuff venders, sellers of consumption cures and importers of "foreign wines and choice teas."[3]

How much of his surroundings Mr. Adams takes in as he makes his way uptown can never, of course, be known. He has walked these streets a thousand times, and he is focused, in any case, on the business at hand.

On that chill autumn day, the newspapers are still filled with sensational details of the death of the "Beautiful Cigar Girl," Mary Rogers, whose brutalized corpse was found floating off the New Jersey shoreline several weeks before and whose murder, despite the concerted efforts of the city constabulary and the ingenious speculations of Edgar Allan Poe, will forever remain unsolved. Other events, too, occupy the papers, including the upcoming murder trial of Alexander McLeod, a Canadian lawman whose arrest by U.S. authorities for the killing of an American citizen has provoked threats of war from the British government. But these and other penny-press sensations will shortly be supplanted by the case in which the unwitting Mr. Adams is about to be fatally involved.[4]

On the corner of Ann Street, along Mr. Adams's route, stands Scudder's American Museum, a run-down repository of seashells, minerals, stuffed birds, and other natural-history specimens. Within a few months, it will be purchased by Phineas T. Barnum, who will transform it into a gaudy showplace crammed with astounding artifacts, believe-it-or-not exhibitions, and bizarre anatomical "curiosities." At present, Barnum has not the slightest awareness of Mr. Adams's existence—though, like the rest of the population, he will soon come to take an absorbing interest in the printer.[5]

The time is somewhere around 3:30 p.m. Near the Rotunda on Chambers Street, Mr. Adams is spotted by an acquaintance, a clerk at City Hall Place named John Johnson, who has just emerged from the post office. The two men have already spoken several times that day. Intent on his affairs, Mr. Adams does not notice the clerk, who watches as the printer strides purposefully in the direction of Broadway.[6]

It is almost 4:00 p.m. when Mr. Adams arrives at his final destination.

Catercorner to City Hall, the Granite Building is an unimposing structure by today's standards but "large and rather glooming-looking" to the eyes of Jackson-era New Yorkers.[7] Mr. Adams enters unnoticed, proceeds directly to the dimly illuminated stairwell, and climbs to the second floor.

Minutes pass. Outside on Broadway—oblivious to the horror transpiring just out of sight—the swirling human tide hurries along.

PORTRAIT OF JOHN C. COLT.

FRAIL BLOOD

1

The neighborhood of his birth would later become known as Asylum Hill, after the Connecticut Asylum for the Education and Instruction of Deaf and Dumb Persons, the nation's first institution of its kind. In 1814, however, it was still called Lord's Hill, an apt name for a place so steeped in Puritan tradition—though, in fact, it derived from the original owners of the land: the descendants of Captain Richard Lord, one of the early heroes of the colony.[1] In succeeding decades, various luminaries—among them Mark Twain and Harriet Beecher Stowe—would make their home on Lord's Hill, drawn by the tranquil charm of this rural district of Hartford. The infant born in a farmhouse there on July 19, 1814, would himself grow up to be one of the century's most eminent figures, a man whose name would become synonymous with the nation's burgeoning industrial might: Samuel Colt.

He came by his enterprising spirit honestly. His maternal grandfather, Major John Caldwell, was one of Hartford's leading citizens: first president of its bank, first commander of its volunteer horse guard, a founder of the deaf asylum, and one of the commissioners responsible for building the statehouse in 1796. He was also the richest man in town, a shipbuilder and canny businessman who—like many another God-fearing New England merchant—made a fortune in the West Indies trade, shipping produce, livestock, and lumber to the Caribbean slave plantations in exchange for molasses, tobacco, and rum.[2]

To his other grandfather, Lieutenant Benjamin Colt, Samuel owed some of the mechanical aptitude that would make him one of the world's great inventors. Admired throughout the Connecticut Valley for his handiwork, Benjamin had been a blacksmith of unusual skill and ingenuity who owned a wider variety of tools than any metalworker in the region. History would credit him as manufacturer of the first scythe in America.[3]

The children of these two worthies, Christopher Colt and Sarah Caldwell ("Sally" to her family and friends), had met in Hartford in 1803, when—according to one possibly apocryphal account—the strapping six-footer had stopped the runaway buggy in which the young woman was trapped.[4] An attraction immediately developed between the pair, both in their early twenties at the time. Despite his many virtues, however—his manly bearing, indefatigable energy, and striving ambition—Christopher Colt did not appear to be a particularly suitable candidate for the hand of Sarah Caldwell, patrician daughter of Hartford's leading citizen.

To be sure, Christopher claimed an illustrious background of his own, tracing his lineage to Sir John Coult, an English peer in Oliver Cromwell's day who gained everlasting renown in his country's civil wars. During one ferocious battle—so the story goes—he had three horses killed under him, shattered his sword, and still led his troops to victory. Knighted for his heroism, Coult adopted a coat of arms emblematic of his exploits: a shield with three charging steeds above the family motto, *Vincit qui patitur*—"He conquers who endures."[5]

At the time of his meeting with Sarah, however, Christopher—a recent arrival from his native Massachusetts who had left home to seek his fortune in Hartford—was in dire financial straits. Indeed, the members of the city council, wary of indigent newcomers who relied on the public dole, had resolved to expel him from town.[6] Impressed, however, with young Colt's personal qualities, Major Caldwell took the youth under his wing. Before long, thanks to his strict adherence to the Franklin-esque values of industry, frugality, and perseverance—coupled with a zeal for commercial speculation—Christopher Colt had accumulated a sizable fortune of his own. In April 1805, with the blessing of his mentor in Hartford's booming mercantile trade, he and Sarah were wed.

Their first child, Margaret, was born a year later. Seven more followed at regular intervals. Of this substantial brood, two would die in childhood, two others in the bloom of their youth. The survivors would comprise a judge, a textile pioneer, the legendary Colonel Colt, and a brilliant accountant responsible—in the language of nineteenth-century sensation-mongers—for the most "horrid and atrocious" murder of his day.

2

Of his three brothers, Sam was closest to the eldest, John Caldwell Colt, four years his senior.[1]

Much later, at the height of John's notoriety, commentators would offer radically different views of his boyhood character. According to his harshest critics, he was a "willful, cunning, and revengeful youth," ruled by "violent passions" over which he had "no great control." Bridling at parental authority, he displayed rank "insubordination from childhood upwards," refusing to submit to "the common restraints of the family, the school room, and the law of God."[2]

Other people, whose loyalty to John never wavered, described him in far more flattering terms as a rambunctious but fundamentally good-hearted boy, who reveled "in air and freedom" and would "do anything for a frolic." "His juvenile characteristics," insisted one acquaintance, "were a fondness for boyish sports, extreme bravery, and great generosity of character . . . His daring was remarkable." Though given to all sorts of juvenile pranks, "there was nothing vicious about his sportfulness."[3]

In his own published statements, John recalled himself as a headstrong youth—"rash and foolishly venturesome"—whose boldness often bordered on sheer recklessness and whose penchant for risk taking frequently put his life in danger. Besides numerous hunting and riding accidents, there were at least five separate occasions when his fearlessness nearly got him killed.

At the age of five, for example, while playing near a cider press, he lost his footing and "plunged head foremost" into the vat full of juice. Only the quick actions of a playmate, "a stout young girl" who saw him go under, saved him from drowning.

Several winters later, he nearly drowned again, this time while playing on a frozen river. He was "jumping up and down on the ice" when it gave way beneath his feet. "Swept by the current some sixty feet under a sheet of ice," he was carried into open water, where he managed to catch the limb of a fallen tree and drag himself onto the bank.

Another time, he was "playing tricks with" his favorite horse, which retaliated by throwing him from the saddle and delivering a near-crippling kick to his hip. And then there was his "awful encounter" with an enraged buffalo, part of "a caravan of animals" that arrived in Hartford with a traveling show. Sneaking into the creature's pen, young John found himself face-to-face with the "shaggy-throated beast" that "forthwith plunged at me, nailing me fast against the wall between his horns." He was rescued by the keeper's assistants, who immediately leapt at the buffalo and began to "belabor him with their clubs."

The most memorable of all John's juvenile mishaps, however, occurred when he was eight. His favorite pastime at that age was playing soldier. His doting mother—whose father had fought with distinction in the Continental army—was happy to encourage her little boy's "military mania" and supplied him with the means to "rig out a little troop of boys" with outfits and toy rifles. The centerpiece of their company was a miniature brass cannon. One day, John, with the help of a companion, loaded the little weapon with an excessive charge of powder. When John put a light to the fuse, the cannon exploded.

Somewhat miraculously, neither John nor his playmate suffered serious injury, though their eyesight was temporarily impaired. "How we escaped with our lives," John later recalled, "is a wonder."[4]

Whether Samuel Colt was present when his older brother detonated the toy is unclear. Some biographers speculate that the four-year-old boy did, in fact, witness the event, which had a powerful effect on his imagination, sparking his lifelong fascination with armaments. If so, the repercussions from that small blast would be felt, in time, throughout the world.[5]

· · ·

Besides the bond they shared with each other, both boys were deeply attached to their older sisters, Margaret and Sarah Ann. Throughout his exceptionally peripatetic life, John would carry keepsake locks of their hair; while the adult Sam, after finally achieving his hard-won fame and fortune, would hang framed mementoes of his sisters in his private room at Armsmear, the baronial estate he constructed in Hartford.[6]

Beyond their importance to their brothers, little is known about the two young women. Margaret, the firstborn of the Colt children, was described by an acquaintance as a warm and loving spirit who took simple joy in the "pleasant things" of "this beautiful world." The same observer recalled Sarah Ann as a pretty young girl "with profuse flaxen hair, clear blue eyes, and sweet smile" who "affectionately depended" on her older sister.[7] Apart from this testimony, verifiable facts about the sisters are scant. One salient detail of their early lives, however, is part of the historical record. In 1814, at the respective ages of eight and six, Margaret and Sarah Ann were enrolled in an unusually progressive private school run by their neighbor, Lydia Howard Huntley.

In later years, Lydia Huntley Sigourney (as she was known following her marriage) would achieve national fame as an author. Wildly prolific, she would publish sixty-seven volumes before her death in 1865. Some were novels, some memoirs, some histories and biographies. Her reputation, however, rested primarily on her poetry.

Dubbed the "Sweet Singer of Hartford," she poured out an endless stream of popular verse, most of which consisted of cloyingly sentimental tributes to the newly deceased. Of the nearly one hundred pieces collected in her 1822 *Poems,* for example, more than half are mawkish elegies with titles like "The Dying Mother's Prayer," "Anniversary of the Death of an Aged Friend," "Babe Bereaved of Its Mother," "Voice from the Grave of a Sunday-School Teacher," and "Death of a Young Lady at the Retreat for the Insane." In an age that made a fetish of bereavement and mourning, however, it was precisely Mrs. Sigourney's morbid preoccupations, rendered in verse and drenched in a saccharine piety, that made her so widely beloved—the country's best-selling poet before Henry Wadsworth Longfellow.[8]

Though she began writing poetry at a precocious age, her earliest ambition was to keep a school. Her childhood reveries (as Sigourney writes in her autobiography) were replete with "vivid pencillings of the delight, dignity, and glory of a schoolteacher." During her playtime, she would arrange her "dolls in various classes, instructing them not only in the scanty knowledge I had myself attained, but boldly exhorting and lecturing them on the higher moral duties."[9]

She first got a chance to realize her dream in 1811, when she and a friend started a seminary for young girls in Norwich. Three years later, at the behest of her acquaintance Daniel Wadsworth—the wealthy Hartford arts patron who would go on to found the Wadsworth Atheneum—she established a new private school for the daughters of his well-to-do friends. The inaugural class was limited to fifteen pupils, a number that was eventually enlarged to twenty-five. Among the members of this "select circle of young ladies" were Margaret and Sarah Ann Colt.

In contrast to other teachers of her era—who believed that girls should be schooled solely in such "womanly arts" as needlework and watercolors—Sigourney had little use for the "ornamental branches." Her stated pedagogical goal was the cultivation of both the intellect and "moral nature" through "rational education." To that end, she devoted each hour of the school day to one of the "simple, solid branches of culture": history, geography, rhetoric, grammar, arithmetic, orthography, and natural and moral philosophy.

To refine their diction, she had her pupils recite "select passages of poetry," devoting "much attention to the meaning of the sentences" so that they might make "the spirit of the author their own" and thus "more accurately interpret his style." To assist them in developing rigorous habits of mind, she frequently quizzed them on the dates of significant world events: "In what year of the world did the ark rest upon Mount Ararat? Who was called, 1,921 years before the Christian era, to go forth alone from his people and his father's house? Who was Queen of Assyria, and who the Judge of Israel, when Troy was destroyed, 1,184 years before Christ?"[10]

Sigourney also placed great emphasis on the acquisition of "clear and precise penmanship." Each girl was given a blank book with marble-paper covers and "long foolscap pages" and required to make daily entries in their finest handwriting.

Two of these notebooks—one belonging to Margaret Colt, the other to her younger sister, Sarah—still survive.[11] Margaret's is distinguished by a bold, exuberant script and pages that are illustrated with bright floral designs. By contrast, Sarah's notebook is written in a cramped, tightly controlled hand and is utterly devoid of decoration. To a startling extent, moreover, it consists of transcriptions of exceptionally death-haunted poems: "The Orphan," "The Loss of Friends," "The Grave: A Poem." This is perhaps unsurprising, given her teacher's own morbid inclinations. Even so, there is something unsettling about the little girl's funereal tastes. And in view of the calamities that were about to befall the Colt family, it is hard not to read a number of her selections—"Death of an Affectionate Mother," "The Beautiful Burial Plot," "Consumption" ("There is sweetness in woman's decay, / When the light of beauty is fading away")—as sadly prophetic.

*A*n epitome of the risk-taking, entrepreneurial spirit of his age, Christopher Colt had, by dint of his "innate ability, hard work . . . and sheer willpower," made a swift rise to wealth and local eminence.[1] A successful importer and retailer of assorted merchandise, from dry goods and glassware to cutlery and crockery, he had also opened a thriving distillery with his father-in-law. By 1818, Christopher held a number of positions in local institutions, serving, among other offices, as treasurer of the Hartford County Agricultural Society and as a trustee of the Society for Savings, the first savings bank in the state.[2]

One of the vice presidents of the latter was the prosperous hardware merchant Charles Sigourney. In 1819 the recently widowed Sigourney, having been introduced to Lydia Howard Huntley by their mutual friend Daniel Wadsworth, declared his feelings for her in a letter "of touching eloquence and the fairest chirography." Though the twenty-eight-year-old poetess had, by then, resigned herself to spinsterhood—to the untroubled existence, as she put it, of "a quiet school-dame . . . addicted to maiden meditations"—she accepted his proposal. Retiring from teaching, she moved into her husband's splendid hilltop home and took up the life of a prosperous housekeeper, supervising the three female servants while herself performing a variety of domestic tasks, including the keeping of the household accounts. She also served as hostess to the frequent "pleasant parties of friends . . . for whom it was our rule to make ice-cream and other varieties of refreshments within our own premises."[3]

Christopher and Sarah Colt were among the regular guests at these gatherings. Evoking those early halcyon days of her marriage in her posthumously published autobiography, *Letters of Life*, Lydia Sigourney recalled the Colts as "the handsomest couple" in their neighborhood: he "a gentleman of fine form and countenance and amiable manners," his wife "a model of dignified beauty." Their home, opposite to the Sigourneys' own splendid "hill-residence," was "a spacious and pleasant mansion."

Having ascended to the upper ranks of Hartford society, Christopher Colt was determined to give his eldest boy an education befitting the son of a gentleman. Accordingly, in 1819, nine-year-old John was sent to Hopkins Academy in his father's hometown, Hadley, Massachusetts.

Housed in a fine three-story brick building erected in 1817 at the then substantial cost of nearly five thousand dollars, the school featured two classrooms on the ground floor and, on the second, five additional rooms "used for recitations and to contain scientific apparatus and the beginning of a library." The third floor consisted entirely of a spacious gallery known as Academy Hall. There, on a stage raised four feet above the floor, "embryo orators spouted poetry and read compositions at the afternoon rhetorical exercises, debates were held on abstruse subjects, exhibitions were given, lecturers spoke words of wisdom, and diplomas were awarded to those who had attained 'ripeness and dexterity' in all sorts of learning." Tuition at the academy—which, under the preceptorship of the Reverend Daniel Huntington, placed heavy emphasis on the knowledge of Latin and Greek—was three dollars per quarter, plus an additional dollar and a half a week for board, "including room rent and washing."[4]

Besides a sound education, John's parents evidently hoped that their unruly son would derive other benefits from his time at Hopkins Academy. The former pastor of the Congregational Church in North Bridgewater, the Reverend Mr. Huntington was reputed to be a strict disciplinarian who brooked no frivolity in his charges. Surely a course of study under this "grave master" would help tame John's "volatile spirit." Their hopes were quickly dashed.

Bridling at the constraints of an institution that, according to its bylaws, demanded complete "subjection" to its "authority and government," John devoted himself largely to troublemaking. The threat of public "degradation"— the prescribed punishment for misbehavior—only seemed to incite him to even more flagrant acts of rebelliousness.[5] He became, in the words of an

early biographer, "the ringleader of all mischief." Utterly indifferent to the study of dead languages, John sought to excel not in his schoolwork but "at swimming, skating, horseracing, hunting, and fishing."[6]

After one year, his father withdrew him from the academy. Besides the evident futility of subjecting the boy to a classical education, another consideration entered into the decision. Even the modest expense of less than eighty dollars per annum had suddenly become prohibitive for Christopher Colt.[7] Like millions of his countrymen, he had suffered a precipitous reversal of fortune.

• • •

In the immediate aftermath of the War of 1812, the United States experienced a period of unprecedented economic expansion, a heady era of booming commerce, soaring land values, and rampant speculation. Five years after the end of hostilities, however, the economy crashed. Exactly what caused the panic of 1819—the first such crisis in the nation's history—is still a subject of debate among scholars. Its devastating consequences, however, are beyond dispute. Banks failed, property values plunged, jobs evaporated, the ranks of paupers swelled at an alarming rate. Times were so hard that, according to one contemporary newspaper report, desperate young men turned to robbery not to profit from the loot but to get thrown into prison, where they could at least be assured of regular meals and a roof over their heads. All together, an estimated three million people—roughly one-third the population—were adversely affected.[8] Among that staggering number was the family of Christopher C. Colt.

Sam Colt was only six years old when his father went bankrupt. He was playing under the piano in the front parlor when Christopher came in and informed his wife that he had "lost the bulk of his property." Though the news had dire implications for herself, Sarah's first thoughts were for her children. "My poor little ones!" she cried, wringing her hands as her "eyes dimmed with tears." It was a memory that would haunt Sam for the rest of his life.[9]

In the midst of this family crisis, John, back home from the Hopkins Academy, was still finding ways to make trouble. Somewhere around this time—the exact date is unclear—he and a friend decided to take revenge on a neighbor who had caught them stealing apples from his orchard and

had administered a severe whipping to John's friend. The neighbor, a surly old farmer and veteran of the Continental army, owned a prize horse that he rode proudly on militia muster days. Not long after the incident in the apple orchard, John and his friend set about collecting "a vast supply" of burdock burrs. They then snuck into the animal's pen and pelted it with the burrs until its tail and mane were hopelessly ensnarled. Unable to comb out the burrs, the farmer was forced to shear off the hair, making the horse too unsightly to ride in the next parade. That John and his friend carried their vengeance to such an extreme—"even to the persecution of an innocent horse," as one outraged commentator wrote—inspired widespread indignation in the community.[10]

It was shortly after this episode that John was sent to live with an uncle, a farmer in Burlington, Vermont. While his year under the stern discipline of the Reverend Mr. Huntington had done little to improve the boy's character, the rigors of farm work—the unceasing round of plowing and planting, mowing and hoeing, repairing fences and retrieving strays—had a beneficial effect. The refractory boy blossomed into a responsible man. On one memorable occasion, he was entrusted with a particularly challenging task. A blizzard had left the local roads buried beneath drifts seven feet high. When the storm finally subsided, a group of neighbors turned out to clear the roads. Thirteen oxen were hitched to a snow drag with two horses in the lead. Perceiving "an excellent opportunity of trying what John was made of," his uncle assigned him the job of riding the foremost sorrel. Though the horse threw him a half dozen times while negotiating a treacherous hill, the boy remained undaunted and acquitted himself "in the best manner." "John is made of good stuff," his uncle reported to Christopher soon after this event. "You need not give yourself any uneasiness about him."[11]

By the time this letter was sent, its recipient had already turned to a new trade: yarn and cloth manufacturing. Equipped with newfangled technology—water-powered spindles and looms—the nascent New England textile industry was spared the worst effects of the depression of 1819.[12] True to his family motto—"He Conquers Who Endures"—Christopher Colt took the loss of his fortune as a mere setback. A fresh opportunity awaited in the mills. To persist in the face of adversity was, as the proverb assured him, the key to success.

As it happened, his capacity to endure suffering was about to be sorely tested. Fate had another, even more devastating blow in store for him.

In May 1821, his wife delivered her eighth child, a boy christened Norman Upton Colt. By then, however, she had already suffered the first bouts of bloody coughing that signified the onset of pulmonary tuberculosis—consumption, the "white plague." She died on June 6 at the age of forty.

The infant, sickly from the day of his delivery, survived for only a year. His burial took place on May 5, 1822—the anniversary of his birth. His passing was—predictably—commemorated in verse by Lydia Sigourney, who rarely squandered a chance to rhapsodize on the death of a newborn:

> DEATH *found strange beauty on that polished brow,*
> *And dashed it out. There was a tint of rose*
> *On cheek and lip. He touched the veins with ice,*
> *And the rose faded. Forth from those blue eyes*
> *There spake a wishful tenderness, a doubt*
> *Whether to grieve or sleep, which innocence*
> *Alone may wear. With ruthless haste he bound*
> *The silken fringes of their curtaining lids*
> *For ever. There had been a murmuring sound*
> *With which the babe would claim its mother's ear,*
> *Charming her even to tears. The Spoiler set*
> *The seal of silence.*
>   *But there beamed a smile*
> *So fixed, so holy, from that cherub brow,*
> *Death gazed, and left it there. He dared not steal*
> *The signet-ring of Heaven.*[13]

The Grim Reaper, in this typically tear-jerking piece, may have been humbled by the holiness of the infant's "cherub brow." But neither Death nor his favorite female poet was done yet with the offspring of Christopher and Sarah Colt.

4
─────

*N*ot long before she succumbed to the white plague, Sarah Colt
bestowed on her little son Samuel a cherished keepsake: a military horse pistol that her father had wielded in the Revolutionary War.
That, at any rate, is one version of the story. Another is that she bought him
the old firearm as a reward for learning to read. According to a third, Sam
found it among the discards in a "gunsmith's junk pile." And some biographers claim that he got it in a trade from his younger brother Christopher,
Jr., reputedly a sharp dealer even in early boyhood.[1]

Though these tales differ in detail, all agree that the gun was inopera-
tive when Sam acquired it and that—in a precocious display of mechanical
genius—he tinkered it back into working order with spare parts from "some
generous gunmaker's scrapbox." One famous anecdote portrays the seven-
year-old seated "under a tree in a field with the pistol taken entirely to
pieces, the different parts carefully arranged around him, and which he was
beginning to reconstruct. He soon, to his great delight, accomplished this
feat." Like the stories of Newton and the apple and Washington and the
cherry tree, there is a hagiographic quality to this tale of little Sam Colt and
his broken-down flintlock—appropriately enough for a figure who would
one day be compared to the Deity Himself.[2] Whether it corresponds in any
way to actuality is another matter. In any event, the truth is impossible to
verify.

There *are* some documented facts about this period in the Colt family
history. Following Sarah's death, the running of the household fell to
Christopher's widowed sister, Lucretia Colt Price, who had lived with the

family for a number of years. In March 1823, she was relieved of her domestic duties when Christopher took a second wife, Olivia Sargeant, daughter of a prosperous Hartford mechanic.

Two years after this happy event, another tragedy befell the Colt family, at least as devastating as the loss of Sarah. In July 1825, Margaret, the oldest child, fell victim to the scourge that had claimed her mother. She was only nineteen at the time and just months shy of her long-planned marriage—"snatched," as Lydia Sigourney put it, "in her bloom and in her bridal hour."

In her inevitable tribute, Mrs. Sigourney lavishes her usual maudlin attention on the presumably poetic details of Margaret's slow decay: her struggles "for that slight breath that held her from the tomb," her "wasting form" like "a snow-wreath which the sun marks for his own," her "emaciate hand" raised "in trembling prayer." Describing the young woman's funeral, Sigourney pictures the mourners gathered at the gravesite. There are the grieving companions of Margaret's youth—"a train of young fair females with brows of bloom / And shining tresses." There is her stricken fiancé, E. B. Stedman—the "pale lover," who, "'ere the fading of the summer rose," had "hoped to greet her as a bride." And finally there are the young woman's surviving siblings: "those who at her side were nursed / By the same mother."[3]

Though precise dates are impossible to ascertain, it would appear that their sister's funeral was one of the last times, for years to come, that the children of Christopher and Sarah Colt would all be gathered in one place. Their lives were about to undergo a major upheaval.

• • •

If Freudian theorists are to be believed, the figure of the evil stepmother, so familiar from the Brothers Grimm, is rooted in unconscious childhood fears of maternal rejection. Less psychoanalytically inclined scholars, on the other hand, see the prevalence of wicked stepmothers as a reflection not of infantile fantasy but of historical reality. Two hundred years ago, women of procreative age died at an alarmingly high rate. Husbands frequently remarried and sired children with their new wives, who, in the natural way of things, treated the offspring of their predecessors less tenderly than their own.[4]

Christopher's new wife, Olivia, was no fairy-tale ogress. But with her husband struggling to reestablish his finances, she was obliged to impose a strict new regime on the household, beginning with the discharge of the servants. Within five years of her marriage, moreover, she had given birth to three babies of her own.[5]

Having been raised as pampered members of the local gentry, the children of Christopher's first marriage suddenly found themselves in radically reduced circumstances, expelled from the ranks of the social elite. Apart from the youngest, nine-year-old James, they were now expected to earn their own keep. Christopher, Jr.—who had worked up a small business running errands for the neighbors—was permitted to remain at home, adding his earnings to the household funds.[6] The others were sent into the world.

Within months of Margaret's death, her younger sister, Sarah Ann, was farmed out to relatives who, by all accounts, treated her little better than a menial.[7]

John, who had begun to entertain dreams of a military career, hoped to enter West Point. His new stepmother, however, made it clear that such an ambition was beyond the family's means. Instead he was sent to work at the Union Manufacturing Company in Marlborough, Connecticut, a textile mill that produced the blue cotton stripe fabric used to clothe slaves in the Southern plantations. John so excelled at his work that, within a year, he was promoted to assistant bookkeeper, familiarizing himself with the so-called double entry system of accounting favored by New England merchants.[8]

As for Sam, he was indentured to a farmer in Glastonbury, Connecticut. History records few details of his departure from the family home. Most of his biographers, however, agree on one point. When he left, he took his gun.[9]

_H_owever deep the bonds of affection between them, whatever traits of character and temperament they shared, Samuel Colt and his big brother, John, differed radically in at least one crucial regard. By the time he reached adolescence, Sam had already conceived his life's purpose and pursued it with a fierce determination for the rest of his days. Nothing would deflect him from his goal. Though he would travel widely, his wanderings were always in the service of a single ambition. His aim (to use the obvious metaphor) was as narrowly focused as the view through a marksman's sight.

By contrast, to chronicle John Colt's career is to chart a distinctly meandering course. Though possessed, like his younger brother, of seemingly boundless energies and a bold enterprising spirit, there was a haphazard quality to his pursuits. In search of success, he would lead a nomad's existence, trying his hand at assorted moneymaking schemes around the country. In the original meaning of the term—"following a winding or erratic course, rambling, roving"—John Colt's life was distinctly devious. Whether the word also applied to him in its more common sense—cunning, crooked, untrustworthy—would, in later years, be a subject of heated debate.[1]

. . .

John Colt saw Manhattan for the first time in 1826, when he accompanied his father there on a business trip. The previous fall, at a ceremony to mark the opening of the Erie Canal, Governor De Witt Clinton had prophesied that the 350-mile waterway would transform New York City into the country's "emporium of commerce." Less than a year later, that prediction was already coming true, as barges laden with the bounty of America's heartland made their way to the great, booming port.[2]

The burgeoning metropolis—"with its domes and spires, its towers, its cupolas and steepled chimneys"—impressed the sixteen-year-old boy as a wonderland. He was particularly struck by the hum and bustle of the South Street docks, lined with merchants' shops and warehouses and bristling with the masts, spars, and rigging of countless sailing ships and packets.[3]

A month and a half after he returned to his job at the Union Manufacturing Company, John vanished, only to turn up three weeks later in Albany, New York. Though the facts are sketchy, he appears to have run off to New York City before making his way northward by steamer, evidently in the vague hope of realizing his dream of entering West Point. A chance encounter with a family acquaintance at a hotel in Albany alerted his father to John's whereabouts.

By then, Christopher Colt had moved his wife and family to a cottage in Ware, Massachusetts, where he had become the sales agent for the Hampshire Manufacturing Company, makers of cotton and woolen yarn and cloth, as well as "machinery, castings and gearings" used in the production of textiles.[4] Writing to his son in Albany, Christopher urged the sixteen-year-old to return home and come work at the mill. Though John's supply of cash was, by then, running perilously low, he refused, informing his father that he was determined to further his education.

To lure his prodigal son back home, Christopher acceded to his wishes, offering to pay for his tuition at an academy near Hartford. John promptly enrolled, pursuing his studies with a diligence that "astonished everyone." After just one quarter, however, Christopher—apparently under pressure from his parsimonious new wife—withdrew his financial support and demanded that John "return home in the next mail stage."

• • •

John's sister, Sarah Ann, was living at home again, earning her keep by teaching at a female seminary.[5] The two were now the oldest children in the Colt household—the ones with the clearest recollections of their privileged past. The memories of their indulgent mother—and of the luxuries they took for granted while she was alive—only heightened their resentment of Olivia.

Still bent on completing his studies, John seethed when his stepmother urged him to abandon his academic ambitions and return to his job in Marlborough. Under the family's current straitened circumstances, she informed him, John must "dismiss his extravagant expectations" and reconcile himself to a life of "privation." The most he could expect from his parents was a meager allowance—a "mere pittance."

Given the state of their finances, Olivia's extreme frugality was surely a matter of simple prudence. To John, however, her lectures "upon the necessity of not rendering himself a burden to his parents" rankled bitterly.

His anger was compounded by the plight of his older sister. Brought up in a world of wealth and "fashionable society," Sarah Ann was now reduced to a life of extreme deprivation, "cut off from indulgences and opportunities of seeing and being seen freely granted to other young ladies, even some of inferior standing." On the few occasions that she ventured a complaint, her stepmother would remind her of the family's "narrow means" and insist that Sarah stop "thinking about dress and frivolous parties and so forth." Sarah soon learned to bite back her unhappiness, sharing her feelings only with her brother, who was "cut to the very soul by what he regarded as an indignity to his only remaining sister."

Eventually John could no longer endure the situation. Approaching E. B. Stedman—Margaret Colt's bereaved fiancé, who had remained close to the family after her death—John unburdened himself to the young merchant and revealed his intention "to quit his father's house and never more to be indebted to him for support." The sympathetic Stedman responded by "placing fifty dollars in his young friend's hands" and exclaiming, "Should you ever need assistance, let me know; and while I have a dollar, I'll divide it with you."

Sometime in 1827—the exact date is unknown—seventeen-year-old John Colt departed from home, becoming, as one newspaper later put it, a "voluntary exile from the parental roof."[6]

His sister, Sarah Ann, would choose a different mode of escape.

6

In the agrarian past, when farming "was as much of a trade to be learned as that of cobbler, miller, or blacksmith," it was standard practice for the sons of New England yeomen to undergo formal apprenticeships. For terms of varying duration, boys were indentured to local farmers who, in exchange for the unstinting services of their young charges, agreed to provide them with room, board, and a modicum of basic education while training them in the traditional "art of the husbandman."[1]

According to the terms of one typical indenture from the 1820s, the apprentice agreed to serve his master "well and faithfully" and "his lawful commands everywhere at all times readily obey." In addition:

> He shall not waste the goods of said master, nor lend them
> unlawfully to any; at cards, dice or any unlawful game he
> shall not play; fornication he shall not commit, nor matri-
> mony contract during said term; taverns, ale-houses or
> places of gaming he shall not haunt or frequent; from the
> service of his said master he shall not absent himself, but in
> all things and at all times he shall carry himself and behave
> as a good and faithful apprentice ought, during the whole
> time or term aforesaid.[2]

In later life, Sam Colt had little to say about his year in Glastonbury, other than to remark that "he did not find there a very gentle master and certainly was in no danger of being spoiled by over-indulgence."[3] That the eleven-year-old boy was subjected to unfamiliar rigors is not surprising. Even under the best of circumstances, farming was a grueling affair. The journal of one of Sam's contemporaries offers a vivid glimpse of the numbing monotony that constituted early nineteenth-century farm life:

July	28th	I mow'd ½ the day, ½ plow'd hops.
	29th	I plow'd and hoe'd hops.
	30th	I sow'd some turnips. It rained.
	31st	I helped Father plow with my oxen.
August	1st	I was haying.
	2nd	I was plowing my stubble. It rain'd.
	3rd	I went and plow'd corn.[4]

Even Sundays did not offer much relief from the grinding tedium. Though Sam's master, a "robust Christian," strictly observed the biblical prohibition against work on the Sabbath, certain indispensable chores—carrying firewood, feeding the livestock, milking the cows—were still demanded of the boy. Attendance at church, where the minister would typically deliver a sermon of several hours' duration, was mandatory. And the "blue laws" inherited from New England's Puritan founders still forbade any activity resembling fun. (As late as 1837, certain Connecticut towns enforced a law declaring "that no one shall run of a Sabbath day, or walk in his garden or elsewhere, except reverently to and from church.")[5]

By most accounts, Sam did manage to sneak away on an occasional Sunday afternoon for a ramble in the countryside. Legend has it that he would bring his prized flintlock pistol and that, on one occasion, he yielded to temptation and discharged the gun, shattering "the taut quietude of a Puritan Sabbath."[6]

He also found refuge in the pages of a book. Though Sam—as per the provisions of his indenture—was sent to a local schoolhouse to learn the three Rs, he would always be an indifferent student (as the rudimentary spelling abilities he carried into adulthood would attest). Nevertheless, he was reputedly enthralled by a volume belonging to his Glastonbury master. This was a massive *Compendium of Knowledge*, one of three books that constituted the entire household library (the others being the family Bible and a farmer's almanac).

Like other works of its kind, the volume that so fascinated young Sam Colt contained information on a dizzying range of subjects, from Greek mythology to colonial American history, from beekeeping to poultry breeding, from the proper method for making malt to the correct cure for hoof-and-mouth disease. The chapters that riveted Sam's attention, however, were not the ones on literature or philosophy, horticulture or medicine, astronomy or phrenology. They were the sections that explained the workings of galvanic batteries and the formula for making gunpowder.[7]

•   •   •

His year of servitude over, Sam returned to Ware and went to work at the Hampshire mill alongside his father. Unlike his older brother Christopher, Jr.—who would go on to become a pioneer in the American silk industry—Sam had little interest in textiles per se.[8] But with his unquenchable mechanical curiosity, he was continuously fascinated by the workings of the water-powered manufactory: "the clicking, whirling looms, the darting bobbins . . . the machines replacing what before he had known only as a winter's evening task, spinning and weaving by the fireside."[9] In the person of William T. Smith, supervisor of the mill's "bleeching and colouring" laboratory (in Sam's typically heterodox spelling), he also found a kindred spirit who shared his love of chemistry and who, by most accounts, encouraged the adolescent boy's earliest experiments with homemade explosives.[10]

Sam was able to pursue his interests with a more learned instructor when, after three years at the mill, he went off to nearby Amherst Academy. Founded in 1814, the school (the academic seedbed out of which Amherst College would shortly spring) was an educationally progressive institution that prided itself on, among other accomplishments, its early adoption of that state-of-the-art instructional device, the blackboard. ("It is surprising and delightful to see the interest which it kindles in even the dullest scholar," exclaimed the author of an 1827 report prepared for the board of trustees, who foresaw the day when this pedagogical marvel would become common in the classroom. "By rousing the curiosity and holding the attention beyond all other means, it would almost completely banish that weariness which makes the schoolhouse a place hated to so many children and that *listlessness* and *idleness* which renders that time spent there so often worse than lost.")[11]

In addition to its classical curriculum—ancient languages, moral philosophy, grammar, arithmetic, and so forth—the academy offered courses in
subjects "just beginning to be taught in schools outside of colleges."[12]
Among these was chemistry, taught at the time of Sam Colt's attendance by
a gentleman named Rufus Graves.

One of the founders of Amherst Academy, Graves was an unprepossess-
ing fellow whose "sluggish and phlegmatic appearance" belied his prodigious energy.[13] A Massachusetts native who had earned a divinity degree at
Dartmouth College, he had, in the course of his exceptionally varied career,
run a tannery, helped construct the first bridge over the Connecticut River,
founded the Putnam Drug Company (one of the longest continuously operating businesses in early New Hampshire history), served as lieutenant
colonel in the Sixteenth U.S. Infantry, and been a chemistry instructor at
Dartmouth.

Insofar as Graves remains known at all today, it is among enthusiasts of
the paranormal, the types who relish tales of abominable snowmen, UFOs,
and other such pseudoscientific phenomena. This dubious distinction is
owing to a short piece Graves published in an 1820 issue of the *American
Journal of Science*. Titled "Account of a Gelatinous Meteor," the article describes Graves's observation, on the evening of August 13, 1819, of a "luminous meteor" of "a brilliant white light" that streaked through the sky over
Amherst and crashed beside a nearby house. The following morning,
Graves located the spot where the "fire-ball" had ostensibly fallen to earth
and discovered

> a circular mass of jelly about eight inches in diameter and
> about one in thickness of a bright buff colour with a fine
> nap upon it, similar to that of milled cloth. On removing
> this nap, a buff-coloured pulpy substance, of the consis-
> tency of soft soap, appeared, having an offensive suffocat-
> ing smell, producing nausea and giddiness. After a few
> minutes exposure to air, the buff colour was changed into a
> livid colour resembling venous blood.

Graves's supposedly sensational discovery—which has since been identified as a common species of plant called myxomycetes, or slime mold—did

nothing for his ultimate scientific reputation. It did, however, earn him a place in the history of what folklorists describe as the centuries-old belief in "star jelly," a tradition that runs from Shakespeare's day to the 1950s cult film classic *The Blob*.[14]

Despite his credulity when it came to blood-colored jelly from outer space, Graves was esteemed as a lecturer. As a member of his class, Sam would have witnessed and participated in simple experiments designed to introduce young students to the basic principles of chemistry: combining sulphur with hydrogen, for example, to produce sulphuretted hydrogen gas, the "essence of that nauseous scent" that "is generated in all dirty sinks and other places abounding such filthy substances." Or inserting a piece of burning candle into a glass tube filled with pure oxygen to demonstrate "the necessity for having oxygen diluted with nitrogen; for if the atmosphere were pure oxygen, all combustible substances, when once inflamed, would burn without control to the destruction of all the living beings."[15] From one of the textbooks then in use at Amherst, John White Webster's *A Manual of Chemistry*, Sam also would have learned of a phenomenon that would figure importantly in his adult life: "the feelings of excitement" induced by the inhalation of nitrous oxide.[16]

•   •   •

John Colt's movements in the months following his flight from the "parental roof" are impossible to trace with certainty. By late 1827, he appears to have made his way to Baltimore, where he found work as a mathematics teacher at a ladies' seminary and (though the records on this are ambiguous) may have begun dabbling in real estate investment.[17] Residing at a downtown hotel, he is said to have befriended an elderly engineer by the name of Everett, who—impressed with the young man's "celerity at figures"—offered him a high-paying supervisory job in what was then a booming field: the canal business.

The stunning success of the Erie Canal had set off a wave of canal construction in surrounding regions, particularly in Pennsylvania, where a complex system of waterways would soon crisscross the state. The project to which John was assigned involved a three-quarter-mile stretch of the so-called North Branch Canal, designed to transport coal from the rich anthracite fields just below Wilkes-Barre to urban markets in Delaware, New York, and New Jersey.[18]

Arrived at a place called Longshores, about fifteen miles south of Wilkes-Barre, John found himself faced with a daunting task. "Along the river and into the water, there was to be built with stone an apron eighteen feet wide; and thereupon a wall twenty-two feet high, to constitute the first foundation of the canal. For this end, the side of the mountain had to be pulled down and many other encumbrances removed. Every species of obstacle and labor entered into the stupendous work."

Though still a mere "stripling" of eighteen, John threw himself into the job with an efficiency and zeal that won the admiration of his far more experienced subordinates. "He was a favorite of every engineer. In less than ten days, his sheds were built, his tools all purchased and delivered, and thirty men at work; and in less than a month, a hundred. The section was universally pronounced the best managed on the line."

After seven months—at the "very handsome salary" he was earning from his friend Mr. Everett—John was able to repay the fifty dollars he had borrowed from E. B. Stedman while retaining two hundred for himself. By then it was December 1828. "The cold had become unusually bitter," and John's "duties required exposure to every kind of weather, from day-break to night-fall." Having begun to suffer from recurrent bouts of coughing—a precursor, he feared, to the disease that had already claimed his mother and older sister—John decided to leave.

Everett did his best to retain him, offering to raise his already hefty wage, but John would not be dissuaded. His success at overseeing the complex construction job had kindled his desire to acquire "such technical knowledge as might better qualify him either for an engineer or for a teacher; and he resolved to devote the sum he had earned to a winter's study." Repairing to Wilbraham, Massachusetts, he enrolled at the Wesleyan Academy, then under the leadership of the prominent Methodist minister Wilbur Fisk.

In a speech delivered shortly after he assumed his position in 1826, the Reverend Mr. Fisk had made plain his low opinion of the typical academic institutions of the day, which, in his stern view, were breeding grounds of sin and impiety. At other schools, he proclaimed, the student "meets the filthy conversation of the wicked and learns to blaspheme. He meets the debauchee and learns incontinency. He meets the jovial companion and indulges the social glass. He meets the caviling infidel and learns to sneer at religion. In short, he leaves school more learned but frequently more corrupted, if not wholly ruined."

Vowing that, under his stewardship, the Wesleyan Academy would "better guard the habits and morals of scholars than they are usually guarded in our common schools," Fisk instituted strict "arrangements for good discipline":

> For the most difficult cases they had a prison, and for the worst, the utterly incorrigible, there was a dungeon. The prison was a room furnished only with a hard bed, a single chair, and a naked table; the dungeon was a room with clean straw scattered over the floor. The fare of these prisoners was not such as to tempt them to intemperance. A brief seclusion in these cheerless rooms usually broke the resolution of the most rebellious.

When even these measures failed, there was always the recourse of a public whipping "severe enough to do its work effectively." The Reverend Mr. Fisk generally "inflicted these whippings himself; for his sincere kindness and strict self-control made it safer not to entrust such disagreeable duties to his subordinates."[19]

A few years earlier, it is likely that John himself would have done time in the dungeon or been lashed for his own good by the benevolent-hearted minister. But the intervening time had matured him, and he applied himself diligently to his studies—until disaster once again struck his family.

• • •

Exactly why Sarah Ann Colt chose to end her life is a matter of conjecture. One newspaper reported that she "quarreled with her step-mother, fled to the house of a neighbor, Widow May, and, at the end of two days, procured arsenic and put an end to her life." According to another account, "The uncomplaining but high-spirited and acutely sensitive girl took a morbid view of her doom to labor and regarded it as humiliating, till at length her forti-

THE BOY COLT INVENTING THE REVOLVER.

tude and her mind gave way." Yet a third source claimed that, like brother John, Sarah Ann was subjected to unbearable "persecutior home but, being female, could not, as he did, "fly into the world for ref Instead "she found it in the grave." Her youngest brother, James, or other hand, would always believe that Sarah Ann had become "derar from excessive immersion in her studies—from applying herself "too cl to her books."

As a member of that ill-fated sorority that Lydia Sigourney liked to to as "my dead," Sarah Ann was, of course, memorialized in the sugary "Sweet Singer." The tribute, however, offers no clues as to the cat Sarah Ann's death. Indeed, Mrs. Sigourney avoids the mention of st altogether, remarking only that—by the tenth anniversary of the dis ing of her Hartford school—Sarah Ann had become a "tenant of th row tomb," and comparing the young woman's "brief span" to a spa "drop of morning dew" inhaled by the "noon-day sun."[20]

Whatever the reasons for Sarah Ann's suicide, she must have in dire emotional straits to subject herself to the torments of a poisoning—to the unbearable nausea and vomiting, the uncontro bloody diarrhea, the muscular convulsions and excruciating cramp died on March 26, 1829, at the age of twenty-one.

Of all her siblings, John was most devastated by the death of the "around whom twined every tendril of his heart." In despair, he "flun; his books. His ambition was quenched. Of the future he felt reckles word 'home' filled him with bitterness."

Forsaking his studies, he resolved to leave the country and "pass t of his days in some foreign land."[21]

Part Two

FORTUNE'S TRAIL

1

o say that people cope with grief in different ways may be a platitude, but it's no less true for that. Those who knew Samuel Colt best testify that he cherished the memory of his long-deceased sisters to the very end of his life.[1] To be sure, his reaction to Sarah Ann's suicide was less dramatic than John's. Indeed, to all outward appearances, her shocking death had little impact on him at all. Certainly it did nothing to deflect him from his immediate pursuits. But his reaction says less about the love he bore for her than about the fierce single-mindedness that (as with other men of genius) was one of Sam Colt's most salient traits.

• • •

Exactly when Sam became obsessed with the mechanics of undersea warfare is unknown, though his official biographer claims that water mines—"aquatic pyrotechnics," in the quaint locution of the day—were the great inventor's "first love," predating even his fascination with repeating firearms.[2] Perhaps, as another authority speculates, Sam's interest in these weapons was stimulated by accounts of the so-called Battle of the Kegs, a celebrated Revolutionary War episode in which watertight oaken kegs, packed with gunpowder and rigged with flintlock detonators, were floated down the Delaware River in an attempted attack on British vessels moored in the Philadelphia harbor. The incident was immortalized in a ballad that Sam reportedly heard as a young boy from his grandfather Major Caldwell:

Gallants attend, and hear a friend,
  Trill forth harmonious ditty,
Strange things I'll tell which late befell
In Philadelphia city.

'Twas early day, as poets say,
  Just when the sun was rising,
A soldier stood on a log of wood,
And saw a thing surprising.

As in amaze he stood to gaze,
  The truth can't be denied, sir,
He spied a score of kegs or more
Come floating down the tide, sir.

A sailor, too, in jerkin blue,
  This strange appearance viewing,
First damn'd his eyes in great surprise,
Then said, "Some mischief's brewing.

"These kegs, I'm told, the rebels bold,
  Pack'd up like pickled herring;
And they're come down t'attack the town,
  In this new way of ferrying."[3]

As Sam later testified, he was also aware at an early age of Robert Fulton's experiments with aquatic explosives. Later renowned as the inventor of the commercial steamboat, Fulton was an early proponent of undersea warfare whose experiments with "submarine bombs" (as he called them) were widely publicized in his book *Torpedo War*. Published in 1810, this work included illustrated instructions for the manufacture of copper-encased water mines that would (theoretically) detonate upon contact with an enemy ship. The very first engraving in the book—a picture that, by Sam's own admission, made a deep impression on him as a boy—showed a tall-masted brig being blown out of the water by one of Fulton's devices.[4]

Though there's no way of knowing when Sam himself began to dream

about destroying boats with "submarine bombs," it is clear that by the time
he was fifteen, he was already mulling over the possibility of detonating
gunpowder underwater by means of an electrical current, transmitted from
a simple battery via a tarred copper wire. His first known attempt to put this
idea into practice occurred just six months after the death of Sarah Ann,
during a summer break from Amherst Academy. Displaying the showman's
flair that would serve him so well throughout his career, Sam evidently dis-
tributed a crudely printed handbill trumpeting his intended contribution to
the town's Independence Day festivities:

> SAM'L COLT WILL BLOW A RAFT SKY-HIGH
> ON WARE POND, JULY 4, 1829

Sam's advertisement succeeded in drawing a sizable crowd of spectators,
including a crew of neighborhood apprentices who "walked some way to see
the sight." Unfortunately, the promised spectacle turned into something of
a bust. According to one eyewitness, "an explosion was produced, but the
raft was by no means blown sky-high." Still, however disappointing as a pyrotechnical display, Sam's experiment did produce one significant result.
"Curious regarding the boy's explosive contrivances," one of the apprentices, a brilliant twenty-one-year-old machinist named Elisha K. Root, introduced himself to the young inventor. It was the start of a long
relationship that would have enormous consequences not only for the two
men but for the American industrial system itself.[5]

• • •

By the following spring, Sam found himself dreaming of a life before the
mast—an aspiration cherished, according to the author of *Moby-Dick*, by
countless young men of the time. "Why is almost every robust healthy boy
with a robust healthy soul in him, at some time or other crazy to go to sea?"
observes Herman Melville, another child of privilege whose family suffered
severe financial reversals that ultimately led him to seek a sailor's life.[6]

Writing to her stepson at Amherst Academy in June 1830, Mother
O. S. Colt (as Olivia signed herself) informed him that a family friend, the
Boston textile entrepreneur Samuel Lawrence, had spoken to the owner of
a ship named *Corvo*, which was scheduled to leave shortly for a ten-month

cruise to the Orient. "Mr. Lawrence," Olivia assured Sam, "had no doubt but you could have the Situation desired aboard that Ship . . . provided you qualify your self."

With her stepson about to venture forth into the wider world, Olivia took the opportunity to dispense the kind of counsel that parents have been ladling out to young men since at least the days of Polonius:

> You see then, Samuel, that self-application is necessary to the gratification of your inclination in your favourite pursuit and a thorough knowledge of Navigation will be a great advantage to you in a voyage upon the Seas. It is an uncertain element and all the information you can get on this subject (Should you continue to follow the seas) will be of immense benefit to you—but life is still more uncertain therefore get Wisdom, that Wisdom which is profitable to direct in the life that is now and that which is to come . . .
>
> Now, when making choice of your occupation it is time to pause and reflect . . . Look around—on the one side you see the abodes of Wisdom and Virtue—enter in thru her gates. On the other, that of vice and folly—her habitation looks to misery and wretchedness—pass not by her gates—turn away, pass by on the other side. Give up the low frivolous pursuits of a boy—and determine at once you will pursue the steps of Manhood . . . above all reverence the Supreme Being, never let your lips be polluted by profaning and taking his name in vain.[7]

Olivia's admonition to Sam, urging him to abandon the "frivolous pursuits of a boy," appears to have fallen on deaf ears. Among the cherished relics of the town of Amherst was an old Revolutionary War cannon, an iron six-pounder, that belonged to General Ebenezer Mattoon, who had brought it home from the Battle of Saratoga in 1777. At daybreak on July 4, 1830—just two weeks after receiving Olivia's missive—Sam and two schoolmates, Alphonso Taft (who would become United States attorney general under President Ulysses S. Grant) and Robert Purvis (later a famous abolitionist), snuck onto Mattoon's property. Attaching ropes to the old field piece, they lugged it up to College Hill and proceeded to get a jump on the Independence Day festivities by discharging it.

Awakened from their slumbers, several faculty members, including the Reverend John Fiske, hurried up the hill and ordered the boys "not to fire again." Ignoring the command, Sam placed himself "near . . . the cannon, swung his match and cried out, 'a gun for Prof. Fiske' and touched it off." When the outraged teacher demanded that he identify himself, Sam jeered that "his name was Colt and he could kick like Hell."[8]

Whether Sam was expelled for this escapade or left school voluntarily is unclear. What's certain is that a few days later, he left Amherst Academy for good, his formal education having come to an end with a very literal bang.

• • •

Less than one month later, on the morning of August 2, 1830, the brig *Corvo* set sail from Boston Harbor. Among its passengers were Mr. and Mrs. J. T. Jones of the American Baptist Mission, on their way to Rangoon to convert the heathen Burmese.[9] Also on board—not as a passenger but as a novice crewmember—was Samuel Colt.

At a cost of $91.24—slightly more than $2,000 in current funds—Samuel had been outfitted with a sailor's necessities: seaman's chest and slop clothes, quadrant and compass, boots and bedding, jackknife and almanac, and more. His supplies included a sheaf of stationery so that he could send an occasional letter to his family, none of whom was there to see him off.[10]

Standing in for his father was Samuel Lawrence, who, later that day, sent the following report to Christopher Colt:

> The last time I saw Sam he was in a tarpaulin, check'd shirt
> & duck trousers on the fore topsail yard loosing the topsail.
> This was famous at a first going-off. The Capt & Super
> cargo will give him good advice if required & instruction in
> seamanship, he is a manly fellow & I have no doubt will do

credit to all concerned, he was in good spirits on departure. There were some thousands present to see the missionaries off. Prayers and singing were performed on board.[11]

Not long after Mr. and Mrs. Jones's fellow missionaries completed their farewell services, the anchor was heaved up, the ship got under way, and sixteen-year-old Samuel Colt embarked on what would prove to be the most fateful trip of his life.

8

From his days of boyhood make-believe—when he and his friends formed a troop of play soldiers, with equipment supplied by his mother—to his adolescent dream of enrolling in West Point, John Colt had always been drawn to the military. It is little wonder, then, that after Sarah Ann's suicide, when he sought to throw off his old life and leave for other parts of the world, he decided to enlist in the marines.[1]

He appears to have taken this drastic step with a certain degree of naivety. Shortly after fleeing home, he made the acquaintance of a former member of the corps, who—preying on the young man's gullibility—assured him that the duties of a new recruit were extremely light, "the most irksome of them being to stand guard daily for a prescribed number of hours." For the grief-addled John, this seemed a small price to pay for the chance to "escape the native land which had now become so desolate to him." Making his way to the Gosport marine station at Norfolk, Virginia, he signed up at once, expecting that "after three or four months at the most," he would be off on a voyage that would take him around the world: "to Constantinople—thence to Alexandria—thence to Calcutta—thence to Canton—crossing the Pacific returning homeward through South America."[2]

The reality turned out to be far more disagreeable than he had been led to believe. Though John had endured his share of hardships since his father went bankrupt, he had been raised in genteel circumstances and was unprepared for the rigors of life in the corps: the coarse, barely palatable fare, the even coarser behavior of his comrades, and the harsh, demeaning discipline to which he was routinely subjected. Not long after his first night of sentry duty, he was seized with a "violent fever" and confined to the infirmary. He emerged several weeks later to find that his ship had sailed without him. By then he had awakened to the sobering truth that a military career was "not only a waste of time for him but a waste of his powers and chances." Though John had committed himself to an extended term of service, he resolved to leave the corps.

When his formal request for a discharge was denied, he briefly considered desertion before resorting to a more cunning expedient: a forged letter addressed to the commanding officer of the marine station. Written (presumably) by a Massachusetts farmer named Hamilton, the letter declared that the young recruit who had enlisted under the name John C. Colt was actually the sender's underage son, who had run away from home in his boyish eagerness to see the world. The letter begged that the lad be discharged so that he might be reunited with his aged and ailing parents who had been "rendered wretched" by his absence. John mailed this letter to his brother James, asking him to post it from Ware.

The hoax (as John later described it) succeeded. Shortly after its arrival, he was granted his discharge. Altogether, he had done "three months' service—eleven days and two nights of which he had been on duty, and more than half the rest of the time upon the sick list in the hospital."[3]

. . .

John's aborted experience with the marines marked the end of his nautical ambitions. His life would remain strictly landlocked—though in later years, at the height of his notoriety, a rumor circulated that he had spent some time as a riverboat gambler on the Ohio and Mississippi during the early 1830s. It was even said that, during this interlude, he fought a gun duel with a wealthy planter over an octoroon mistress.[4]

There is good reason to doubt this sensational tale. One thing seems certain, however. If a duel *did* take place, it would have been conducted with the kind of handgun standard for such encounters in those days: the kind that required a painstaking process of reloading after discharging a single shot.

9

*I*n pursuit of what one anthropologist describes as humanity's most characteristic goal—creating ever more efficient weapons with which to dispatch other members of the species—gunsmiths had been attempting to devise a workable repeating firearm for several centuries before Samuel Colt's birth.[1] Various approaches were tried, among the least sensible of which was to load two bullets into the barrel of a gun and fire them successively with dual triggers. More practical (and far less apt to explode in the shooter's hand) was the multibarrel design. Matchlock pistols with several barrels that could be rotated by hand were invented as early as the 1540s. By the eighteenth century, the "pepperbox" pistol—a percussion-cap firearm equipped with up to eight barrels that revolved with each pull of the trigger—represented the state of the art in rapid-fire technology. Unfortunately, while they didn't require constant reloading, they were cumbersome, poorly balanced, and virtually impossible to aim with any accuracy.

The solution to the problem, as gunsmiths recognized from early on, was a pistol with a single barrel and a revolving cylinder that could be loaded with several balls. Though a few specimens of such weapons have been traced to the time of Charles I, it wasn't until 1813 that a Boston mechanic named Elisha H. Collier produced a reasonably effective model: a flintlock pistol with a cylindrical breech that, when turned by hand, allowed a "succession of discharges from one loading" (as he described it). Unable to interest American investors in his invention, Collier moved to London, where he secured a patent and set up shop in the Strand. Though his weapons were expensive to manufacture and somewhat clumsy to operate, they could fire up to eight shots without reloading and were purchased in bulk by the British army. They were in wide use by His Majesty's troops in India when Sam Colt's ship arrived in Calcutta in the winter of 1831.[2]

• • •

"When truth becomes legend, print the legend." The line is from John Ford's 1962 Western *The Man Who Shot Liberty Valance*, one of the classics of a genre whose iconic figures—from Owen Wister's *Virginian* to Jesse James and John Wayne—are impossible to picture without Samuel Colt's invention strapped to their hips. The truth of how he came up with that invention has long been a matter of controversy. One story claims that the idea sprang directly from his sympathy for Southern slave owners. At some point during his early adolescence, according to this tale, young Colt

> happened to be near the scene of a sanguinary insurrection of Negro slaves, in the southern district of Virginia. He was startled to think against what fearful odds the white planter must ever contend, thus surrounded by a swarming population of slaves. What defense could there be in one shot, when opposed to multitudes, even though multitudes of the unarmed? The master and his family were certain to be massacred. Was there no way, thought young Colt, of enabling the planter to repose in peace? No longer to feel that to be attacked was to be at once and inevitably destroyed? That no resistance would avail were the Negroes once spirited up to revolt?
>
> As yet he knew little of mechanics; in firearms, he was aware of nothing more efficient than the ordinary double-barreled pistol and fowling-piece. But even loading and reloading these involved a most perilous loss of time. Could no mode be hit upon of obviating the danger of such delay? The boy's ingenuity was from that moment on the alert.[3]

Dismissing this account as a racist fabrication, various firearm historians insist that Colt conceived his idea after seeing some of Elisha Collier's flintlock revolvers in India. Alternatively, these scholars suggest, he may have viewed some ancient specimens of repeating handguns on display in the Tower of London "when the *Corvo* docked in the Thames" on its return trip to the United States.[4]

Colt himself steadfastly denied that he had been inspired by Collier's weapons. Indeed (so he claimed), he did not become aware of their existence until years later, during a subsequent voyage to England. His idea, he insisted, was wholly original to himself, an epiphany that came to him on board the *Corvo*, when—so the story goes—he was "watching the action of the ship's wheel" and suddenly "realized that the same method of locking the wheel in a fixed position could be applied to a revolving firearm."[5]

This tale became the standard version, the official creation myth recounted throughout the later nineteenth century in books like *Famous Leaders of Industry: The Life Stories of Boys Who Have Succeeded*— inspirational texts intended to teach young men "what an individual can accomplish by ability and indomitable energy and perseverance."[6]

Did the idea for his revolver really burst upon the mind of sixteen-year-old Sam Colt one day as he watched the first mate at the wheel of the *Corvo*? Perhaps so. Still, the story seems a little too pat, like one of those eureka moments so beloved by the makers of Hollywood biopics. It is undeniably true, however, that at some point during the voyage, Colt used his fifty-cent jackknife and a chunk of scrap wood to whittle a crude model of his invention. It was among his effects when the *Corvo* dropped anchor off Boston on a late spring morning in 1831.[7]

10

By the fall of 1831, Sam Colt, barely seventeen years old, had already found his calling. His brother John, four years his senior, was still casting about for his.

After securing his discharge from the marines, John made his way to New York City, where he clerked in the law office of his cousin Dudley Selden, a prominent Manhattan attorney, a future U.S. congressman, and a man who—during John's most desperate hours—would play a critical role in his life. John's duties, which demanded extensive reading in Blackstone and other standard legal texts, reawakened his hunger for formal schooling. At the end of a year, with his cousin's blessing, he headed north to enroll in the University of Vermont.[1]

Though its curriculum covered everything from Greek prosody to moral philosophy to elocution, the university had always stressed the study of mathematics, an emphasis reflected in its official seal, which featured a prominent pictorial representation of the Pythagorean theorem.[2] Besides practical (or, as it was then called, "vulgar") arithmetic, required courses included Logarithms and Algebra, Geometry and Euclid's Elements, Plane and Spherical Trigonometry, and Conic Sections. Though John pursued his studies with no particular professional goal in mind, he did discover a special aptitude for mathematics—a skill that would serve him well in the coming years.

Those years would be filled with a dizzying variety of pursuits as John, after leaving the university in the summer of 1832, wandered the country in search of his fortune. He tried his hand as a fur trader in Michigan. Land

speculator in Texas. Schoolteacher in Kentucky. Soap manufacturer in New York. Dry-goods merchant in Florida. Sales agent for a grocery wholesaler in Georgia. Even party promoter (as it would now be called) in New Orleans, organizing masquerade balls during Mardi Gras season.[3]

Some of these ventures were more profitable than others. (He reportedly pocketed more than thirteen hundred dollars from the galas he staged in New Orleans.)[4] None of them, however, satisfied his larger financial ambitions—or his growing desire to make a mark in the world.

• • •

It was during his summer stay in Louisville that John Colt finally settled on his vocation, the lifework that would—so he was convinced—secure him both wealth and renown. The field he chose was utterly devoid of glamour; even today its practitioners are stereotyped as joyless drones. Colt himself acknowledged that he could think of no other subject that was "calculated to excite so little interest" in the general public.[5] And yet it was a subject that could inspire him to heights of near-poetic eloquence—a field he embraced with a passionate enthusiasm and promoted with a crusader's zeal. That field was accounting.

His knowledge of the subject derived from several sources. It is likely that he was exposed to the basics of business math as early as grammar school, since American children of his era were commonly taught to "cast accounts" as part of their elementary education.[6] In the following years, he practiced bookkeeping as an apprentice in Connecticut, taught practical mathematics in the South, and became adept at balancing ledgers in the course of his varied and far-flung mercantile pursuits. By the time he reached Louisville, he had evidently become proficient enough not merely to undertake a series of public lectures on double entry bookkeeping but also to entertain thoughts of a grand project: a volume, addressed to the young nation's booming population of merchants, manufacturers, and tradesmen, that would offer a simplified way to master the science of accounting.

That summer in Louisville, "he devoted himself exclusively to the subject," reading whatever texts he could get his hands on, making extensive notes, and refining his own approach through lectures and teaching.[7] It quickly became apparent to him that his magnum opus would require a sig-

nificant amount of time to complete. To support himself in the meanwhile, he resumed his former pursuits, "devoting himself to trade and speculation in the West and the South."[8]

• • •

Sometime after his watershed summer in Louisville—the exact date is impossible to determine—John's peregrinations landed him in Cincinnati, where he would live on and off for the next several years.

In the fifty years since its founding, Cincinnati had undergone a remarkable transformation. Beginning as little more than a forest clearing—a rudimentary settlement that "seemed better suited for the raccoons, opossums, and wildcats that infested it than for human habitation"—it swiftly grew into a major mercantile and manufacturing center. By the time of John Colt's arrival, the raw frontier village had blossomed into the largest and most flourishing trading hub in the Ohio Valley:

> The easterner, mingling with the crowds in the Cincinnati streets and observing the handsome buildings, could forget "the nursery slanders about backwoods and boors." A compactly built city stood where before had been merely another Ohio river clearing. The quay, paved with limestone and extending three hundred yards along the river, was jammed during the busy seasons of the year; drays and wagons of every kind brought passengers and freight to and from the landing where steamboats arrived and departed hourly. Overlooking the lower level of the city stood rows of rectangular blocks of houses, occasionally relieved by the gilded spires of the churches, and few conspicuous mansions of the rich. Clouds of smoke poured from chimneys of the Queen City's steam foundries, and behind the city rose the hills, hazy and indistinct, a few houses on their wooded summits.[9]

In this buzzing hive of commerce, John found a receptive audience for his orations on the "practical importance and scientific beauty" of double entry bookkeeping. It was an era when public lecturing served as a form not

only of mass education but also of popular entertainment. Communities throughout the country—as many as four thousand towns, villages, and cities, according to the estimate of one historian—boasted lyceum societies that sponsored regular addresses on a staggering range of topics. In one season alone, for example, the residents of a small city in Maine could attend "lectures on astronomy, biology and physiology, the principles of geology, conversation, reading, the cultivation of memory, popular delusions concerning the Middle Ages, Iceland, the equality of the human condition, the true mission of women, the domestic life of the Turks, the problem of the age, and the origin of letters." Colt's talks on bookkeeping were typical of this phenomenon, the product of an age when the lyceum lecture served "to satisfy the seemingly insatiable craving for 'useful knowledge' " among the American public.[10]

Several of John's speeches would later be published as an appendix to his book. They are revealing documents. Informed by a sweeping erudition, they trace the history of accounting from its reputed origins in the ancient Middle East to its development in medieval Italy, and invoke sources from Seneca and Pliny to Sir Walter Scott and Samuel Johnson. Given the inherent dryness of the subject, the lectures are also remarkable for their sheer fervor.

Colt saw accounting as a branch of knowledge peculiarly suited to America, a young, enterprising country rapidly "advancing to become the greatest maritime and commercial nation in the world." In his lofty view, the teaching and learning of double entry bookkeeping promoted the values and ideals set forth in the Declaration of Independence, allowing the individual to "enjoy the blessing of enlightened life" by helping him achieve "money, property, and possessions." In a society committed to democratic principles and material pursuits, it was a subject that should be "taught in every common school." In contrast to the study of literature—which instilled in the young a dangerous love for "the corrupting fiction of a novel"—the science of bookkeeping had a "daily and indispensable use, valuable alike to the rich and the poor, the young and the old, the statesman and the man of business."

So mathematically elegant, so intellectually stimulating was the system of double entry bookkeeping that young men who devoted themselves to it were certain to have their "views enlarged," their "minds expanded." In addition, it possessed a powerful moral dimension. A knowledge of bookkeep-ing, Colt argued, "fastens upon the mind the respect we owe to others' rights, and the bounden duty man owes to himself and his dependents. It points to justice, honor, and honesty. It is a daily beacon prompting to fru-gality; an hourly admonisher of the ruinous effects of sluggishness, careless-ness, and extravagance."[11]

There was one final benefit to be derived from a mastery of double entry bookkeeping. Colt stressed it repeatedly in his talks. In light of later events, his remarks take on a terrible irony.

According to this "mercantile philosopher" (as Colt styled himself), double entry bookkeeping was the method best suited to document business transactions and thus to provide an irrefutable record of the financial deal-ings between debtors and creditors. As such, it was the surest way to prevent "frauds, collisions, and disputes."

11

*I*n the decades to come, all too many disputes would be resolved not with the help of John Colt's beloved system of double entry bookkeeping but with the invention that his younger brother conceived on board the brig *Corvo*. Indeed, in its most famous incarnation, Sam Colt's six-shooter would be known by a name that proclaimed its uniquely effective ability to settle arguments once and for all: the Peacemaker.

That sleek, lethal implement—"the gun that won the West"—was a far cry from the carved wooden model that Sam brought home from his maiden voyage. Even that rough contrivance, however, represented a revolutionary step in handgun design, "a multishot weapon . . . that allowed its user to automatically rotate the cylinder by the simple action of cocking the hammer."[1]

Given the money they had already invested in his seaman's gear, Sam's parents—particularly his ever-prudent stepmother—expected him to embark on a second voyage without undue delay. A distant relation of Olivia's, Captain Abner Bassett of New London, Connecticut, was happy to offer him a place on board his merchantman, scheduled to depart shortly on an extended voyage.[2] By then, however, Sam had lost interest in the sailor's life. When he crossed the ocean next, he would travel as a businessman, propelled by the dream that would drive him for the rest of his days.

• • •

In February 1832, just eight months after the *Corvo* returned to port, Sam left home again, this time via stagecoach for Washington, DC. Packed among his belongings were a pair of crude but functioning prototypes of his invention—one a pistol, the other a rifle—both equipped with rotating cylinders constructed according to his innovative design. They had been built by a local gunsmith named Anson Chase, hired largely because he worked fast and cheap.[3] Also in Sam's possession was a letter of introduction to Henry L. Ellsworth, a Hartford native shortly to become commissioner of U.S. patents.

Details of this journey are exceedingly sparse; only a single piece of evidence pertaining to it still exists. This document does, however, shed considerable light not only on the purpose of the trip but also on a trait of Sam Colt's that would stand him in excellent stead in the coming years: his salesman's gift for ingratiating himself with men who could advance his ambitions.

The document is a brief note from Henry Ellsworth to Christopher Colt, Sr., reporting on Sam's visit. Dated February 20, 1832, it reads: "Samuel is now here getting along very well with his new invention. Scientific men & the great folks speak highly of the thing—I hope he will be well rewarded for his labors. I shall be happy to aid him. He obtained $300 here at the bank with my endorsement."[4]

Impressed as he was by young Colt's invention, Ellsworth counseled him to put off filing "for a patent until he had improved the experimental models."[5] Sam realized that to perfect his firearm would require far more money than the loan he had obtained with Ellsworth's backing. (Indeed, over the next three years, he would invest "a total of $1,362.73 in the production of ten pistols, seven rifles, and one shotgun"—an amount equivalent to more than $34,000 in today's money.)[6] And so, sometime in late 1832, the eighteen-year-old inventor embarked on a career that has always proved extremely lucrative to its most successful practitioners. He became a popular entertainer.

•   •   •

First identified by Joseph Priestley in 1773, nitrous oxide—"laughing gas"— became known to the world through the work of Sir Humphry Davy, the great British chemist who began to experiment with the substance twenty-six years after its discovery. Working at a research facility called the Pneumatic Institute—established to explore the therapeutic use of certain gases in the treatment of consumption—Davy spent fourteen months inhaling from six to twelve quarts of the gas four or five times a week, often while sealed inside an airtight "breathing chamber." His ecstatic accounts of the "sublime emotions" he experienced during this period—reported to the Royal Institution of London in 1802 and published in his treatise, *Researches, Chemical and Philosophical; Chiefly Concerning Nitrous Oxide*—set off a craze for public demonstrations of the "exhilarating gas" in both England and the United States.

In mid-nineteenth-century America, such demonstrations became a big part of show business, conducted before sell-out crowds in various small-town and big-city venues: hotel ballrooms, Masonic halls, lyceums, young men's associations, dime museums. Presenting himself as a highly qualified scientist, chemist, or physician, the lecturer would invite willing audience members onto the stage and, by means of an oversized rubber bladder, administer a "potent dose" of the gas to the volunteers. Their resulting behavior—laughing, singing, dancing, declaiming, leaping about the stage, and, in general, making public spectacles of themselves—served as a rich source of amusement for the spectators, well worth the standard twenty-five-cent admission.[7]

That Sam Colt would turn to performing as a way to earn money seems completely in character. His flair for the theatrical had been evident since childhood, most notably in the raft-blowing experiment he had staged with such ballyhoo on the Fourth of July, 1829. In later years, his phenomenal success would owe much to his genius for showmanship and self-promotion. A brilliant manipulator of "myths, symbols, and stagecraft," he turned himself into America's first industrial superstar, "a man whose personality became so widely associated with his product that ownership provided access to the celebrity, glamour, and drama of its namesake."[8] Given his early fascination with chemistry—fostered by his friendship with William T. Smith, supervisor of the bleaching and dyeing lab at the Hampshire mill—it is equally unsurprising that he would set himself up as a laughing gas lecturer.[9]

Employing the ancestral (and presumably more high-toned) spelling of his family name, Sam assumed the role of "the Celebrated Dr. Coult of New York, London, and Calcutta." Decked out in frock coat and high hat, and sporting a newly grown mustache and beard to make him look older than his eighteen years, he embarked on a tour of the eastern seaboard. Arrived at his destination, he would drum up excitement with a newspaper ad. The following announcement of an 1833 appearance in Lowell, Massachusetts, is typical:

Dr. Coult (late of New York, London, and Calcutta) respectfully informs the Ladies and Gentlemen of Lowell and vicinity, that he will lecture and administer Nitrous Oxide, or Exhilarating Gas, this evening, Nov. 29, at the Town Hall. The peculiar effect of this singular compound upon the animal system was first noticed by the English chemist, Sir Humphrey Davy. He observed that when inhaled into the lungs, it produced the most astonishing effects on the Nervous System; that some individuals were disposed to involuntary fits of laughter, others to recitation, and that the greater number had an irresistible propensity to muscular exertion, such as leaping and running, wrestling, boxing & c., with innumerable fantastic feats. In short, the sensations produced by it are highly pleasurable, and are not followed by debility.

Dr. C. being a practical Chemist, no fears need be entertained of inhaling an impure Gas; and he is willing to submit his preparation to the inspection of any Scientific Gentlemen.

Dr. C. has exhibited the extraordinary powers of this Gas in many cities in America, to numerous audiences of Ladies and Gentlemen of the first respectability. He has administered it to more than 20,000 individuals and has taken it himself no less than 1,000 times.

The persons who inhale the Gas will be separated from the audience by means of a network, in order to give all a better opportunity of seeing the exhibition. Dr. C. will first inhale the gas himself, and then administer it to those who are desirous of inhaling it.

Such individuals as wish to inhale the gas in private parties, will be accommodated by applying to Dr. C. at the Merrimack House.

Tickets 25 cents each to be had at the principal Hotels
and at the door. Seats may be secured between the hours of
12 and 3 o'clock. Doors open at 6 1/2 o'clock; entertainment will commence precisely at 7.[10]

Colt seems to have been a hit wherever he played. A newspaper item
about his appearance at Trowbridge's Albany Museum in October 1833
conveys the excitement that typically attended his performances:

> We never beheld such an anxiety as there has been during
> the past week to witness the astonishing effects of Dr.
> Coult's gas. The Museum was crowded to excess every
> evening; and so intense was the interest which was mani-
> fested that the doctor has been compelled to give two ex-
> hibitions every evening.
>
> The effect which the gas produces on the system is
> truly astonishing. The person who inhales it becomes com-
> pletely insensible, and remains in that state for about three
> minutes, when his senses become restored, and he sneaks
> off with as much shame as if he had been guilty of some lit-
> tle mean action. No person will begrudge his two shillings
> for the gratification of half an hour's laugh at the ludicrous
> feats displayed in the lecture hall.[11]

Precisely how much money Sam earned during his time on the road is
unclear, though all his profits went directly to the various gunsmiths at work
on his models. For three years, he lugged his equipment—bottles, retorts,
funnels, hoses, and his big India-rubber gasbag outfitted with a wooden
spigot—from city to city. Besides Lowell and Albany, he played Baltimore
and Boston, New Haven and Philadelphia, Natchez and New Orleans,
Vicksburg, Mississippi, and Portland, Maine. His journeys eventually took
him as far north as Halifax, Nova Scotia, and westward all the way to
Cincinnati.[12]

Cincinnati's Western Museum was established in 1820 with the high-minded goal of serving as a "citadel of scientific knowledge." Originally located in the Cincinnati College Building, it began as an assemblage of natural history odds and ends: glass-encased displays of fossils, seashells, stuffed birds and reptiles, geological specimens, Egyptian antiquities, Indian artifacts, and the like. There was also a small library of scientific treatises and a collection of color sketches by the museum's assistant curator and resident taxidermist, the young artist-naturalist John James Audubon.[1]

Unfortunately, the public seemed less interested in these edifying exhibits than in the novelties offered at a competing establishment, a supposed "fine arts" museum called Letton's that featured, among other attractions, waxwork effigies of historical figures, a horseshoe reputedly dating back to the sixteenth century, a mummified mermaid, an armless woman, and an "Enormous Elk."[2] Within two years of its founding, the Western Museum went bankrupt.

Its fortunes revived when it passed into the hands of an enterprising French émigré named Joseph Dorfeuille. Relocating the museum to a heavily trafficked intersection by the waterfront, he proceeded to transform it from a somber scientific institution into the kind of popular showplace that, as one English commentator observed dryly, defined the notion of museum in nineteenth-century America:

> A "Museum" in the American sense of the word means a
> place of amusement, wherein there shall be a theatre, some

wax figures, a giant and a dwarf or two, a jumble of pictures, and a few live snakes. In order that there may be
some excuse for the use of the word, there is in most instances a collection of stuffed birds, a few preserved animals, and a stock of oddly assorted and very dubitable
curiosities; but the mainstay of the "Museum" is the "live
art," that is the theatrical performance, the precocious
manikins, or the intellectual dogs and monkeys.[3]

Within months of taking charge, Dorfeuille had reinvigorated business
by installing such crowd-pleasing attractions as a seven-legged pig; the absolutely authentic aboriginal war club used to slay Captain Cook; the tat-
tooed head of a New Zealand cannibal; a waxwork tableau depicting the
butchering of a wife by her hatchet-wielding husband; and "the head, right
hand, and heart of Mathias Hoover, a murderer of local renown," preserved
in alcohol-filled jars.[4]

It was another exhibit, however, that turned the Western Museum into
a bona fide sensation, a must-see attraction for visitors to the Queen City.
This was an elaborate funhouse display variously known as "Dorfeuille's
Hell," "Dante's Inferno," and the "Infernal Regions." The apparent brain-
child of Mrs. Fanny Trollope—the British novelist and caustic observer of
American manners, then residing in Cincinnati—this "stupendous and
colossal entertainment" was realized by the museum's young waxwork mod-
eler and chief inventor, Hiram Powers, later to become America's most celebrated sculptor.

Born and raised in Vermont, Powers had migrated to Ohio with his
family in 1819 at the age of fourteen. Two years later, he found work as a
stock clerk in a Cincinnati grocery store, where, in his spare moments, he
gave vent to his creative urges by sculpting mounds of butter into hissing
rattlesnakes, gaping loggerhead turtles, and other "horrid forms." When the
grocery failed, Powers went to work at a local clock and organ factory, displaying an aptitude that soon got him promoted to head mechanic. Among
his accomplishments during this period was the construction of a mechanical organ equipped with life-sized angelic automatons that "moved, sounded
trumpets, and rang bells."[5]

During a visit to Dorfeuille's museum, Powers was so taken with a replica of Jean Antoine Houdon's marble bust of George Washington—then the most popular piece of statuary in America—that he promptly enrolled in a local artist's studio, where he soon mastered the art of making plaster casts. Before long, he came to the attention of Dorfeuille himself, who hired him as the museum's full-time "wax-figure maker and general mechanical contriver."

Powers's skills as both sculptor and technician found their fullest expression in the creation of the Infernal Regions. An antebellum precursor of the kind of "animatronic" spook house epitomized today by Disneyland's Haunted Mansion and similar theme park thrill-rides, this lurid spectacle—located in the museum's cramped, darkened attic—offered customers an effects-laden tour of the horrors of hell, complete with automated demons, writhing sinners, swirling smoke, artificial flames, and a "continuous clamor" of hair-raising sounds. To provide an extra—and quite literal—jolt, an electrified iron grating was installed between the spectators and the moving wax figures, so that (as Mrs. Trollope put it) "should any daring hand or foot obtrude itself within the bars, it receives a smart shock that often passes through many of the crowd."[6]

While this mechanized spectacle quickly established itself as the museum's biggest draw, Dorfeuille continued to offer live entertainment as well, including the ever-popular administration of nitrous oxide, whose amusing effects on audience volunteers were celebrated by one anonymous poetaster:

> Have you ever been at the museum
> When D—— was giving the gas?
> By jokers, it's funny to see 'em
> When candidates plenty he has.
>
> Some fence, some caper and shout
> And some of them act like a fool,
> And others will tragedy spout—
> I suppose they have learnt it at school.[7]

Early on (as this bit of newspaper doggerel indicates) Dorfeuille himself "gave the gas," though he had evidently quit performing by the time "Dr. Coult" arrived in Cincinnati.

We know of Sam Colt's appearance at the Western Museum from a letter sent to him many years later by none other than Hiram Powers, who began a long-lasting friendship with the six-gun inventor in Cincinnati. By the time this letter was composed in 1851, Powers was living in Florence, Italy, where he had won international renown as the creator of *The Greek Slave*. A life-sized marble statue of a chained female nude, this piece achieved a level of popular success that no other American sculpture has ever rivaled (at least partly, no doubt, because it afforded Victorian gentlemen the chance to ogle a naked, nubile woman under the pretext of contemplating fine art).

In his letter to Colt, Powers reminisced about a memorable incident at the Western Museum:

> I shall never forget the *gas* at the old museum, nor your sly glances at the ropes stretched around the columns, when about to snatch the gas bag from the huge blacksmith, who glowered so threateningly at you, while his steam was getting up—nor his grab at your coat tail as, froglike, you leaped between the ropes—[8]

Since Powers's letter constitutes the only record of Colt's visit to Cincinnati, there is no way of knowing exactly what transpired on the trip, beyond the comical episode involving the intoxicated blacksmith. Still, it is safe to assume, as have various historians, that Sam spent a good portion of his time there in the company of his brother John, who was not only residing in the Queen City during this period but was himself an occasional lecturer at Dorfeuille's.[9]

• • •

While maintaining himself through public speaking, teaching, and assorted mercantile pursuits, John continued to work on his textbook. To illustrate the basic principles of his method, he included hundreds of sample ledger entries. Many of these were drawn from his own experiences. One entry, for example, refers to "sundry notes" owed to Edmund B. Stedman, the fiancé of his late sister Margaret. Another mentions "bills payable" to Robert Trumble, a college friend from John's days at the University of Vermont.

Other friends and relations whose names appear in the book include his cousin John Caldwell; his business associate Joseph Law; and his youngest brother, James.[10] Thanks to this practice, Colt's "treatise on book-keeping" is an unexpectedly autobiographical work, offering provocative clues to his personal life.

One item has struck scholars as particularly intriguing. In a section labeled "Inventory of my Property with which I commence business," Colt includes the following:

Rec'd from the executors of my father-in-law's estate,
   as follows:
Sundry Notes, amounting to . . . .$ 4,500
A deed for 1,000 acres of Texas land valued at 5,000
Cash—deposited 10,000
                                         19,500[11]

Based on this notation, biographers of the Colt family have speculated that, sometime during his travels around the Southwest, John had acquired a wife with property in Texas.[12] What became of her—assuming that she existed at all—is unknown. Death, divorce, or abandonment are the likeliest possibilities. Whatever the case, John appears to have been free of any marital entanglements during his residence in Cincinnati. Certainly there was nothing to prevent him from pursuing a romance with an adventurous young woman named Frances Anne Frank, stepdaughter of another of Joseph Dorfeuille's competitors.

• • •

While certain scholars insist that the idea for "The Infernal Regions" originated with Mrs. Trollope, others attribute it to Frederick Frank, proprietor of an eponymous showplace located above a drugstore on the southwest corner of Main and Upper Market streets. Like Letton's, Frank's establishment had begun as a "gallery of fine arts" before being converted into a garish dime museum. For the price of admission—a quarter for adults; fifteen cents for children under ten—visitors were treated to the usual array of "unprecedented attractions," from anatomical curiosities, to a "cosmoramic tableau" of "the bustling streets and markets of Cincinnati," to live performances by the likes of thirteen-year-old Master Kent, "the greatest Juba dancer living," and Mr. Jenkins, "the celebrated Singer and Delineator of Yankee Eccentricities."[13] According to some historians, Frank was also the first Cincinnati showman to present a lurid exhibition of the torments of hell, featuring waxwork figures of cavorting "imps, devils, and goblins."[14]

Performing daily at Frank's Museum was his twenty-one-year-old step-daughter, Frances Anne, an enchanting (if "uninstructed") singer who accompanied herself on the organ. In addition to her "sweet, rich" voice, Frances was endowed with other natural charms:

> Her form, of the medium height, was perfectly symmetri-cal, though inclining to fullness. She had the foot of Cin-derella, and hands and fingers long and exquisitely turned. To a fine bust, she added a countenance stamped with the heroic—the forehead broad and high—the complexion animated and transparent—the eyes large, full, black, and fiery—the hair very dark brown and luxuriant.[15]

Despite her youth, Frances had already been married twice and was the mother of an infant girl. At fifteen she had eloped with a riverboat gambler, then divorced him after two years of wandering "from wretchedness to splendor and from splendor back to wretchedness." Shortly thereafter, she entered into a marriage of convenience with a "young German of consider-able wealth and rank." That union—which produced Frances's child—ended when her husband died after squandering his fortune "in three years of reckless luxury."

Whether John met Frances while visiting the museum as a customer or appearing there as a lecturer is unknown. In any event, he was immediately "enraptured by her beauty and manner" and "found no difficulty in engag-ing her in conversation." They immediately formed a close and increasingly intimate friendship.

Seated on the museum's balcony overlooking the "vast quay of Cincin-nati," they shared the stories of their "strange, wild" lives while gazing out at the glorious vista: "the moving city of steamers,—the strangely fashioned flat and keel boats,—the ever bustling crowd thronging the water's edge,—the gentle Ohio and its beautiful banks,—on the opposite Kentucky shore,

the picturesque city of Covington, and in the far distance beyond, hills rising upon hills, and landscapes of varied loveliness." Before long, the two
had become lovers.[16]

Their relationship continued for several years. When John was away on
one of his frequent business trips, they were "constant correspondents";
when he was in town, "they were constant visitors." As the time passed, it
became increasingly evident that Frances had marital designs on John and
was prepared to deploy all of her "allurements" to "make him hers."

One evening, for example, they were out for a ride at dusk along the
banks of the Ohio. Stopping "at a brook where they were accustomed to let
their horses drink," Frances suddenly announced, "No man can outswim
me!" When John took up the challenge, she alighted from her steed,
stripped off her clothing, and plunged into the water. John—after watching
her for a moment as if in a "reverie"—followed suit. Meeting "his fair antagonist midway across the stream," he raced her to the opposite shore; where-
upon "Frances sprang to the bank and stood there, another Venus from the
ocean foam," allowing John to contemplate her naked form in the moon-
light.

Despite all the favors she bestowed on him, however—which included
a constant stream of "little presents wrought by her own hand"—it became
increasingly clear that John had no intention of becoming Frances's third
husband. Their relationship grew increasingly strained, particularly after
Frances informed him that she was thinking of becoming a professional
thespian. In keeping with the view of the theatrical profession prevalent
in Victorian America—when actresses were seen as little better than
harlots—John sent her a tongue-clucking letter, warning her that if she pursued such a path, she would not only "be set down as a bad woman" but "be
ranked among the most worthless."[17]

Mortified by John's priggish tone, Frances "felt as though she had been
baffled and repelled." She sent no reply to his "offensive letter." When
John—"piqued by her silence"—sent a reproachful follow-up, she ignored
that one as well. Finally, after one more failed attempt to get in touch with
her, John, acting very much "like a chagrined lover," "gathered the elegant
little presents she had wrought" and sent them back to her, while demanding the return of his own letters.

Although they managed to patch up this quarrel when he returned to

Cincinnati, the incident effectively marked the end of their love affair. Soon afterward, John made an extended trip to New York City. When Frances wrote "for permission to join him" there, he promptly sent a curt letter of refusal.

Just hours after she received this note, Frances showed up at the home of her sister and brother-in-law, Susan and Joseph Adams. As Mr. Adams would later testify, Frances appeared to be in a state of extreme agitation, plying them with such "strange and confused questions" that he and his wife grew alarmed and urged the young woman to lie down. Flinging herself onto the bed, she lay there in a stupor for several hours before rousing herself and begging her sister to stay by her side.

While Susan attempted to comfort her, Joseph hurried off to find a physician. In the meantime, Frances's closest friend, a woman named Lawton, was summoned to her bedside. Throughout the evening, as Frances grew increasingly "frenzied," her attendants applied mustard poultices to her ankles and stomach and tried to administer calomel and other medications, which Frances refused to swallow. Finally, crying out that her vision was failing, she urged Mrs. Lawton to get a pencil and paper and take down the following letter:

> You say right. I do not love you; for women love but once, and the idol I worship is beyond my reach; but still, I love him yet; but I am grateful for the many favors I have received from you, and the interest you have displayed in my welfare. I have pretended to love you dearly, but in my heart I did not. I have ever admired your talents and respected your person, but your last two letters were of such a nature as to kill even those feelings. You will never see me again; for, a few short hours, and I will be in heaven. Forgive me, for I am dying now.

To Mrs. Lawton and the others gathered at the scene, this message seemed so "unaccountable" that "they set it down to mere fever-dream incoherence."

As midnight approached, Frances "seemed entirely to lose all perception of what was passing. She called in a hurried, frenzied manner for her brother-in-law and sister but could not distinguish any one." She lingered

until early the following afternoon, when she "died with a few short struggles." That the vital young woman had been carried off with such shocking
swiftness struck her survivors as an inexplicable calamity until a note found
among her possessions revealed the truth: "that this extraordinary girl had
taken one hundred and fifty grams of opium upon receiving the last letter"
from John C. Colt.[18]

*I*n early 1834, Sam began an extended run at the Baltimore Museum and Gallery of Paintings. Touted in contemporary guidebooks as a "grand repository of sublime works" both natural and man-made, this establishment offered the usual hodgepodge of curiosities, diversions, and wonders. Its most popular attraction, created by a "profound Italian physician and artist" named Joseph Chiappi, was an "obstetric and anatomical cabinet" featuring wax representations of the female reproduction system—an ostensibly edifying display that (like the sleazy "miracle of birth" exploitation films of a century later) served up sexual titillation in a scientific guise.[1]

It was during this engagement that Sam—dissatisfied with the model weapons he had been receiving from Anson Chase—secured the services of a new and more sophisticated technician, a Baltimore gunsmith named John Pearson. Their relationship, though productive, proved to be thorny. While Pearson labored ten hours a day in a cramped and underheated workshop, Sam—out on the road with his act—bombarded him via mail with a steady stream of demands and directions.

The older Pearson bristled not only at his young employer's high-handed tone but also at Sam's habitual failure to meet his financial obligations, including Pearson's salary. In letters that grew increasingly bitter over the course of their two-year business arrangement, Pearson complained that his day-and-night labors had gotten him nothing but "vexation and trouble" and that Sam's treatment of him was an "insult."

"The manner you are using us is too bad," he railed in one of his letters.

"Come up with some money. I am in a devil of a humor and not without a cause." In reply, Sam (who, as one scholar drily remarks, "was about as good at spelling as at meeting his debts") did his best to placate Pearson: "make your expenses as lite as possible . . . Don't be allarmed about your wages, nothing shal be rong on my part, but doo wel for me & you shal fare wel."[2]

Charging as much as fifty cents per person for admission to his show (a considerable sum at a time when a complete multicourse dinner at Delmonico's original restaurant in New York City could be had for twelve cents), Sam traveled through South Carolina and Georgia, keeping Pearson mollified—and "at the grindstone"—by sending him whatever money he could spare: seventy-five dollars in February 1835; another fifty in March.[3]

One month later, Sam returned to Baltimore, having finished his tour with a swing through Virginia. His performances in Lynchburg and Richmond would be his last. The celebrated Dr. Coult was laid permanently to rest. Henceforth, Sam Colt would devote himself, with absolute singleness of purpose, to the fashioning of a far more heroic persona—one that would eventually take its place in the pantheon of America's industrial demigods.

• • •

Taking rooms in Baltimore, Sam secured both a larger workplace and a helper for Pearson, then set about supervising the construction of a pair of patent models: one pistol, one rifle. They were completed to his satisfaction in early June. On the seventeenth of that month, he traveled to Manhattan to show them to his cousin (and potential investor) Dudley Selden, the distinguished Manhattan attorney for whom John had briefly clerked several years earlier.

Deeply impressed with the invention—and worried that it might fall prey to the piratical practices of foreign manufacturers—Selden advised Sam to patent it first in Great Britain and France. Accordingly, in the third week of August 1835, Sam—flush with loans from several family members—set sail for England.

He was gone for just under four months. From a legal standpoint, the trip was an unqualified success. When his ship, the *Albany*, arrived back in the United States in early December, Sam had his foreign patents safely in hand. According to his most reliable biographer, he brought home another acquisition as well: a sixteen-year-old wife.[4]

Historians describe her as a person of "striking beauty" but extremely "humble origins" who "could barely read or write." The precise circumstances of their courtship (such as it was) remain shrouded in mystery, though she and Sam reportedly met in Scotland. Since he was there for only a week or two between visits to London and Paris, he clearly leaped into the marriage with the kind of haste that, as Dr. Franklin wisely observes, causes couples to repent in leisure.

The truth of that old saw was proven in the case of Sam Colt himself. Indeed, by the time he returned to America with his bride, he already appears to have been beset by second thoughts. Perhaps, as his biographers have speculated, Sam's initial sexual infatuation quickly gave way to a sobering realization: that he had saddled himself with an unschooled, socially awkward young wife who was unlikely to help advance his ambitions. In any event, from the moment his ship docked in New York Harbor, Sam Colt "kept the marriage a secret from the rest of the family, and the world at large."[5]

14

*A*ccording to the myths of the world, there are times when all heroes must prove themselves by performing miraculous tasks—overcoming obstacles and ordeals that would defeat lesser mortals. To accomplish their quests, they must scale impossible mountains, sail peril-filled seas, descend into the lairs of monsters, negotiate nightmarish mazes, cross bottomless chasms over bridges no wider than knives. Like the classic figures of mythology, Sam Colt, too—according to the official chroniclers and keepers of his legend—had to surmount a succession of challenges and tribulations as he fought his way to his ultimate goal. That perilous "road of trials," so full of crises and reversals, started shortly after his return from Europe.

• • •

Things began promisingly enough. After Sam's American patent came through in February 1836, he and his investors lost no time in forming the Patent Arms Manufacturing Company for the making of "arms, machinery, and cutlery." In March, under prodding from influential friends, the New Jersey legislature granted the fledgling operation a charter of incorporation. While construction commenced on an imposing four-story factory on the banks of the Passaic River in Paterson, Sam and his partners leased an old gristmill nearby and set up shop on the ground floor. A gifted craftsman named Pliny Lawton—formerly Christopher Colt's head machinist at the Hampshire mill in Ware—was brought in as superintendent. Lawton set about at once devising machines for the mass production of the guns, which, until then, had been crafted individually by hand.[1]

It soon became clear, however, that Sam's great expectations were wildly optimistic; that—as inspirational guides were forever reminding young go-getters—the "road to success was never smooth, straight, nor strewn with flowers."[2] On a trip to Washington, DC, that spring, he did manage to generate some favorable publicity in the *Washington Post,* where a writer named F. S. Burns testified that he had "tried the newly improved pistol of Mr. Colt and found that it shot exceedingly well—in my opinion it will prove a very great improvement in firearms."[3] But Sam's hopes of winning a far more important endorsement—that of President Andrew Jackson—were quickly dashed.

Jackson, of course, had an intimate, lifelong knowledge of firearms. Aside from his military heroics—most famously during the Battle of New Orleans, when he and his ragtag forces wreaked havoc on the massed British regulars—he had fought several gun duels in his younger days and still carried the bullets from two of these deadly encounters in his shoulder and chest. Moreover, just a few weeks before Sam's arrival in the capital, Old Hickory had escaped with his life when a would-be assassin attempted to discharge a pair of pistols at his chest, both of which misfired. As one historian observes, the incident should have given the old warrior "a keen sense of the unreliability of old-time firearms."[4] Nevertheless, when Sam— who had somehow wangled a meeting with the president—demonstrated his invention, Jackson was unimpressed, seeing no need for the army to abandon the kind of single-shot flintlocks that had served him so well against the redcoats.

Other disappointments soon followed. Despite his intense lobbying efforts—which consisted largely of throwing lavish, wine-fueled dinner parties for Washington officials and dispensing the occasional gift—Sam not only failed to snag any government commissions but also incurred the ire of his powerful cousin Dudley Selden. The company's single biggest investor and de facto director, Selden repeatedly rebuked the young inventor on his extravagant—and ethically dubious—ways: "You use money as if it were drawn from an inexhaustible mine," he fumed in one letter. "I have no belief in undertaking to raise the character of your gun by old Madeira." At another point, he blasted Sam's readiness to resort to bribery as "dishonor-able in every way."[5]

When Sam did manage to win a spot for his guns in an army trial con-ducted at West Point in the summer of 1837, the results were disastrous. During one demonstration, his rifle discharged several loads at once, produc-ing a mini-explosion. In another, the hammer broke off. In the end—while conceding that Colt's weapons might have certain limited applications—the ordnance board was "unanimous in opinion" that, owing to their "compli-cated character, liability to accident, and other reasons," his revolvers were "entirely unsuited to the general purpose of the service."[6]

There were some encouraging developments along the way. To boost the reputation of his product, Colt—whose grasp of public relations was at least as impressive as his knowledge of firearms technology—joined the prestigious American Institute of New York City, an organization dedicated to the "encouragement of science and invention." At the institute's annual public exhibition in October 1837, one of Sam's revolving rifles was awarded a gold medal, the first of many that would be bestowed upon him. Pioneering a ploy that would be exploited by countless marketers to follow, he touted the award in his advertisements, the first of which appeared in the December 27, 1837, issue of the *Morning Courier and New-York Enquirer*:

> Colt's Repeating Rifles are now for the first time offered for sale. They have been manufactured at the "Patent Arms Manufacturing Company" at Paterson, and in beauty and workmanship are fully equal to the highest finished Rifles imported from England . . .
>
> The Rifles now offered for sale are even superior to those exhibited at the last Fair of the American Institute, for which the Gold medal was awarded. They are put up in mahogany cases, with all their equipments complete.[7]

Two months later, in a typically splashy bit of showmanship, Sam—having secured the consent of the mayor and the city council—staged a public demonstration of his rifles at Castle Garden on the southernmost tip of Manhattan. Though the rapid-firing repeaters elicited admiring gasps from the crowd, the price of the guns—$150 apiece (equivalent to roughly

$3,500 in current funds)—rendered them prohibitive for the average purchaser. Sales remained stagnant, even as Sam continued to burn through his investors' money at an alarming rate in an effort to drum up business.

More convinced than ever that the very survival of his company depended on volume sales to the government, Sam embarked on a bold venture. In February 1838, just weeks after his Castle Garden exhibition, he personally transported ten cases of his rifles—one hundred pieces altogether—to the Florida Everglades, where U.S. forces were bogged down in a bloody effort to dispossess the native Seminoles from their rightful lands. Fifty of his repeaters were purchased by the Second Dragoons and put into immediate action in the grueling guerrilla war. Their accuracy and rapidity of fire—sixteen shots in thirty-one seconds—won a glowing review from the commanding officer, Colonel W. S. Harney. "I do assure you that sooner I would use any other Rifle myself, I would use none," Harney reported to his superiors in Washington—an endorsement that Sam (a pioneer in the use of expert testimonials for advertising purposes) would be quick to publicize.[8]

Even so, the trip was far from the triumph that Sam had hoped for. Half of his rifles remained unsold. On the return voyage, moreover, Sam's boat capsized in the waters off St. Augustine, Florida. Though he escaped drowning by clinging to the overturned craft for four hours, his luggage—including the trunk containing the army's $6,250 draft—was lost in the surf. By the time he was safely back on land, he had come to regard the whole trip as a "cursed adventure."[9]

Making his way back north, Sam holed up at the Astor Hotel in Manhattan for a few recuperative days before throwing himself back into the hectic business of promoting his guns. In late fall, he returned to Washington for another costly—and ultimately futile—round of courting public officials. During one demonstration on the White House lawn—so the legend goes—"a squad of men armed with Colt's repeating rifles" let off a "fusillade that scared the horses of the President's carriage. The coachman was thrown from his seat trying to control the plunging horses and fell onto a picket fence, impaled."[10] The story is unverified and almost certainly apocryphal, though it does serve as an apt metaphor for Colt's depressing situation at this period of his life, when his high hopes were invariably punctured in the most brutal way.

The same disheartening pattern repeated itself over the next year. In 1839 the company opened a retail shop at 155 Broadway. By this point—thanks in large part to Sam's tireless PR efforts—the public was becoming increasingly aware of the lethal efficacy of his revolvers. One newspaper editorial, for example, proposed a simple test for anyone who doubted their superiority over old-fashioned flintlocks. Should a man find himself "engaged to meet another in single combat, and his antagonist apprise him that he will come armed with one of Colt's repeating pistols, taking his station at forty yards, then to advance and fire at will, the friend of the old system, we think, would hesitate to meet the encounter with a single dueling pistol against one of Colt's."[11] Despite such tributes, however, the high cost of the handguns—twenty-six dollars each versus six dollars for a pair of flintlock pistols—kept sales to a trickle at the Broadway store.

Military contracts remained equally elusive, owing largely to the hidebound attitude of the head of the army's ordnance department: Colonel George Bomford, an officer who "had reached that age and rank at which extreme rigidity sets in" and who (as Sam wrote in his reliably wretched manner) was "dedly oposed" to his newfangled firearms.[12] Matters came to a head in June 1840. With virtually no commercial or governmental demand for Colt's repeaters, the board of directors—whose members had been in more or less constant conflict with Sam over his profligate ways with company funds—made a fateful decision. Sam, in Washington at the time, learned about it in a letter from Pliny Lawton, who informed him that the directors had "resolved to stop a large portion of the works . . . and have been devising means to pay off the workmen." Production had been halted at the Paterson gun mill.

Under the circumstances, the news couldn't have come as a total surprise to Sam. Still, it was a blow. And worse—much worse—was yet to come.

*L*ike other members of the Colt family, John had become actively involved in Sam's enterprise. In late 1837 he served as an
agent for the Patent Arms Company, receiving several thousand dollars'
worth of rifles and holster pistols on consignment, most of which he succeeded in selling "to various dealers and speculators."[1] Even while engaged
in this and other business, he managed to run a small accounting school in
Cincinnati and to put in so much work on his text that it eventually grew
to fifteen hundred pages. By the end of the year, determined to get the book
in print, he gave up his teaching, suspended his commercial dealings, and
devoted himself full-time to putting the manuscript into publishable shape.
In the spring of 1838, it was ready to go to press.[2]

By then, Cincinnati had established itself as a major publishing center—
"the Literary Emporium of the West." As early as 1826, with its population
at just over sixteen thousand, the city's printers were already issuing books
in impressive numbers—nearly two hundred thousand primers, almanacs,
songbooks, religious works, river guides, and more in that year alone. A
decade later, that number had increased tenfold, with two million volumes
pouring off the presses in the course of a single year. By the time John Colt
had finished preparing his textbook, "Cincinnati publishers and dealers
were famous throughout the West."[3]

Preeminent among these was a pioneering bookman named Ephraim
Morgan, a Massachusetts native who had migrated to Ohio with his family
at the age of fourteen. In 1827, after a long apprenticeship as a printer's
devil, he and two partners launched the *Cincinnati Gazette,* the city's first

newspaper. One year later, after quitting the paper in protest over its "policy of carrying advertisements for the return of fugitive slaves," Morgan embarked on a highly successful five-decade career as a bookseller and publisher. By the time he retired, he had seen his printing operation expand from a small, water-propelled mill to an industrial powerhouse with a dozen steam-driven presses turning out millions of volumes per year. In 1836, eager to see his son, James, enter the trade, he helped the young man establish a publishing house with two partners. One of these was William Webster, son of the famous lexicographer. The other was a fascinating character named Nathan G. Burgess.[4]

In later years, Burgess would become renowned as one of America's earliest professional daguerreotypists. Among historians of photography, he is perhaps best known as a practitioner of that peculiarly Victorian craft, the making of artfully arranged postmortem portraits. In an article published in an 1855 issue of the *Photographic and Fine Arts Journal,* he offers detailed instructions on this delicate process, including tips for creating tasteful pictures of dead babies. ("If a portrait of an infant is to be taken, it may be placed in the mother's lap and taken in the usual manner by a side light, representing sleep.")[5]

In 1836, however, the daguerreotype had not yet been introduced to the world, and Burgess was making his living as an agent for an eastern publisher. Traveling to Cincinnati on behalf of his employer, he joined with William Webster and James Morgan in establishing their own company. Within the space of two years, as partners came and went, the name of the firm underwent several corresponding changes: Webster, Burgess & Morgan became Burgess & Morgan, then Burgess & Crane, and finally, in 1838, N. G. Burgess & Co. It was under this imprint that Nathan Burgess brought out the first edition of John Colt's accounting textbook.[6]

Colt had high expectations for his book, anticipating "its adoption far and wide, and thence its providing him with a yearly income for life."[7] And, in fact, his text met with a gratifying reception. A review in the influential trade publication the *Merchants' Magazine and Commercial Review* praised its novel approach and wealth of practical exercises, presented "with such clearness and simplicity as to render all of them perfectly comprehensible even to a child."[8] Prominent educators, merchants, and bankers in Cincinnati, Philadelphia, and New York offered glowing testimonials, hailing

Colt's work as "the best we have ever examined" and "far superior to the treatises in common use."

Several hundred public schools and seminaries were quick to adopt the book, which rapidly went through various revisions and reprintings. Some editions carried an appendix containing several of Colt's public lectures, while others were issued in two separate formats: a larger one (priced at $1.50) for "Teachers and Clerks," and a more compact version (costing $1) for students.[9]

In the end, *The Science of Double Entry Book-Keeping* would go through no fewer than forty-five editions and earn its author a lasting place in the history books. Or rather, in two very different sorts of history books: the kind dealing with the development of the accounting profession in the United States, and the kind chronicling the nation's most notorious homicides.[10]

*S*hortly after the publication of his accounting text, John—adding to his already dizzying array of commercial and speculative ventures—entered into a business partnership with Nathan G. Burgess who, like other publishers of the time, also ran a small book and stationery store.[1] Besides devoting themselves to the marketing of Colt's work, they gambled on a major undertaking, investing a sizable sum to bring out a deluxe edition of a book called *An Inquiry into the Origin of the Antiquities of America* by John Delafield, Jr.

A prominent New York banker actively involved in the city's cultural life, Delafield had apparently become fascinated by pre-Columbian civilizations during a visit to Cincinnati, when he viewed a number of archaeological curiosities on display at Dorfeuille's Western Museum.[2] His book, produced during the breaks between his many other professional and social affairs, marshaled a wide range of highly dubious evidence (including geographical calculations based on the presumed location of Mount Ararat, where "Noah's ark came to rest upon the receding of the Flood") to prove that the aboriginal inhabitants of Mesoamerica were descended from the Cushites of ancient Egypt. Adding to this exercise in pseudo-scholarship was an egregious appendix by an amateur historian named James Lakey that offered "A Brief Inquiry into the Causes of the Superiority of Man in the Northern Hemisphere over Those of the Southern Hemisphere." Quite lavishly produced for its time and place, the volume was illustrated with ten engraved plates, five of them hand colored, plus a foldout facsimile of the

Aztec document known as the "codex Boturini"—measuring no less than nineteen feet in length.[3]

Offered by subscription only, Delafield's book proved to be a major disappointment to its publishers. Its failure wiped away most of the profits from John's accounting text and put the fledgling firm of Colt, Burgess & Co. (as it was now called) into a deep financial hole. Burgess later testified that the two partners lost one thousand dollars—equivalent to roughly twenty-three thousand dollars today—on the venture.[4]

Believing that he might find a larger market for the Delafield book in New York City, Colt relocated to 14 Cortlandt Street, Manhattan, in April 1839, renting a small office that doubled as his residence. For the most part, he devoted himself wholly to his business affairs, single-handedly performing all the "duties of such establishment," including the construction of the wooden packing cases used to ship his wares. The "few friends who frequented his office" would later recall "the array of boxes and profusion of paper strips, and the nails, and the hatchet or hammer, and other tools— and [Colt's] appearance, stripped to his shirt with his sleeves rolled up" as he assembled the crates.[5]

John's efforts on behalf of Delafield's book brought only middling results. The bulk of his income continued to come from his own accounting text, which he found himself continually updating. Evidence suggests that—perhaps because of the extreme financial burden he and Burgess had incurred by bringing out the costly and unprofitable *Antiquities*—John's behavior was increasingly troubled at this time.

Working tirelessly from daybreak to nightfall while living "in the most frugal manner," he began to seek respite from his labors in a local tavern. On one occasion, after a long night of imbibing punch with a friend, he found himself in jail after breaking into a law office on the Battery. His official biographer and leading apologist would later attribute this incident to an innocent "blunder"—a matter of John's having drunkenly mistaken the attorney's office for his own. The explanation would be more convincing if John hadn't found himself in other legal difficulties during this period of his life.[6]

Temporarily abandoning New York, John next opened a bookstore on the corner of Fifth and Minor streets in Philadelphia. While there, he was the target of a lawsuit by the Cincinnati publisher (and father of Nathan Burgess's original business partner) Ephraim Morgan, who accused John of swindling him out of nearly six hundred dollars.[7]

Though the details of this case have been lost to history, one fact about John's life during this interlude in Philadelphia is certain: He became intimately involved with a beautiful, if uneducated, "female in humble life" named Caroline Henshaw, who worked in a corset maker's shop.[8] In early 1841, after six months in Philadelphia, he returned to New York City and took up residence at a boardinghouse in Lower Manhattan run by a Captain and Mrs. Hart. Soon afterward, Caroline joined him there, passing as John's wife. By then, she was several months pregnant.[9]

Even after the Patent Arms Company ceased producing new weapons, Sam Colt clung fiercely to the hope of salvaging his business. That possibility, already remote, grew even more unlikely with the news out of Florida. After putting Colt's repeating carbines to heavy use in the grueling campaign against the Seminoles, Colonel Harney's Second Dragoons—initially so enthusiastic about the guns—had reached a devastating conclusion. "I am very sorry to report that your arms have proved an entire failure when put to the test of actual service," wrote one officer, detailing problems that ranged from exploding cylinders and bursting barrels to accidental discharges and jammed cap primers.

Though Sam insisted that the defects in those models had subsequently been fixed, the damage was done. In February 1841, John Ehlers—a major investor who had managed to take control of the company—sent Sam a dispiriting message: "Our sales are little better than nothing." Within the year, the Patent Arms Manufacturing Company of Paterson would be defunct.[1]

Even before the company underwent its final collapse, however, the ever-resilient inventor, now twenty-seven years old, had begun to focus his prodigious energies on a new project. Or, rather, to redirect them toward an old project he had kept in abeyance while pursuing his gun business: the development of "submarine explosives," an interest of Sam's dating back to his adolescence, when he had attempted to blow a raft "sky high" on Ware Pond as part of the town's Fourth of July festivities.

• • •

The possibility of using underwater mines to defend the nation's harbors had taken on a new urgency in the spring of 1841, owing to increasing tensions between the United States and Great Britain over a crisis that came to be known as the McLeod affair.

Several years earlier, a group of insurgents in upper Canada, intent on establishing a republican government, had attempted an armed rebellion against British rule. Their leader was the fiery reformer, newspaper editor, and former mayor of Toronto, William Lyon Mackenzie. After a few skirmishes—culminating in a rout of Mackenzie's forces in March 1837—the rebel leaders fled to the United States, took refuge on a small island in the Niagara River, and began making preparations for an invasion of upper Canada. To provision themselves, they chartered a little steamer called the *Caroline*, which operated out of Buffalo, and ferried men and munitions to the island from the American shore.

When the insurgents began launching attacks on the Canadian village of Chippewa, the British mustered a large force under the command of a colonel named McNabb, who resolved to cut off the rebels' supply line by destroying the *Caroline*. On December 29, 1837, an expedition of five small boats, carrying a party of heavily armed men, set out for this purpose under the cover of night. Finding the *Caroline* moored to the wharf at Fort Schlosser on the American side of Niagara Falls, the attackers, wielding muskets and swords, clambered on board and drove the crew from the vessel. They then towed the ship out onto the river, set it ablaze, and sent it drifting over the falls. During the melee, one of the *Caroline*'s crew members, a New Yorker named Amos Durfee, was shot through the head and killed.

Three years later, at a tavern in upstate New York, a Canadian deputy sheriff named Alexander McLeod drunkenly boasted that he had not only taken part in the destruction of the *Caroline* but was the man who shot Durfee. He was promptly arrested by New York authorities and indicted for arson and murder. The British government demanded his immediate release on the grounds that, at the time of the incident, McLeod had been "acting in the necessary defense of his country against a treasonable insurrection, of which Amos Durfee was acting in aid at the time." The Supreme Court of the State of New York, however—ruling that "the attack upon the

Caroline was an offense against the laws of the state and the life and property of her citizens, and came within the jurisdiction of her courts"—refused to let him go. The decision to proceed with McLeod's trial aroused widespread outrage among the people of Great Britain, whose government began to mobilize for war.[2]

While this escalating international crisis caused alarm in many quarters, Sam Colt saw it as a godsend, a chance to sell the military—no longer interested in his small arms—on a unique new weapons technology: his so-called submarine battery. This device, the precise workings of which Sam kept shrouded in secrecy, consisted of "a tin tube containing anywhere from one hundred to two hundred pounds of black powder that was anchored to the sea floor at a predetermined depth. To detonate the mine, Colt proposed using a spark created by an underwater electromagnetic cable."[3]

In June 1841, Sam traveled to Washington, DC, set himself up at Fuller's Hotel, and proceeded to compose a letter that—judging from its perfect orthography—clearly was set down on paper for him by someone who could actually spell. In it, Sam boasted that, after years of "study & experiment," he had devised a system for "effectually protecting our Sea Coast"—a method that, "if adopted for the service of our government, will not only save them millions in outlay for the construction of means of defense, but in the event of foreign war, will prove a perfect safeguard against all the combined fleets of Europe without exposing the life of our citizens."

Without entering into specifics, Colt proclaimed that his invention enabled him "to effect the instant destruction of either Ships or Steamers, at my pleasure on their entering a harbor, whether singly or in fleets . . . All this I can do in perfect security and without giving an invading enemy the slightest sign of danger." Emphasizing the economic benefits of his system—which could protect a "harbor like that of New York" for "less than the cost of a single steamship" and required only "one single man to manage the destroying agent against any fleet that Europe can send"—he requested a government appropriation of twenty thousand dollars to arrange a demonstration of his submarine battery before the Cabinet. He then sent the letter to President John Tyler.[4]

It was a particularly hectic time for Tyler, who had ascended to the presidency only months earlier following the untimely death of William Henry Harrison. (The record holder for the shortest presidency in U.S. history,

Harrison had insisted on delivering his two-hour inauguration speech in freezing rain without either a hat or a coat; one month later, he was dead of pneumonia.) When Tyler failed to respond to the letter, Sam turned to two supporters who could provide him with an entrée to the chief executive. One was Senator Samuel L. Southard of New Jersey, previously secretary of the navy under presidents James Monroe and John Quincy Adams. The other was John Howard Payne.

· · ·

Born in 1791, Payne was a prodigy who became obsessed with the stage at an early age. Discouraged by his bluenosed father—who shared the general view of acting as a scandalous occupation—he was shipped off to New York City at the age of fourteen to apprentice to a merchant, in the hope that "hard work" would "cure his unwholesome ambitions." All efforts to quash his "yearning for things theatrical," however, were in vain. Sneaking off to the city playhouses at every opportunity, the stagestruck youth began to write and publish a little paper called the *Thespian Mirror*—a kind of early nineteenth-century fanzine—containing "interesting sketches of contemporary actors, criticisms of plays, and dramatic news items from American and British papers." The publication brought him to the attention of the editor of the *New York Evening Post* and other influential figures who offered to further Payne's education at their own expense. After a year at Union College in Schenectady, New York, Payne embarked on a highly successful acting career, appearing (among many other leading roles) as Romeo and Hamlet alongside Edgar Allan Poe's actress-mother, Elizabeth.

In 1813 Payne left the United States for London, where he enjoyed a brilliant, if relatively short-lived, stage career, formed a deep and lasting friendship with Washington Irving (then residing in England), and (at least according to rumor) wooed the recently widowed Mary Shelley. When his popularity as an actor began to wane, he turned to playwriting.

In 1823, as part of an operetta called *Clari, the Maid of Milan*, he composed the lyric that would make him immortal: "Home, Sweet Home." The song—whose second line quickly became proverbial ("Be it ever so humble, there's no place like home")—was a genuine cultural phenomenon, achieving "a wider circulation and a more universal appeal than any other ever written," according to the rapturous account of one of Payne's early biographers:

In the days of its greatest popularity, it is said that every English speaking person in the civilized world could hum the air . . . It became the world's answer to pain and unrest, its refuge from sorrow and sin. It was a sermon on every lip, a prayer in every heart. Nothing ever written outside the Bible and a few grand old hymns is believed to have had wider influence for good. It checked tendencies to stray, it hallowed the fireside and sanctified the marriage altar. To estimate fully its far-reaching influence is as impossible as to calculate the productive quality of a single sunbeam, the attraction of a single star, or the fixed processes of spiritual elements. Every man's home was blessed by it.[5]

After nineteen years abroad, Payne returned to the United States and embarked on a theatrical tour through the South and the West to raise money for an ambitious project: a weekly international arts and literary journal. Precisely when and where he became acquainted with Sam Colt is unclear, though historians speculate that they crossed paths on the performance circuit, most probably in Cincinnati, where they may have been introduced by John Colt, himself a close acquaintance of the actor. A surviving letter of Payne's—expressing his interest in investing in Colt's revolver—leaves no doubt that the two had become friends by the time the Patent Arms Manufacturing Company was established.[6]

When Sam Colt came to Washington to lobby for his submarine battery in June 1841, Payne was living in the city, writing for the *United States Magazine and Democratic Review*, a publication with a long list of eminent contributors, including Nathaniel Hawthorne, William Cullen Bryant, John Greenleaf Whittier, and Ralph Waldo Emerson. With his gift for friendship, Payne (who would soon be appointed the U.S. consul to Tunis) had established a large network of social connections, including Robert Tyler, an amateur poet and son of the chief executive. When Sam's initial attempt to contact the president failed, Payne sent a letter to Robert, warmly recommending Colt and insisting that the young inventor's latest proposal was "thoroughly entitled to attention."

In a matter of days, Sam received an invitation to meet with President Tyler and Secretary of the Navy George E. Badger. Though Tyler merely listened politely, Badger's interest was piqued, and in late July, Sam received word that an upcoming naval appropriation bill would include a sizable allocation for the development of his harbor defense system.[7]

By early September 1841, Sam was back in Manhattan, where he put up in his favorite hostelry, the City Hotel on lower Broadway—just a short distance from the lodgings then occupied by his brother John and John's pregnant mistress, Caroline Henshaw.

FINDING THE BODY IN THE BOX

Part Three

THE SUBLIME OF HORROR

18

*J*ames Gordon Bennett didn't invent the penny press. That distinction belongs to Benjamin Day. Before Day founded the New York *Sun* in 1833, urban newspapers catered largely to the mercantile and professional elites. Somber to the point of deadliness, they devoted themselves primarily to commercial news, financial affairs, and political propaganda on behalf of whatever party they were established to serve. They were also priced beyond the means of the average reader. Sold mainly by subscription, the big-city papers—the *Daily Advertiser,* the *Courier and Enquirer,* the *Journal of Commerce*—cost ten dollars a year. Individual issues could be purchased only at the publisher's office for six cents a copy—this at a time when the daily wage for the typical workingman was eighty-five cents.[1]

Day's innovation was to create an inexpensive paper sold on the streets, free of political partisanship, and featuring the kinds of stories that have always appealed to ordinary people. Whereas the contents of traditional dailies consisted largely of commodity prices, ship sailings, legal notices, ads for wholesalers, political editorials, and a smattering of small items about subjects like tariffs, congressional doings, and the federal banking system, Day's penny paper devoted significant space to such titillating topics as steamboat disasters, suicides, and local crimes. The paper was a runaway success.[2]

It was James Gordon Bennett, however, who turned the penny press into a vehicle of unabashed sensationalism—a precursor of the "yellow" papers that would flourish in the Gilded Age and the tabloid journalism that helped define the following century. An emigrant from Scotland, Bennett subsisted briefly as a teacher in Halifax before making his way down to Boston, where he scratched out a living as a proofreader in a printing house. Three years later, he moved to New York City, where a chance encounter led to a job with the *Charleston* (S.C.) *Courier.* During the next ten years, he wrote for various newspapers, honing a brash and entertaining style that—in a pattern that would characterize his entire career—tickled the public while incensing his high-minded peers.

In 1835, after several failed ventures as a publisher, he used his last five hundred dollars to launch *The New York Herald,* a four-page penny paper aimed at "the great masses of the community" (as Bennett proclaimed in the inaugural issue). Expanding on Day's crowd-pleasing formula, Bennett "fed his readers a steady diet of violence, crime, murder, suicide, seduction, and rape in both news reporting and gossip." In its first two weeks of existence, the *Herald* published accounts of "three suicides, three murders, a fire that killed five persons, an accident in which a man blew off his head, descriptions of a guillotine execution in France, a riot in Philadelphia, a kangaroo hunt in Australia, and the execution of Major John André half a century earlier."[3]

What turned the *Herald* into a phenomenon, however, was Bennett's lip-smacking coverage of the Helen Jewett murder case. A former servant girl, born Dorcas Doyen, from Augusta, Maine, Jewett was axed to death in a stylish Manhattan brothel in the spring of 1836. Though the slaying of prostitutes was nothing new in the city—according to one historian, "twenty girls had perished in the twenty-two brothels in a single block during the preceeding three months"[4]—Bennett immediately recognized that the Jewett case contained elements that lifted it above the merely sordid: not only illicit sex and brutal murder but also a beautiful victim with a mysterious past and a handsome young suspect named Richard Robinson from a highly respectable old-line Connecticut family.

On the day after the discovery of Jewett's savaged body, Bennett— under the blaring headline "Most Atrocious Murder"—devoted nearly an entire page to an account of the crime. He followed this up with a pioneering piece of investigative journalism, personally visiting the crime scene and describing the "ghastly corpse" in rapturous detail:

I could scarcely look at it for a second or two. Slowly I
began to discover the lineaments of the corpse as one
would the beauties of a statue of marble. It was the most remarkable sight I ever beheld—I never have, and never expect, to see such another. "My God," exclaimed I, "how
like a statue. I can scarcely conceive that form to be a
corpse." No vein was to be seen. The body looked as
white—as full—as polished as the purest Parisian marble.
The perfect figure—the exquisite limbs—the fine face—
the full arms—the beautiful bust—all—all—surpassed in
every respect the Venus de Medicis according to the casts
generally given of her.[5]

Thanks to Bennett's relentlessly exploitive reporting, the story became
a nationwide sensation, America's prototypical media circus. While his
many critics deplored his tawdry techniques—one competitor declared that
Bennett had "no more decency than a rutting pig," while Walt Whitman
described him as both a "reptile marking his path with slime" and "a midnight ghoul, preying on rottenness and repulsive filth"—the public couldn't
get enough of his product.[6] By the time Robinson's trial ended,[7] the *Herald*
had become the city's leading newspaper, confirming its publisher's view
that nothing was better for business than murders of a particularly lurid
stripe. "Men who have killed their wives, and committed other such everyday matters, have been condemned, executed, and are forgotten," wrote
Bennett, "but it takes a deed that has some of the sublime of horror about it
to attract attention, rally eloquence, and set people crazy."[8]

• • •

As Bennett recognized, it took the right mix of ingredients to render a
crime irresistible to the public. New Yorkers had to wait another five years
for a case as juicy as the murder of Helen Jewett.

On the New Jersey side of the Hudson River, on the Hoboken shore,
lay a pastoral spot known as Elysian Fields, "a cleared place of about three
or four acres, surrounded on three sides by trees and open on the other to
the river." Easily accessible by steamboat from the Barclay Street launch in

lower Manhattan, this idyllic glade—as lovely, according to one contemporary observer, "as a nook of Paradise before Satan entered its gardens"—
offered city dwellers a delightful refuge from the heat, stink, and congestion
of the metropolis on stifling summer days.[9]

On the scorching afternoon of Wednesday, July 28, 1841, a young
music instructor named Henry Mallin, along with his friend James Boulard,
was strolling north along the grassy riverbank, having debarked at the
Hoboken ferry landing shortly after 3:00 p.m. As they gazed into the rip-
pling waters, they received what Mallin later described as an "evil shock."
There, bobbing in the river about three hundred yards from shore, was a
human body. Dashing to a nearby dock, they leapt into a scull, rowed out to
the body, and—after securing it with a length of rope—towed it back to
land.[10]

The corpse was that of a drowned female who, to judge by her ghastly
condition, had been decomposing in the water for several days. She was
wearing a torn white cotton frock, a bright blue scarf, "light colored" shoes
and gloves, and a leghorn straw bonnet. Despite her grotesque appearance—
the purplish-black skin, the bloated face, the "frothy blood" leaking from her
mouth—she was quickly identified as Mary Cecilia Rogers, a young woman
familiar to readers of the popular press. Indeed, she was already something of
a local celebrity—though her fame while alive was as nothing compared to
the grim immortality that death would bestow.

•   •   •

Invariably described in the contemporary accounts as a young woman of enchanting appearance—a "raven-tressed" beauty possessed of a "dark smile"
and a "hypnotically pleasing" figure—Mary Rogers had first come to the
public's attention several years earlier while working at a popular Broadway
"tobacco emporium" owned by an enterprising young merchant named
John Anderson. Though his customers represented a broad range of social
types—from young clerks and "sporting gents" to luminaries like Horace
Greeley, Washington Irving, and James Fenimore Cooper—they had one
thing in common: They were all men. Calculating (correctly) that a pretty
face behind the counter would be a boon to his business, the canny proprietor had hired the eighteen-year-old Mary in 1838 to serve less as a salesgirl
than as a sexual magnet.

The strategy worked. Anderson's profits soared as throngs of male admirers flocked to his shop to "preen and squawk before the young lady." Dubbed the "Beautiful Cigar Girl" in the city papers (many of whose reporters were also patrons of the store), Mary became a prototype of the modern celebrity, known for being known. Her charms were extolled in newspaper articles—one of which likened her to a luminous candle set out to catch the moths "that flutter around so attractive a center"—and celebrated in doggerel verse:

> She's picked for her beauty from many a belle,
> And placed near the window, Havanas to sell,
> For well her employer's aware that her face is
> An advertisement certain to empty his cases.[11]

In 1840, two years after entering Anderson's employ, Mary quit the shop to manage a boardinghouse leased by her sixty-year-old mother, Phebe. Located at 126 Nassau Street, in the heart of the city's booming printing and publishing trade, the three-story redbrick building catered to a clientele of young, single workingmen. A number of them, including a cork cutter named Daniel Payne who had become romantically involved with Mary, were residing there on Sunday, July 25, 1841, when the "comely young woman"—after announcing that she was on her way to make a Sabbath visit to an aunt—left the house at around 10:00 in the morning and was never seen alive again.

• • •

Less than an hour after the drowned and disfigured body was dragged onto the shore, Hoboken coroner Dr. Richard H. Cook arrived on the scene. The results of his autopsy were of so shocking a nature that newspapers could only hint at the more lurid details. Before being dumped in the river, Mary (so Cook concluded) had been beaten, gagged, tied, and ultimately strangled to death with a strip of fabric torn from her underskirt. Even more appallingly, bruises on her "feminine region" left no doubt in the coroner's mind that the "unfortunate girl" had been gang-raped: "brutally violated by no fewer than three assailants."[12]

Because of the heat and the body's already advanced state of decay, a temporary burial was quickly arranged. Encased in a rough pine box, Mary's corpse was placed in a shallow grave not far from where it had been brought ashore. Two weeks later, it was disinterred and taken back to New York City for a second examination. By then her remains presented what James Gordon Bennett described as a spectacle "more horrible and humiliating to humanity" than the "most imaginative mind could conceive":

> There lay, what was but a few days back, the image of its Creator, the loveliest of his works, and the tenement of an immortal soul, now a blackened and decomposed mass of putrefaction, painfully disgusting to sight and smell. Her skin, which had been so unusually fair, was now black as that of a negro. Her eyes so sunk in her swollen face as to have the appearance of being violently forced beyond the sockets, and her mouth, which "no friendly hand had closed in death," was distended as wide as the ligaments of the jaw would admit, and wore the appearance of a person who had died from suffocation or strangulation. The remainder of her person was alike one mass of putrefaction and corruption on which the worms were reveling at their will.[13]

The sheer ghoulish verve of this description is typical of Bennett's shameless style. Trumpeting Mary's death as "one of the most heartless and atrocious murders that was ever perpetrated in New York," he filled his paper with graphic descriptions of the injuries inflicted on the "poor girl," feverish speculations about the identity of her "brutal ravishers and murderers," and outraged attacks on the local police force for its failure to make an arrest.

As Bennett intended, the case became the talk of the town, generating an unprecedented wave of public excitement. "I can call to mind no similar occurrence producing so general and so intense an effect," one contemporary wrote. "For several weeks, in the discussion of this one absorbing theme, even the momentous political topics of the day were forgotten."[14] Besides Bennett, other enterprising spirits found ways to profit from the tragedy. Daguerreotypists peddled souvenir "likenesses" of the victim, while hack journalists turned out instant true-crime pamphlets containing full "particulars of the murder" accompanied by prurient accounts of Mary's love life—the various "attempts at courtship and seduction brought about by her manifold charms."[15]

Typical of the sites of sensational murders, Elysian Fields quickly became a ghoulish tourist attraction. Crowds of the morbidly curious flocked to the crime scene and picnicked on the very spot where Mary's corpse had been dragged ashore. One headmistress of a Manhattan girls' school even brought her little charges there on a field trip, under the pretext of delivering a lesson on the "wages of sin."[16]

All this frenzied interest could not fail to attract the attention of the writer who regarded the death of a beautiful young woman as "the most poetical topic in the world": Edgar Allan Poe. Living in Philadelphia at the time of the murder, Poe followed the story closely in the local press, particularly in the *Saturday Evening Post,* which "reprinted nearly all of James Gordon Bennett's coverage from the *Herald.*"[17] Besides his general fascination with the macabre, Poe reputedly had a more personal reason for taking a keen interest in the case. Four years earlier, while residing in Manhattan, he himself had supposedly been a frequent visitor to John Anderson's tobacco emporium and was acquainted with the Beautiful Cigar Girl.[18]

Whatever the truth of this story, it is undeniable that Poe, who kept a close eye on the news for potential source material, quickly came to see the literary and commercial possibilities of the Mary Rogers case. Before long, he would turn it into a classic work of fiction, a sequel to his trail-blazing detective story "The Murders in the Rue Morgue," starring C. Auguste Dupin, the progenitor of Sherlock Holmes and every amateur sleuth to follow. Called "The Mystery of Marie Roget," the story is such a thinly disguised version of the actual events that it amounts to little more than a transposition of the facts to a Parisian setting. To ensure that readers don't miss the connection, Poe helpfully points out at the start of the tale that its details will be known to anyone familiar with "the late murder of Mary Cecilia Rogers at New York."[19]

· · ·

In the weeks following the murder, the police focused their attentions on one suspect after another. Daniel Payne, Mary's fiancé at the time of her death, was rumored to have killed her in a jealous rage when she abruptly broke off their engagement. A young sailor named William Kiekuck—a former boarder at the Rogerses' lodging house—fell under suspicion because (according to the coroner's report) her bonnet had come undone during the murder, then was retied beneath her chin with a "sailor's knot." A neighbor named Joseph Morse—a philandering, wife-beating cad and a regular at Anderson's Tobacco Emporium—was arrested in Worcester, Massachusetts, after fleeing New York in the wake of the crime. Another of Mary's male acquaintances, one Archibald Padley, was taken to the city prison and subjected to a prolonged interrogation on evidence so slight as to be virtually nonexistent.[20]

In rapid succession, each of these suspects was cleared and released from custody. By the end of August—despite a one-thousand-dollar reward raised by private citizens and the promise of a pardon by Governor William Seward for any accomplice who would come forward and identify the killer—the police were no closer to a solution.

It was not until the middle of September that the public learned of a sensational development in the case. At its center was a widow named Frederica Loss, proprietor of a popular roadhouse not far from where Mary's body had been discovered. Several weeks earlier, while out collecting sassafras bark, Mrs. Loss's two sons, twelve and sixteen years of age, had reportedly come upon some articles of Mary Rogers's apparel—including a silk scarf, petticoat, and handkerchief monogrammed with her initials—within a dense thicket of beech trees and briar shrubs. The little hollow within the thicket "was stamped about, and the branches were broken, and the roots bruised and mashed, all betokening that it had been the scene of a very violent struggle."[21]

Mrs. Loss immediately reported the discovery to the police, though it didn't hit the papers until Friday, September 17, when James Gordon Bennett devoted an entire page to the story, complete with a woodcut engraving of Mrs. Loss's inn under the headline "The House Where Mary Rogers Was Last Seen Alive." According to Bennett, the evidence at the scene confirmed his own pet theory that Mary had been murdered by a gang of "miscreants." Giving free rein to his most lurid speculations, he declared, "It appeared . . . as if the unfortunate girl had been placed upon the middle of a broad stone, her head held forcibly back, and then and there horribly violated by several rowdies and ultimately strangled."[22]

As it happened, on the very day that New Yorkers were poring over this harrowing story, another "awful atrocity" was taking place in their midst. Before long, it would supplant the Mary Rogers case from the papers. It would also provide Edgar Allan Poe with the raw material for another classic work of fiction—this one not a tale of mystery and detection but of sheer grotesque horror.

19

*D*espite his distinguished name, Samuel Adams was sufficiently obscure that virtually no records exist of his sadly abbreviated life. The few surviving documents show that he was born in Providence, Rhode Island, in 1811 and, as a boy, apprenticed in the printing establishment of Smith & Parmenter at no. 9 Market Street.

Along with such weighty tomes as the *History of the General or Six Principle Baptists, in Europe and America*, Smith & Parmenter published both the popular newspaper the *Literary Cadet and Rhode-Island Statesman* and the weekly quarto the *Toilet, or, Ladies' Cabinet of Literature*. Like other publishers of the time, they also worked as job printers, offering "to execute any business in the printing line," including "books, show-bills, cards, shop bills, lottery tickets, and blanks of every description, at the shortest notice, and in the first style."[1]

In 1826 the senior partner of the firm, Samuel Jenks Smith, wed a popular poet named Sarah Louisa Hickman, author of a frequently anthologized verse, "White Roses" ("They were gathered for a bridal! / And now, now they are dying, / And young Love at the altar / Of broken faith is sighing"). Three years later, Smith and his wife left Rhode Island for Cincinnati. Sometime around 1832—the exact date is unclear—they moved to New York City, where Smith founded a weekly periodical, the *Sunday Morning News*.[2] Whether Smith was instrumental in bringing his former apprentice to New York City is also unclear, though it is certain that, by 1836, Samuel Adams was residing in Manhattan and running his own printing business at no. 38 Gold Street with an older partner, Frederic Scatcherd.

Though they began modestly enough by producing such works as M. Purvis's catchily titled pamphlet *On the Use of Lime as Manure*, Scatcherd and Adams were soon turning out a range of handsomely made books, including editions of James Boswell's *Life of Samuel Johnson*, Alexis de Tocqueville's *Democracy in America*, Joseph Rodman Drake's *The Culprit Fay, and Other Poems*, and *The Gospel Good News to Sinners* by Henry James, Sr. Within two years of its founding, the firm had gained such a high reputation among the literati of New York that, upon the announcement of the forthcoming publication of William L. Stone's *Life of Joseph Brant*, the critic for *American Monthly Magazine* could confidently assert that "as it is to be issued from the elegant press of Messrs. Scatcherd and Adams, the public may expect a beautifully printed book."[3]

In 1839, however, the firm suffered a severe blow when Frederic Scatcherd died of consumption. By then Adams was wed to the former Miss Emeline Lane and was residing at no. 23 Catherine Street, a short walk from his printing shop. With the loss of his more experienced partner—and with the country in the throes of the worst financial crisis since the Panic of 1819—Adams fell on difficult times. By the summer of 1841, he was behind in his mortgage payments, owed money to his workers, and was being threatened with a lawsuit by a creditor.[4]

Feeling increasingly besieged, he began to take a belligerent tone with customers behind on their payments. One of these was a young merchant named Lyman Ransom. During the preceding two years, Ransom had hired Adams to do roughly $1,500 worth of jobbing work—advertising circulars, handbills, and so on. Though Ransom had never failed to pay his debts, he had fallen a bit behind and owed the printer $110 on a note due August 31, 1841. A week before then, he showed up at the Gold Street office to ask for an extension.

Adams immediately flew into a rage. After enduring several minutes of verbal abuse—during which Adams alternated between bitter accusations that "everybody was trying to cheat him" and pitiable laments that he was desperate for money "and could not pay his hands"—Ransom offered his gold watch as partial payment. A handsome piece engraved on the back with an image of the U.S. Capitol Building, it was worth $100, according to Ransom. Adams agreed to take it at a value of $85, with the balance of the unpaid bill due in cash. Several days later, the beleaguered printer attempted to sell the watch to a neighbor named Nicholas Conklin for $95.[5]

With his business in trouble, Adams clung to the work thrown his way by the various organizations he belonged to. Thanks to his membership in the Brick Church on Beekman Street, for example—where he and Emeline also sang in the choir—he was hired to print the *Missionary Herald*, the monthly publication of the Board of Foreign Missions of the Presbyterian Church.[6] By joining the Apollo Association for the Promotion of Fine Arts in the United States—an organization dedicated to nurturing American artists and fostering an appreciation of their work among the general public—he was able to secure the job of printing its biannual exhibition catalogues.[7]

Precisely how he became acquainted with John C. Colt is another of the many mysteries surrounding Samuel Adams's life. What we do know is that they met sometime around 1838 and that, by the summer of 1841, Colt had contracted with Adams to produce the ninth edition of *The Science of Double Entry Book-Keeping*.[8]

20

On the northwest corner of Broadway and Chambers Street, across from City Hall Park and less than a block away from Anderson's Tobacco Emporium, stood an imposing edifice called, for self-explanatory reasons, the Granite Building. A full four stories high, it would later be converted into a popular hotel named the Irving House before being occupied by Delmonico's restaurant in the decade leading up to the Civil War.

In the fall of 1841, it housed a variety of tenants, many connected to the arts. On the top floor was the gallery of the Apollo Association, where, from nine in the morning until nine at night, visitors could view works by some of the nation's most prominent artists, among them William Dunlap, Rembrandt Peale, Asher Durand, and Thomas Sully. The sculptor Harris Kneeland kept a studio in the building, as did Edward Augustus Brackett, whose statuary display *The Binding of Satan* opened for public exhibition in the spring of that year. Several early daguerreotypists, including John Johnson, Alexander Simon Woolcott, and Augustus Morand, rented space in the building, as did assorted picture-frame makers and dealers in artists' materials.

Other tenants were engaged in more prosaic pursuits. A number of stores, including a pharmacy, a bookseller, and a "fancy goods" shop, occupied the ground floor, while a phrenologist named Dr. E. Newberry conducted his quackery upstairs on the third. On the second floor was the office of a gentleman named Asa H. Wheeler, a teacher of bookkeeping and penmanship who tutored private students in his rooms.[1]

Wheeler, as he would later testify, had known John Colt for three years.

Indeed, along with other respected figures in the field, he had supplied a written testimonial for Colt's accounting text that was prominently featured in advertisements for the book ("I would recommend this work to such as wish to gain a knowledge of the principles of Book-keeping, and as a book of reference for the experienced").[2] In early August, Colt had come to the Granite Building to ask Wheeler about renting the smaller of his two adjoining rooms for six weeks. Wheeler was amenable to the arrangement, and the two agreed that Colt was "to pay . . . ten dollars at the end of four weeks, and five more at the end of six—making fifteen dollars in all."[3]

Colt's room, its lone window facing Chambers Street, was a dreary place—a solitary "uncarpeted office . . . of a dusty, haggard sort of appearance," as Herman Melville later pictured it.[4] Its sole furnishings were a few comfortless chairs, a plain table, a trunk, and a wooden box measuring roughly three feet long and two feet in height and width. The latter had been constructed by Colt himself, who assembled all the shipping crates for his books. A combination hatchet-hammer, the tool he employed for that purpose, lay on one corner of his table.

Though he would later deny it, Colt, like Samuel Adams, was under intense financial pressure in the fall of 1841. Proud and prickly under the best of circumstances, he had become increasingly surly in his dealings with demanding creditors. In early September, for example, a clerk named George F. Spencer arrived at Colt's office to collect an overdue payment on behalf of his employer, a bookseller named Homer Franklin. Colt responded by hurling profanities at Spencer and threatening to "pitch him out of the window." Around the same time, when a hotel keeper named Howard demanded settlement of an unpaid bill, Colt reportedly flaunted a scar on his arm. "Take care what you say," he had warned, darkly intimating that he had gotten the scar "from killing a man who had once dunned him for money."[5]

Asa Wheeler himself was involved in a nasty run-in with Colt over money. When Wheeler approached his tenant at the start of September and asked, in a perfectly civil tone, for his fifteen-dollar rent, Colt had exploded into such a violent temper that Wheeler was taken aback. Mild tempered by nature, Wheeler let the matter drop, feeling that "it was not worth getting wrathy about." Once Colt had calmed down, he offered Wheeler a number of his textbooks in payment, and the two "were on familiar terms again."[6]

To a great extent, Colt held Samuel Adams to blame for his financial predicament. Earnings from his textbook largely depended on the business he was able to transact at the big trade sales held periodically in New York, Philadelphia, Cincinnati, and Boston. Strictly limited to members of the industry, these were major auctions where publishers could dispose of their merchandise with maximum efficiency, and booksellers from around the country could acquire their stock at bargain prices.[7]

Because of production delays with the new edition of his book, Colt had already missed a recent trade sale conducted in New York City by the auction house of Bangs, Richards & Platt. That lost opportunity made it all the more urgent for him to have his books ready for an upcoming event in Philadelphia. Unfortunately, there had been problems with the binding of the book. For the previous three years, Colt had employed a binder named Ballou. Adams, however, had a business arrangement with a different binder, a fellow named Charles Wells. Though Colt was perfectly satisfied with Ballou, regarding him as "one of the finest men in the world," he had agreed—at Adams's urging and from "the purest feelings of charity" toward the financially strapped printer—to give the job to Wells.[8]

As of Thursday, September 16, however, the books—which had to be shipped off to Philadelphia at once if they were going to be part of the impending trade sale—were still not back from the bindery. Colt was determined to visit Charles Wells first thing in the morning and demand that the work be completed immediately. In the meantime, he was in a dark mood. Earlier that day, preparing to construct new shipping crates for his books, he had borrowed a handsaw from Mercy Octon, wife of the building's superintendent. When another tenant, a picture framer named Charles Walker, knocked on his door a few hours later and asked to use the saw, Colt (as Walker later testified) "came to the door, opened it but a very little way . . . and told me to go to hell."[9]

21

On Friday, September 17—the day that James Gordon Bennett broke the news about the discovery of Mary Rogers's belongings in the thicket in Weehawken, New Jersey—John Colt paid an early morning visit to Charles Wells's bindery at no. 56 Gold Street. Colt was relieved to learn that four hundred copies of his accounting text would be ready in time for the upcoming Philadelphia trade sale.

In the course of their conversation, Wells—whose financial affairs were closely tied to Samuel Adams's—inquired about Colt's outstanding printing bill. Colt assured him that the money would be forthcoming just as soon as he received the proceeds from the Philadelphia sales. After discussing a few other trivial matters, Colt departed.[1]

• • •

Several hours later, around noontime, Samuel Adams rose from the table where he had been dining with his wife, Emeline, and made ready to leave their home. He was dressed in a black coat and vest, a white cotton shirt, a black, high-collar neck band known as a stock—a standard item of men's fashion during that period—and gambroon pantaloons. On the little finger of his left hand he wore a gold ring, and in his vest pocket he carried the engraved gold watch he had taken as collateral from his delinquent customer, Lyman Ransom.

His wife, as she later stated, did "not know where he intended to go when he left home."[2]

• • •

Not long afterward, Mr. Adams appeared at his office, where he attended to various business matters. At some point, a clerk named John Johnson, employed at City Hall, dropped by to pick up a batch of documents that had been printed for his employer and exchanged a few words with Mr. Adams before taking his leave.

An hour or so after his departure, the shop foreman, Hugh Monahan, brought Mr. Adams the proof sheets for the October issue of the *Missionary Herald*. After checking them over, Adams left to deliver them to the office of the Board of Foreign Missions at the Brick Church on Beekman Street. As it happened, the City Hall clerk John Johnson, also a member of the church, was at the office too, having stopped by on a small errand. He would later identify the time of Adams's arrival as approximately 2:00 p.m.[3]

• • •

Adams remained at the headquarters of the Board of Foreign Missions for less than fifteen minutes. He then proceeded to Charles Wells's bookbinding shop, where he learned about John Colt's earlier visit. Colt, said Wells, was "very anxious to the get books off to Philadelphia as soon as possible."

"Go ahead and ship them," Adams replied. "I am to get the proceeds."

Wells did not conceal his surprise. "There must be a misunderstanding between you," he said, explaining that Colt also "expected to receive the proceeds."

Upon hearing this news, Adams became visibly agitated—"vexed and excited," as Wells later described it. Exclaiming that he would "go see Colt" at once, he hurried from the office.

The time, Wells subsequently testified, was "about three o'clock."[4]

• • •

Situated in the northeast corner of City Hall Park was a circular brick building called the Rotunda. It had been erected in 1817 by the artist John Vanderlyn upon his return from Paris, where—thanks to financial support from his patron, Aaron Burr—he had gone to study in the atelier of the neoclassicist François Antoine Vincent. During the first years of its existence, Vanderlyn's imposing New York City gallery housed a number of his panoramic paintings, including *Panoramic View of the Palace and Gardens of Versailles* and *The Battle of Waterloo*, as well as his depictions of Adam and Eve in a state of semi-undress. Though the scandal created by the public display of these partially nude figures drew the predictable crowds of gawkers, Vanderlyn's enterprise—often considered the city's first art museum—proved a "complete financial failure. " The "unfortunate artist was forced to surrender his property to the city," which employed it "successively as the home of the Court of Sessions, the Naturalization Office, and the Post Office."[5]

Shortly after 3:00 p.m. on September 17, the City Hall clerk John Johnson, having completed an errand at the Rotunda, was emerging from the building when he spotted Samuel Adams walking briskly up Centre Street toward Broadway. Johnson had already seen and spoken to the printer twice that day, first at Adams's shop, then at the Board of Foreign Missions office. This time Adams "took no notice" of the clerk. A look of grim determination on his face, the printer strode toward the corner of Broadway and Chambers.

"I turned and looked after him," Johnson later said, describing the last time he ever set eyes on Samuel Adams. "He kept on."[6]

lmost certainly, the noise that Asa Wheeler and his pupil heard from the neighboring room did not sound precisely as they later described it: "like the clashing of foils, as if persons were fencing."[1] Though a lethal weapon was involved, the noise was generated by the impact of blade against bone, not metal on metal.

There are good reasons why the two men might have been mistaken. Immersed in their lesson, they were not paying close attention to the goings-on next door. The intervening wall would also have distorted the sound. And though it was a cold and drizzly day, the Broadway-facing windows of Wheeler's office had been raised, filling the room with the ceaseless clamor of the great thoroughfare and obscuring any noise from next door.

Still, while it might not have sounded exactly like the striking of swords, the sound was sufficiently jarring to startle them from their work.

"What was that?" said Wheeler, looking up from the sheet of ruled paper on which he had been inscribing a basic bookkeeping exercise for his student.

Seated beside him on the bench, Wheeler's student—a sixteen-year-old named Arzac Seignette, who was there for his first day of lessons—replied that he had no idea.

Rising from the bench, Wheeler crossed his room and stepped into the hallway, Seignette following close behind. The time was around 3:15 p.m., Friday, September 17.

With his ear pressed to Colt's door, Wheeler listened intently. Silence. Kneeling, he put his eye to the keyhole, but the drop was down on the inside of the door. In his right hand, he still clutched the steel pen he had been using when he and Seignette were interrupted by the strange noise. Inserting the tip of the pen into the keyhole, he slid the drop aside and peered into Colt's room.

From his highly restricted viewpoint, he could make out "a man with his coat off bent over a person who was lying on the floor." According to his later accounts, he watched for a full ten minutes, until the stooping figure straightened up and moved to a table "on which there were two men's hats."[2]

Quickly, Wheeler rose and—instructing Seignette to keep a close eye on Colt's door—hurried up to the top floor, where he knocked on the door of the landlord, Charles Wood. Receiving no response, Wheeler tried the doors of several other occupants, but no one was in, "it being the dinner hour."

As he was descending the stairs, he encountered Law Octon. An elderly African-American fellow who resided on the third floor with his wife, Mercy, Octon worked as the building superintendent and served as a deacon in the Zion Baptist Church.[3] At Wheeler's urging, Octon accompanied him to Colt's office and—using the pen to open the drop—looked through the keyhole. Octon, however, could see nothing and, after a few fruitless minutes of peeping, returned to his apartment.

Convinced that Colt was inside, Wheeler tiptoed down the flight of stairs, then returned with a heavy tromp and rapped sharply on Colt's door—a ploy, as he subsequently explained, "to make Colt think he had a caller and open the door." The stratagem did not work. No one answered.

By then several more of Wheeler's students had shown up, along with John Delnous, a twenty-six-year-old bookkeeper who was interested in renting Wheeler's second room at the end of Colt's tenancy. Wheeler immediately explained what had happened. At first, Delnous laughed off his suspicions. True, there had evidently been a strange commotion in Colt's room, followed by a peculiar, prolonged silence. Still, there might be an innocent explanation. Wheeler was so convinced that something was seriously amiss, however, that when he asked Delnous to go find a police officer, the younger man agreed.

He returned to say that the "officers were all presently engaged but one of them, named Bowyer, promised to come within a half hour."[4]

In those days, before the creation of a professional police department, the city was "inadequately protected" by an "archaic system" that had barely evolved since colonial times. Thirty-one constables and a hundred city mar-shals made up the bulk of the daytime force. At night, the policing of the city fell to a "patchwork corps" of watchmen, made up of moonlighting day laborers—stevedores, mechanics, teamsters, and the like. These part-time de-fenders of the public order—who patrolled the streets after dark and stood guard in sentry boxes—wore no uniforms. Besides a thirty-three-inch wooden club, their only badge of office was a distinctive leather helmet resembling a fireman's old-fashioned headgear and varnished to the hardness of iron. While not precisely laughingstocks, these amateur lawmen were, as one early historian puts it, not held "in especial reverence or dread" by the city's crimi-nal element, who derisively referred to them as "Leatherheads" and made them the butt of assorted pranks. A favorite was "upsetting a watch-box with a snoring Leatherhead inside it or lassoing the sentry-box with a stout rope and dragging it along with the imprisoned occupant inside it."[5]

Along with Delnous and a pair of students named Riley and Wood, Wheeler waited in his office for Bowyer's arrival. Given the dismal state of law enforcement at that period, however, it is no surprise that Officer Bowyer never showed up.

When dusk fell, Wheeler tried again, sending the two students out into the streets in search of a policeman. They returned a short time later with a message from the neighborhood officers, who explained that they had no authority to enter Colt's room and suggested that Wheeler continue to keep watch. Soon after, Riley and Wood left for the night. Delnous went out to refresh himself with a cup of tea, returning at around 7:30 p.m.

He and Wheeler sat together in the office until 9:00, at which point the exhausted older man took his leave. About a half hour later, Delnous, who had promised to keep vigil all night if necessary, was suddenly roused to at-tention by a sound from the hallway. As he would eventually describe it, he

> heard someone unlock Mr. Colt's door from the inside, come out, lock it again, and go away. The person returned in about five minutes, and in about five minutes more, I heard someone in Mr. Colt's room tearing something re-sembling cotton cloth. The next sound was the rattling of water—after that, some person scrubbing the floor, contin-ually putting his cloth in the water and rinsing it.[6]

Afterward, all was silence again in Colt's room. Delnous continued to listen closely until weariness overcame him. Stretching out on the bench by Wheeler's worktable, he promptly fell asleep.

•   •   •

Normally, John Colt was back at the boardinghouse room he shared with his mistress Caroline Henshaw by 10:00 p.m. On the night of September 17, however, he was later than usual. Tired of waiting up for him, the pregnant Caroline went to bed.

She woke up to see him standing at the foot of the bed, slipping on his nightshirt.

"What time is it?" she asked.

"A little after eleven," he said.

"Why are you home so late?"

"I was with a friend from Philadelphia," said John. "He leaves by boat tomorrow morning. I should go see him off."

A short time later, he blew out the candle and slipped into bed. By then, Caroline had already fallen back to sleep.

When she opened her eyes the next morning, John was already dressed and about to leave. Through the lace-curtained window, she saw that it was still dark outside. Peering at the clock that stood upon the bed table, she saw that it was not quite 5:30.

"Where are you going so early?" she asked.

"To the boat," he said. "I might be back soon, or I might not."

When breakfast was served downstairs several hours later, however, John had still not returned.[7]

•   •   •

In his later testimony, John Delnous could not say whether the sound he heard issuing from the neighboring room at around 6:00 in the morning of Saturday, September 18, was "the first noise I heard after I awoke, or the noise that awakened me." He had no doubt, however, about its source.

The noise from John Colt's office, Delnous would state, was "as of someone nailing a wooden box, which sounded as if it was full."[8]

23

Around daybreak that Saturday, the rain began to fall.

Shortly after 8:00 a.m., Law Octon returned to the Granite Building from an early morning errand. As he approached the staircase, he looked up and saw, standing on its end at the top of the first-floor landing, a pine box measuring roughly three feet long and two feet in height and width. A moment later, John Colt emerged from his office, "laid hold of the box," lowered it onto its side, and—with his face toward the crate and his back to Octon—began grappling it down the stairs, "placing his shoulder against the box to prevent it from going too fast." Octon waited at the foot of the staircase until Colt made it all the way down with his burden, then headed up to begin his custodial chores for the day.[1]

• • •

At the same time, a young man named John B. Hasty arrived at the Granite Building. Hasty lodged at a rooming house whose proprietress, in addition to her duties as landlady, managed "the business of carving, gilding, and making picture frames." He had come to deliver a message on her behalf to one of the artists who rented studio space in the building, a portrait painter by the name of Verbruyck.

As Hasty stepped from the street into the entranceway, he saw, as he later recalled, a man in his shirtsleeves taking a large wooden box down the first flight of stairs "with his back towards the street and supporting the box

as it came downstairs." Hasty waited until "the man had got the box downstairs and placed it on the right side of the entryway," near a door belonging
to a corner drugstore called Slocum's. Hasty then climbed to the fourth floor
and knocked on Verbruyck's door. When no one answered, he went back
downstairs, passing Law Octon—"an elderly light colored man" in Hasty's
description—who was sweeping the hallway of the second floor.

When he reached street level, Hasty saw the shirt-sleeved gentleman
still standing in the entry beside the crate. Hasty "asked the man if he knew
where Mr. Verbruyck was." The man gave a brusque reply, saying "that he
did not live in the building." As Hasty made his exit, he glanced down at
the box and "observed that it was marked on the outside with blue ink."[2]

• • •

A few minutes later, Law Octon came downstairs again and saw the box "in
the entryway of the first floor, between the banister of the stairs and the
apothecary's store." Colt, standing there with "no coat or vest," was searching the street through the open doorway. He seemed, Octon said afterward,
"to be looking out for a cartman."[3]

• • •

Long before the advent of truckers and moving vans, the job of hauling
goods from one place to another in old New York was handled by professional cartmen. Members of this trade, numbering about three thousand in
1841, were licensed by the city council, which set the rates they were allowed to charge and fixed the size and shape of carts "in order to insure standard loads."

Cartmen who specialized in household moves required spring carts and
other equipment "suitable for transporting furnishings, pictures, looking-
glasses and other valuables." The ordinary "catch cartman," however—who
waited at a curbside cart-stand or roamed the streets ready "to grab the first
job that was offered"—drove a more rudimentary vehicle: little more than
a seatless wooden sled mounted on a pair of wagon wheels and hitched to a
dray horse. Standing atop their carts in their long white frock coats, heavy
black boots, and broad-brimmed hats, these hardy workingmen—"a cross
between the cab driver and teamster of today"—were a common sight in
nineteenth-century New York.[4]

• • •

At approximately 8:45 a.m. on that raw, drizzly Saturday, Richard Barstow, a thirty-four-year-old licensed cartman, was driving east on Chambers Street when he spotted a man—hatless, in shirtsleeves—beckoning to him from the doorway of the Granite Building. As Barstow pulled his dray horse to a halt, the man hurried over.

"Are you busy?" he asked. According to the cartman's subsequent testimony, he was a slender gentleman of approximately Barstow's age with thick curly hair and dark whiskers.

"Not particularly," said Barstow. "Why?"

The man explained that he wanted to have a crate delivered to a ship docked at the foot of Maiden Lane. Since Barstow was headed in that direction anyway, he agreed to take it.

Another cart was already parked lengthways at the curb in front of the building. It belonged to a fellow carter named Thomas Russell, who regularly hauled paintings to and from the Granite Building for the Apollo Association. Backing his own cart in front of Russell's horse, Barstow dismounted and followed the shirtsleeved gentleman into the Chambers Street entrance of the building.

There between the staircase and a door opening into Slocum's pharmacy sat a big pine crate. Assisted by Russell, Barstow loaded the box—which weighed, according to his estimate, "from one hundred and fifty to two hundred pounds"—onto his cart. As he did, he noticed that the box "was directed to the care of some person at New Orleans."

Stepping back to the doorway where the coatless gentleman had watched the proceedings in silence, Barstow asked him "to what ship I was to carry the box." The man replied that "he did not know the name of the vessel" but would follow Barstow and point it out to him.

Stepping onto his cart, Barstow took hold of the reins and began to drive slowly toward Maiden Lane. From time to time, he glanced back over his shoulder and saw the gentleman walking behind him beneath a green umbrella.[5]

On the bustling wharf at the foot of Maiden Lane, where tall-masted merchant ships from every port lay at anchor, Barstow came to a halt beneath the jutting bowsprit of a New Orleans–bound packet named the *Kalamazoo*. All around, men "swarmed from the warehouses to the boats with cargo of all descriptions, each box, bale, and barrel identified by its fragrance—rum, leather, coffee, tea, tar, hemp, spices."[6] Barstow, as he stated a few days later, "pointed to the vessel to know if that was the one, and the gentleman nodded assent."

Backing up his cart, Barstow took hold of the box and dropped it onto the wharf, "the same as I would a box of sugar." The gentleman then reached into his pocket, extracted some coins, and handed them wordlessly to Barstow, who, glancing down at his palm, saw that the money amounted to two shillings and sixpence. Barstow had intended to ask for three shillings but something about the look on the gentleman's face told the carter that haggling would be "more trouble than it was worth." With a flick of his reins, Barstow "cleared out," leaving the man standing beside the crate on the wharf.[7]

• • •

At around 9:30 a.m., just as Barstow was driving his cart away from the wharf, Asa Wheeler arrived at the Granite Building. Up in his office, he spoke to John Delnous, who had heard Colt wrestling the crate downstairs and—peering down from the first-floor landing—had seen him leave with the cartman.

Hurrying to the top floor, Wheeler rapped on the door of the landlord, Charles Wood. This time, Wood was home. Explaining what had transpired the previous day, Wheeler proposed that they search Colt's room. Wood was reluctant to take such a drastic step, advising "that it was a very delicate subject to meddle with." At Wheeler's urging, however, Wood handed over his master key.

Back downstairs before Colt's door, Wheeler listened for any sounds from within. Satisfied that Colt was still gone, he opened the lock, "stepped one foot in and looked around." He saw at once that the packing box that normally sat in the office was missing. He also noticed that the floor looked freshly scrubbed, particularly around the area where he'd seen the kneeling figure. And there were strange marks he had never seen before—"oil and ink spilled around the base of the floor and thrown in spots on the wall."

Stepping back into the hallway, he locked the door, returned the key to Wood, then retired to his office.[8]

. . .

He was seated at his worktable a half hour later when someone knocked on his door. Opening it, Wheeler found himself face-to-face with John Colt.

Colt surprised him with an unexpected question. Did Wheeler's key fit his door? he wanted to know.

"I'm not sure," Wheeler said. "Why?"

Colt said something about leaving his own key at home. Could he try Wheeler's?

Wheeler handed him the key and watched as Colt crossed to his door and tried the lock.

Satisfied that the key didn't work, Colt returned it to Wheeler, then stepped into the latter's office and began to chat "about bookkeeping and writing." He seemed, as Wheeler said later, "very talkative indeed"— unnaturally so for a man who was often rather standoffish. It took a while before Wheeler managed to get a word in. "Mr. Colt," he finally asked, "what was that noise in your room yesterday?"

Colt's expression seemed to harden for a moment before he arranged his features into a puzzled look. "You must be mistaken," he said. "I was out all afternoon."

"There most certainly was a noise," Wheeler insisted. "My pupil and I both heard it, and it quite alarmed us."

For a moment, Colt merely looked at Wheeler through narrowed eyes. Then, without another word, he turned on his heels and left the room.[9]

. . .

Caroline Henshaw was in the parlor of the rooming house conversing with another boarder when she saw John come through the front door and make for the stairs. A few minutes later, she excused herself and made her way up to their bedroom. The time was around 10:30 a.m.

When she stepped into the room, she saw John getting undressed. Assuming that he was changing his clothes, she took a seat by the window and stared out at the rain. When she looked back, she was startled to see John in his nightshirt, his street clothes draped over the back of a chair.

After using a washcloth to bathe his neck with liniment, he climbed into bed. No word had yet passed between them. Concerned that he might be sick—"it being unusual for him to go to bed in the day"—Caroline rose from the chair and walked to the bed.

Immediately she noticed a large black-and-blue mark on the side of his neck. She began to ask him about the strange bruise—"if it was a pinch or something of the kind"—but before she could finish her sentence, he raised one hand and pushed her away from the bed.

Retreating to the seat by the window, she busied herself with sewing, looking up from her stitchwork every now and then to glance at John. He remained in bed until dinner hour, though "he did not appear to sleep much. He seemed restless."

For the next two or three nights, John continued to apply liniment to his neck before coming to bed—not something he normally did. And there was something else Caroline noticed too. As a general rule, John slept with the neck of his nightshirt open. Now, however, as she would eventually testify, "he slept with his nightshirt pinned up."[10]

24

*I*f the noise coming from John Colt's room on Friday afternoon had struck Asa Wheeler as strange, the one he heard on Monday morning was, in its way, just as peculiar. Colt, arriving at his office at around 10:30, unlocked the door, stepped inside, and broke into song. Wheeler had never heard Colt sing before, certainly not so spiritedly. It was as though he were performing for Wheeler's benefit—to demonstrate that he was a man without a care in the world.

Wheeler, who had come to work about an hour earlier, had been keeping an ear cocked for Colt's arrival. Now, using a piece of bookkeeping business as a pretext, he rapped on the door separating their rooms and was instantly invited inside.

He found Colt seated at his desk, a long Havana clenched in his teeth and a phosphorus match in one hand. Would Wheeler care to join him? Colt asked, lighting the cigar.

Wheeler, who occasionally took a pinch of snuff but was not a smoker, declined.

Colt, as Wheeler would later recall, "observed that he had a very bad habit of smoking." Indeed, he indulged to such "a great extent" that he had "begun to spit blood." With a motion of the hand, he drew Wheeler's attention to a spot on the wall where, Wheeler noted, "there were thirty or forty dark specks."

After chatting for a few minutes about the matter that had ostensibly brought him there, Wheeler "referred again to the noise" he had heard the previous Friday.

"To tell you the truth, Wheeler," Colt said somewhat sheepishly, "I upset my table, spilled my ink, and knocked down the books, making a deuced mess. I hope it didn't disturb you."

Wheeler made no reply, though he thought it odd that Colt—who originally claimed not to have been in the office at all that afternoon—had so completely changed his story. A few moments later, he returned to his own room.[1]

Over the next few days, he and Colt encountered each other frequently in the hall and exchanged pleasantries as if everything were perfectly normal. Every morning, however, in the privacy of his office, Wheeler pored over the newspapers, looking for any item that might confirm his suspicions.

He found it on Wednesday.

• • •

In 1841 the New York *Sun*—now under the proprietorship of Moses Yale Beach, brother-in-law of the paper's founder, Benjamin Day—consisted of four oversized pages, each seven columns wide and crammed with paid notices and advertisements: row after row of real estate offerings; announcements for steamboat and packet departures; reward postings for runaway apprentices, lost hogs, and stray cows; situation-wanted classifieds for dry-goods clerks, housemaids, and governesses; and ads for a vast assortment of goods and services.

On Wednesday morning, September 22, amid ads for Michaux's Freckle Wash, Clirehugh's Ventilating Wigs, Fisk's Novelty Cook Stove, Glenn's Indian Hair Oil, Levitt's Artificial Teeth, and Dr. Quackenbush's "fine Swedish leeches (sold wholesale or retail on favorable terms)," the following notice appeared on page two:

> Any information respecting Mr. Samuel Adams, Printer, who left his place of business on Friday, September 17, about 3 o'clock, P.M. will be thankfully received by his relatives and friends at no. 23 Catherine St., or cor of Ann and Gold, who are unable to account for his sudden disappearance. From an investigation of his business, there does not appear to be an assignable cause for his absence; the

only conjecture is that he has met with some violence, but when or in what manner is still a mystery. [2]

No sooner had Asa Wheeler spotted this notice than he threw on his coat, hurried from the building, and bent his steps toward Catherine Street. The foul weather that had arrived on Saturday morning still held the city in its grip, and heavy rain pelted from the sky.

No. 23 Catherine Street turned out to be the abode of Samuel Adams's father-in-law, Joseph Lane, who was not at home when Wheeler got there. Leaving word that he had important information to convey, Wheeler returned to the Granite Building. He remained in his office until early evening, but Lane never showed up.

· · ·

Seated in his office that same afternoon, the bookbinder Charles Wells was so immersed in his paperwork that he did not hear the front door open. A moment later, someone laid a hand on his desk. Looking up, he saw John Colt standing there, rain dripping from the brim of his tall beaver hat.

His face wrought into a look of deep concern, Colt explained that he had just seen the newspaper notice regarding Samuel Adams. "It's very strange," he said. "What could have become of him?"

"I don't know," said Wells. "The last I saw of him, he said he was going to see you."

Colt made no direct reply to this observation. "I hope nothing's happened to him. He's a fine man. Always treated me well," he said.

The two men spoke briefly about the impending Philadelphia trade sale. Then—repeating his "hope that nothing has happened"—Colt turned and hurried out into the rain.[3]

· · ·

The following day, the *Sun* carried another notice on its second page:

> The Mysterious Disappearance of Mr. Samuel Adams, Printer, continues a mystery, as every pains have been taken by his friends to ascertain any cause, but hearing nothing, his friends and family would still wish that any

person who might have seen him after 3 o'clock, Friday the 17th, would give notice of the same at 23 Catherine St. as it is feared that he has met with some violence.[4]

By then, other newspapers had picked up the story. That morning, both the *Morning Courier and New-York Enquirer* and the *New-York Weekly Tribune* ran identical items:

> Mr. Samuel Adams, printer, at the corner of Ann and Gold Streets, left his office on Friday last to do some business at the Office of the Missionary Herald and has not since returned or been heard of by his friends. Great concern is felt for his fate. His pecuniary affairs were not embarrassed, he had some money with him and was a man of exemplary moral and religious character. It is hardly possible that he should have gone off voluntarily, if in his right mind. Any information of him directed to Mr. J. A. Lane, no. 23 Catherine Street, or to Mr. Adams' printing office, corner of Ann and Gold Streets, will be gratefully received by his afflicted family.

James Gordon Bennett published a very similar item in the *Herald*, although—with his usual flair for the sensational—he printed it under the eye-catching heading "Supposed Murder!"[5]

Later that day, Joseph Lane finally appeared at Asa Wheeler's office. With him was one of the missing printer's employees: a fellow by the name of Loud, who had brought along Samuel Adams's most recent accounting ledger. The three men spent some time examining the records with particular attention to any transactions involving John Colt. They then went across the street to City Hall and proceeded directly to the office of the mayor, Robert Hunter Morris.

A popular and efficient administrator who was ultimately elected to three consecutive terms, Morris, by the charter and laws then in effect, was head of the city police. In the coming years, he would draft the law replacing the antiquated watchman system with a professional force. Now, after listening with mounting concern to the suspicions of Wheeler and his companions, Morris accompanied the three men to the Granite Building, where he interviewed several witnesses, including Law Octon.

Early the next morning, Friday, September 24, a messenger arrived at the home of Police Magistrate Robert Taylor with a note from Morris, summoning Taylor to City Hall at once. As soon as he arrived, Morris filled him in on the situation. The two then made their way across Broadway to the Granite Building, accompanied by a pair of police officers, A.M.C. Smith and David Waldron.

A note was tacked to Colt's door, saying that he was out but would return soon. Posting the two officers at the foot and the head of the staircase, Morris and Taylor waited inside Wheeler's office. A short time later, Colt arrived. As he unlocked his door, Morris stepped into the hall, introduced himself and his companion, and said that they "wished to see him inside his room."

"We all went in and closed the door," Morris recalled at a later date. "I then told him he was arrested on suspicion of killing Mr. Adams."[6]

25

After being read "the affidavits on which the arrest was founded," John was searched for weapons by Officer Waldron. He cooperated willingly, emptying his pockets and stripping off his frock coat to demonstrate that he carried neither pistol nor knife.[1]

In the meantime, Waldron's fellow officer, A.M.C. Smith, was dispatched to the Broadway office of the distinguished New York chemist Dr. James R. Chilton.[2] By the time Chilton arrived, Colt's hatchet-hammer had been found beneath some sheets of old newspaper on his desk.

While Colt and the others looked on, Chilton made a careful examination of the implement. Holding it up to the light, he "observed a red stain in the eye of the hatchet, apparently blood. There was also a similar spot on the hammer end." In addition, there were fresh ink stains on the wooden handle that appeared to have "been put on intentionally." Inspecting the handle closely, he could see "a reddish appearance through the ink."

Chilton then turned his attention to the rest of the room, noting the many fresh stains and ink spots on the walls and floor. After scraping some reddish-brown particles from a wall and removing a small section of floor-board with Colt's borrowed handsaw, Chilton carried his samples—including the hatchet-hammer—back to his laboratory for chemical analysis.[3]

Not long after his departure, John was escorted across the street to the mayor's office, where he asked to see his counsel—his cousin and former employer, Dudley Selden. An officer was sent to the latter's residence but returned a short while later to say that Selden wasn't at home. John was then taken to the Halls of Justice and locked in a holding cell—the beginning of a lengthy incarceration in the recently completed edifice whose architectural resemblance to an ancient Egyptian mausoleum had earned it the nickname "the Tombs."

. • •

That evening, Morris and Magistrate Taylor divided up their duties. The mayor assumed responsibility for tracking down the mysterious crate that John Delnous and others had seen carted away from the Granite Building under Colt's supervision. To that end, Morris composed a brief notice and had it conveyed to the office of the *Morning Courier and New-York Enquirer*. The notice—which appeared on page two the following morning, wedged between a reward posting for the return of a lost Irish setter and the announcement of an upcoming concert by Signor John Nagel, "Composer and Violinist to the King of Sweden and Pupil of Paganini!"—read as follows:

> The person who early on Saturday morning last, 18th, took a Box from the building on the north corner of Broadway and Chambers St. or any person who have seen a Box taken from said place at that time, will please call immediately at the Mayor's office, in the City Hall.
> —ROBT. H. MORRIS, Mayor[4]

In the meantime, Magistrate Taylor undertook the task of locating Colt's lodging place. By Saturday morning, he had ascertained the address. In the company of Officer Smith, he proceeded to the boardinghouse at no. 42 Monroe Street and, upon inquiring for Mrs. Colt, was introduced to the young woman who (as Taylor later put it) "was passing for his wife."

At the request of the two lawmen, Caroline—who had sat up all night in an increasingly frantic state, wondering what had become of John—led them upstairs to her room, where, beneath the bed, Taylor found a well-worn carpetbag containing a few oddments of clothing, nothing of any apparent significance. When he demanded to know where John kept his other possessions, Caroline "drew from a recess" a small locked trunk, which Taylor and Smith transported back to the Upper Police Office and opened in John's presence.

Inside, along with various letters, books, and advertising cards for *The Science of Double Entry Book-Keeping*, they found a few mementos of John's earlier life: his discharge papers from the Marine Corps and, lovingly preserved inside a folded piece of paper, locks of hair from his deceased mother and sisters.

There was something else, too—an item rather haphazardly wrapped in a sheet of newsprint. It would later be shown to Caroline, who would testify that she had never seen it before.

It was a gold pocket watch, handsomely engraved on its back with an image of the U.S. Capitol Building.[5]

26

Though the mayor was the official head of the city's licensed cartmen, their day-to-day affairs were overseen by the superintendent of carts, an officer paid five hundred dollars annually to ensure, among other things, "that all carts were in good working order and complied with city regulations."[1] In 1841 that position was held by a gentleman named William Godfrey.

On Saturday morning, September 25, while Magistrate Taylor was paying his visit to Caroline, Robert Morris sent for Godfrey. By the time he arrived at City Hall, Godfrey had already seen the mayor's notice in the *Morning Courier and New-York Enquirer* and knew why he'd been summoned. He suggested that they seek out Thomas Russell, who—so Godfrey explained—spent much of his time at the Granite Building performing jobs for members of the Apollo Association. Perhaps he might know something about the crate.

While the mayor attended to some urgent business, Godfrey headed across Broadway, where, as expected, he found the cartman stationed outside the Granite Building. In reply to the superintendent's queries, Russell explained that he had helped a colleague load just such a box onto a cart the previous week. Though he didn't know the fellow's name, he felt sure that he could recognize his horse.

With Godfrey beside him, Russell drove toward the waterfront and, before long, spotted the other cartman on Peck Slip. Godfrey immediately recognized him as Richard Barstow. After hearing the superintendent's description of the box, Barstow said that he "recollected it clearly" and proceeded to lead Godfrey to the *Kalamazoo*, still docked at the foot of Maiden Lane. There Godfrey learned from the first mate, Bill Coffin, that—having been delayed because of the bad weather—the ship was set to sail that very afternoon. Hurrying back to City Hall, Godfrey conveyed the information to the mayor, who "took immediate measures to detain the ship" in port.[2]

• • •

Shortly before 9:00 the following morning, Sunday, September 26, Mayor Morris arrived at the Maiden Lane wharf and boarded the *Kalamazoo*. He was accompanied by Magistrate Taylor, officers Smith and Waldron, the cartmen Richard Barstow and Thomas Russell, their supervisor, William Godfrey, and a crew of stevedores.

Under the direction of the ship's young second mate, Bill Blanck, the stevedores began to remove the cargo from the forward hatch. Along with other crew members of the packet, Blanck had been aware of a putrid odor emanating from below decks for several days. He had attributed the smell, however, to the effects of the poison that been scattered throughout the hold to clear the ship of vermin. Now, as the cargo was unloaded, it became increasingly clear that dead rats alone could not possibly account for the fetor.

They found the box three layers down, close to the bottom tier. Addressed in blue ink to "R. P. Gross, St. Louis, to care of Mr. Gray, New Orleans," it was identified by Barstow as the one he had hauled from the Granite Building the week before. Several of the men hoisted it onto the middle deck, where the lid was knocked off. The stench that arose caused several of the men, Thomas Russell among them, to flee aloft without looking inside.

Those who remained—most pressing handkerchiefs to their noses—saw a semi-naked, grotesquely contorted male body, trussed up with rope and partly covered with a piece of window awning. The exposed flesh was greenish with decomposition and—at least according to several of the witnesses—sprinkled with salt. Maggots swarmed everywhere.

Fetching some chloride of lime, the chief mate sprinkled the disinfectant powder over the corpse. The wooden lid was nailed back on, the crate hoisted to the top deck, then lowered over the side of the ship. By then a crowd of curiosity seekers had gathered at the wharf. They watched as the crate was lifted onto Barstow's cart and followed along as it was conveyed to the Dead House in City Hall Park.

There the lid was removed again, the corpse lifted from the box and placed on a rough wooden table. The rope was cut and the twisted body straightened out. So repulsive was its condition—so overpowering its stench—that no one could be found to wash it until a fellow named James Short, an attendant at the public alms house, agreed to do so for a fee of six dollars (the equivalent of one hundred fifty dollars in today's money).[3]

By the time Short had completed the task, Dr. C. R. Gilman, physician to the city prison, and his assistant, Dr. Richard S. Kissam, had arrived at the Dead House. At around 1:00 p.m., they began their postmortem examination of the carrion remains of Samuel Adams.

• • •

Their grim work was completed about two hours later. Not long afterward, Coroner Jefferson Brown convened an inquest in the old alms house. Until late in the evening, the jurors heard testimony from a string of witnesses, including Asa Wheeler, Law Octon, John Delnous, Dr. James Chilton, Richard Barstow, Thomas Russell, Mayor Morris, and Magistrate Taylor. They also heard from the *Kalamazoo*'s second mate, Bill Blanck, who had been taken to the Tombs earlier in the day. There, he had identified John Colt as the "man with the swarthy face, black side whiskers, and piercing black eyes" who had left the crate at the ship.[4]

Far and away the most shocking testimony came from Dr. Gilman. His summation of the autopsy was rendered all the more disturbing by his tone of bland clinical detachment—particularly his insistence on referring to the savaged victim as "it."

"It was a man rather under the middle size, stout rather than fat," Gilman began. "It measured five-feet-nine-and-a-half inches in height. It was very considerably decayed in all its parts. I should think it had been dead seven or eight days. Its head was so much decayed that the scalp could be pushed off by the rub of a finger."

Before the corpse was stuffed into the box, Gilman explained, it had been "tied with a rope around the knees and carried to the head. The thighs were strongly bent up and the head a little bent forward." Gilman then of-

fered a graphic description of the fatal injuries, all of which had been inflicted on the victim's head:

> The skull was fractured in several different places. The right
> side of the forehead, the socket of the eye, and a part of the
> cheekbone were broken in. On the left side the fracture was
> higher up. The brow had escaped, but above that the fore-
> head was beaten in. The two fractures communicated on the
> center of the forehead, so that the whole of the forehead was
> beaten in, also the right eye and a part of the right cheek.
> On the other side of the head, directly above the ear, there
> was a fracture, with depression of the bone—it was not de-
> tached, it was dented in. This fracture was quite small.
> There was also a fracture on the left side of the head, a little
> behind and above the ear, in which there was a round, clean
> hole, as if made by a musket ball, so that you might put your
> finger through it. There was no fracture on the back part of
> the head. When I examined the cavity of the skull, I found
> some pieces of bone, about the size of a half dollar, beaten in
> and entirely loose among the pulpy mass, which was the
> brain. The lower jaw was also fractured.

Apart from a shirt—which had been "ripped up and was hanging like a
gown from the arms"—the body was unclothed. Whoever had perpetrated
the atrocity, however, had overlooked one telltale piece of evidence that
Gilman had removed from the corpse and now displayed to the jurors: "a
small plain ring on the little finger of the left hand."[5]

The ring—along with some scraps of clothing that had been stuffed inside the crate—was identified by the final witness of the day, Emeline
Adams, who was also shown the gold watch discovered in John Colt's
trunk. She confirmed that her husband possessed a watch "precisely like
it—that he had gotten it for a debt very lately." He was carrying it, she declared, "when he left home after dinner" on the day he disappeared.[6]

It was late in the evening when the coroner's jury returned their verdict: "that the body was that of Mr. Samuel Adams and that, in their belief,
he came to his death by blows inflicted by John C. Colt."[7]

27

Though the Mary Rogers case was still the city's biggest crime story in the days leading up to John Colt's arrest, it was far from the only one. Murders, rapes, assaults—some of startling brutality—were regularly reported in the penny press.

In Hempstead, Long Island, a woman named Hall was killed by her African-American gardener, Alexander Beck, who fractured her skull with a shovel in an apparent fit of religious delirium. Another Long Island resident, a boat builder named Jesse Ryerson, had his throat cut by a journeyman worker named Smith, who dumped the victim's body into Hempstead Bay.

A few days later—in what the *Herald* immediately trumpeted as "Another Mary Rogers Case"—the corpse of a "good-looking young girl about twenty years of age," dressed "in a calico frock with purple fringes and muslin underclothes, but neither bonnet nor shoes," was found floating in the Hudson River. Even as her body was being transported to the Dead House, the trial of eighteen-year-old William Phelps, "accused of murdering George Phelps during a robbery," was getting under way in Brooklyn.

In Lower Manhattan, William Bolton—a twenty-year-old "soaplock" (slang for a dandyish youth who affected the style later called sideburns)— was arrested after attempting to rape "a stout, athletic Irish wench named Mary Farrell" as she entered her backyard to use the privy. Bolton, according to the *Herald*, "so far succeeded in his object that he seized her, laid her on the ground, and was preparing to have carnal knowledge of her when two other women extricated her from the clutches of the ravisher."

From farther afield came reports of the hanging of sixty-five-year-old Samuel Watson of Williamston, North Carolina, who was executed for the murder of a neighbor, Mrs. Fanny Garrett. "There was a plum orchard between their residences," reported the *Herald*, "and she was stooping, in the act of gathering plums, when he deliberately shot her dead, assigning as a cause that she was a witch and had conjured him." Shortly before his death, the twice-married Watson also confessed that he had "caused the death of both his wives."

That same week, another elderly Southerner, seventy-year-old John Davis, went on a rampage in a Greenville, South Carolina, boardinghouse when another lodger disturbed him from his sleep. Leaping from his bed, Davis "commenced an indiscriminate slaughter," stabbing "six men with a knife, two of whom—T. J. Larder, Esq., and Mr. Samuel Brawley—were killed."

Perhaps most shocking of all was a reported case of parricide in Bridgewater, Massachusetts, where twenty-year-old Henry Gunn brained his elderly father with a hatchet, then absconded with "money and valuables worth about $40,000," leaving the bloody weapon in a woodpile behind the house, its blade clotted with "tufts of hair from the head of the murdered man."[1]

None of these outrages, however, proved to be more than a passing diversion for readers of the sensational press. Once the Colt-Adams story broke on the morning of Monday, September 27, they were immediately forgotten.

Though multicolumn banner headlines didn't exist in 1841, the city papers trumpeted the news as loudly as their small-print format permitted.[2] Each of the dailies ran a version of the same attention-grabbing headline: "Awful Murder" (*New York American*), "Frightful Murder" (*Morning Courier and New-York Enquirer*), "Terrible Murder" (*Tribune*), "Another Shocking Murder" (*New-York Commercial Advertiser*), "Horrible Murder of Mr. Adams" (*Sun*), "Shocking Murder of Mr. Adams, the Printer" (*Herald*). The accompanying stories offered detailed accounts of the killing and the discovery of the victim's crated remains in the hold of the packet *Kalamazoo*.[3]

The case was an instant sensation, the talk of the town—"the subject of conversation among all classes of the community," as one newspaper put it.[4] By Monday afternoon, the site of the "awful murder" had already become the city's hottest attraction. Two floors above Colt's office, the Apollo Association's fine arts gallery had drawn so few visitors in the first years of its existence that, at its third annual meeting, the membership talked of shutting it down.[5] Now the same public that couldn't be lured to the Granite Building for its cultural offerings came flocking there in droves for a glimpse of the crime scene. Throughout the day, the northwest corner of Broadway and Chambers was so packed with curiosity seekers that pedestrians had to detour around the crowds.[6]

Even as the gawkers blocked the foot traffic on Broadway, craning their necks for a better view of Colt's second-story window, the man himself was being escorted from his cell to the office of Police Magistrate Taylor. There, attended by Dudley Selden and two other attorneys, Robert Emmett and John A. Morrill, he was examined by Taylor, who asked him his name, age, place of birth, and occupation. Colt replied firmly to these pro forma questions, hesitating only when asked if he was married. After a brief consultation with his lawyers, he replied, "I decline answering under the advice of my counsel."

"What have you to say to in relation to the charge against you?" asked Taylor.

"I decline answering any further questions by advice of my counsel," Colt repeated. "But I am innocent of the charge."

Newspapers described Colt's appearance and behavior during this examination in dramatically different, if not completely contradictory, ways. Most agreed that he was an "exceedingly prepossessing" man: about five feet nine inches tall and "very well made," with curly, dark brown hair and full side whiskers. Some, however, found his good looks marred by his eyes, reported to be of that "brown-colored class that cannot easily be read, and that are generally found in the faces of all scoundrels, schemers, and plotters."[7]

As for his mien, several accounts emphasized Colt's "remarkable composure," "singular coolness," "peculiar nonchalance"—a trait presumably in keeping with the "calculating deliberation" he had exhibited in his attempts to hide the evidence. Indeed, in the view of more than one observer, it was the callous way that Colt had gone about trying to "conceal the deed," even more than the murder itself, that made his crime an "enormity without parallel."[8]

This picture of Colt as a cold-blooded creature was reinforced by a widely printed story that the only emotion he had displayed at the examination was a flash of self-pity. "I don't think they treat me well with regard to my meals," he reportedly complained to Taylor before being led back to his cell. "They don't bring my dinner on a clean plate but on one that had been used before."[9]

In sharp contrast to this image of Colt as a man of "extraordinary coolness of nerve," other accounts depicted him as profoundly distraught during his brief appearance before Magistrate Taylor. "His face was of a ghastly paleness," wrote the reporter for the Commercial Advertiser, "his eyes deeply sunk into his head and fearfully wild in their expression. The few hours since the verdict of the inquest had been rendered had evidently been those of intense suffering, of deep mental anguish. The prisoner made a strong effort to maintain his composure, but the effort was clearly visible." Indeed, according to the same report, Colt was in such an "overwrought frame of mind" that "every means had been taken to prevent his committing self-destruction—a result he evidently contemplates."[10]

Of all the journalists in the city, James Gordon Bennett lavished the most loving attention on the Colt-Adams story, perceiving it from the start as a potential circulation booster on the order of the Helen Jewett and Mary Rogers cases. In Tuesday's issue of the Herald, for example, he ran a full-profile woodcut portrait of Colt—a highly unusual feature at a time when the typical newspaper page consisted of row upon row of eye-straining type, unrelieved by any illustrations. He was also the only journalist to describe Samuel Adams's burial on Monday, and to run a remarkable (if highly suspect) story about Adams's wife, Emeline. According to Bennett (who provides no source for his believe-it-or-not anecdote),

> some days before Adams was murdered, his wife dreamed that she saw him dead—murdered and script naked and put into a box, and his clothes thrown into a privy. She awoke and burst into tears; but finding her husband asleep by the side of her, she said nothing about it. The next night, she dreamed the same thing, and next day concluded to tell her mother of it; but finally laughed it off as

an idle dream. There is no doubt of the truth of these facts, and to say the least of it, it was very remarkable.[11]

Bennett, moreover, lost no time in exploiting the public's prurient interest in Colt's unsanctified relationship with Caroline Henshaw. Picking up on John's evasive replies to questions about his marital status, other papers had referred to "the female who has been kept by him for some time."[12] Bennett alone, however—resorting to proper French at a time when the word *pregnant* was considered too vulgar for public utterance—added a titillating detail. Colt's female companion, Bennett revealed, "is by him *enciente* and the period of her *accouchement* is near."[13]

It was Bennett who also provided the most extensive coverage of Colt's arraignment, which took place in the Court of Oyer and Terminer on Tuesday afternoon. Standing before the bench, Colt appeared "firm, calm, and collected" as the clerk began reading the true bill indictment, a formulaic document combining tortured legalese with a Bible-steeped view of human motivation:

> The Jurors of the People of the State of New York in and for the body of the City and County of New York upon their oath present that John C. Colt late of the Third Ward of the City of New York in the County of New York aforesaid Laborer, not having the fear of God before his eyes but being moved and seduced by the instigation of the Devil on the seventeenth day of September in the year of our Lord one thousand eight hundred and forty one with force and arms at the Ward, City and County aforesaid in and upon one Samuel Adams in the peace of God and of the said People then and there being feloniously, wilfully, and of his malice aforethought did make an assault and that the said John C. Colt with a certain hatchet of the value of six cents which he the said John C. Colt in his right hand then and there had and held, the said Samuel Adams in and upon the right side of the head of him the said Samuel Adams then and there feloniously, wilfully

and of his malice aforethought did strike and cut, giving to him the said Samuel Adams then and there with the hatchet aforesaid in and upon the right side of the head of him the said Samuel Adams one mortal wound of the breadth of three inches and of the depth of six inches of which said mortal wound he the said Samuel Adams then and there died.

And so the Jurors aforesaid upon their oath aforesaid do say that he said John C. Colt, him the said Samuel Adams in the manner and form aforesaid feloniously, will-fully, and of his malice aforethought did kill and murder, against the form of the statute in such case made and pro-vided and against the peace of the People of the State of New York and their dignity.

Jamming the courtroom for the proceedings were more than two dozen of the city's most eminent lawyers, a reflection (in Bennett's words) of the "intense excitement that this most extraordinary and unparalleled case has occasioned, even among the legal fraternity."[14]

It wasn't just the gruesomeness of the killing, the macabre method of body disposal, or the spicy hints of illicit sex that made the case so riveting. Another tantalizing ingredient was the same one that, in future years, would help turn figures like Professor John Webster, Lizzie Borden, Nathan Leopold and Richard Loeb, O. J. Simpson, and others into media celebri-ties: namely, their social prominence. However much Bennett and his com-petitors differed in their initial depictions of John Colt's demeanor, all agreed on one point: that the accused was "descended from one of the most eminent families of the state of Connecticut," being "the grandson of the Hon. John Caldwell of Hartford and son of Christopher Colt, a respected textile manufacturer of that place." And none failed to mention that his brother, Samuel, was the "well known inventor of Colt's celebrated firearms."[15]

28

From the moment he embarked on his firearms business, Sam Colt had been forced to deal with a virtually uninterrupted series of crises. His brother's arrest for murder, however, was, by a considerable measure, the worst. And for Sam, it couldn't have come at a less opportune time.

Since his meeting in June with Secretary of the Navy George Badger, Sam had been awaiting the passage of the naval appropriation bill with its promised allocation for the development of his harbor defense system. As late as September 5, he had received word from a Washington friend that the bill would most likely be "taken up and passed" within a matter of days. By then, Sam, brimming with confidence, had already drafted a prospectus for his Submarine Battery Company, approached a small group of investors, and sold five hundred shares at fifty dollars each.[1]

Less than a week after he received his friend's encouraging news, however, Washington was shaken by a political upheaval. On September 11, Naval Secretary Badger—along with the rest of the Cabinet, excepting Secretary of State Daniel Webster—resigned in protest over President Tyler's fiscal policies.[2] Badger's replacement, a Virginia judge named Abel P. Upshur, knew nothing of the agreement struck between his predecessor and Colt. Suddenly Sam found himself without a governmental sponsor.

It was at this very moment, when the federal funding he was counting on seemed about to fall through, that Sam returned from an out-of-town business trip to find the city abuzz with news of his brother's arrest.

From the start, Sam was his brother's most stalwart defender. Despite the precarious state of his own finances, he assumed responsibility for John's legal fees, offering each of the attorneys a thousand-dollar retainer—"five hundred in cash and ten shares par value in the Submarine Battery Company."[3]

At the same time, Sam never lost sight of his own business interests. Throughout John's ordeal, he pursued his current project with the tireless drive that, to his later hagiographers, exemplified his "unconquerable spirit"—the "indomitable energy and perseverance" that, "when the dark clouds of adversity rested upon him," allowed him to "overcome all obstacles and emerge triumphantly into the light of day."[4]

Even while providing moral and material support to his brother, Sam bent his efforts "towards getting an early action by the Navy Department on his submarine battery appropriation."[5] To one influential friend in Washington, he sent a letter expressing the urgency of the situation: "Circumstances of a nature too painful to relate have rendered it of vital importance that I should raise a som [sic] of money at once," he wrote, urging the recipient to do everything possible to expedite the bill. He also wrote directly to the new secretary of the navy, Abel Upshur, describing the harbor defense system, suggesting "that the Naval ordinance appropriation was his by right and intent," and conveying his "hope that matters would be permitted to continue in their original course."[6]

While Sam, however rattled by the crisis, remained characteristically dogged in pursuit of his goal, newspapers reported that the scandal of John's arrest had produced a devastating effect on the family patriarch. According to a widely disseminated story, originally published in the *Hartford Review*, Christopher Colt, Sr., "the father of J. C. Colt, the supposed murderer of Samuel Adams," had "become insane." Pulling out the sentimental stops, the article described Christopher as "an aged man, whose years have been embittered by the folly of his son, and this last horrible act has 'filled up the measure of sorrow' which will soon lay him in his grave."[7]

As affecting as it is, the story is nothing more than empty rumor, typical of an era when the penny papers did not scruple to print colorful gossip as sober fact. However distressed Christopher undoubtedly was over his eldest son's plight, he retained his sanity and lived another nine years, dying at the respectable age of seventy. What is perhaps most striking about this article is the fact that it was reprinted as far away as Wisconsin: testimony to the fascinated interest—the "excited curiosity," as one newspaper put it—that, by early October, the Colt-Adams case had already generated.[8]

• • •

It was, in fact, from his local St. Louis newspaper that another member of the clan, James Colt, learned the shocking news.

Like both John and Sam, the twenty-three-year-old James had traveled widely from an early age. At fourteen, he had left home and made his way to Washington, DC, in the hope of becoming a naval cadet. Failing to receive an appointment—and fearing that he was prone to the consumption that had claimed the lives of his mother and older sister—he proceeded south to Savannah, Georgia, where he was employed by a merchant named G. B. Lamar, a cousin of Mirabeau Lamar, future president of the Republic of Texas.

In 1835, in the company of another Lamar relation, James traveled to Velasco, Texas. There he became acquainted with Colonel James Walker Fannin—a comrade of Jim Bowie and William Travis—whose botched attempt to bring a troop of reinforcements to the Alamo would cast serious doubts on his leadership. Impressed with young Colt, Fannin offered him a position as aide-de-camp and dispatched him on a mission to New Orleans. James had just arrived in the city when news reached him that Fannin and roughly four hundred of his men, after surrendering to an overwhelming Mexican force at the Battle of Coleto, had been marched back to Goliad and executed on the order of General Antonio López de Santa Anna.

By the summer of 1836, James was back in Hartford, where he undertook the study of law. In the following years, he spent time in Philadelphia and New York City before being admitted to the bar in 1840. That fall, along with a partner named Alan Dodd, he headed west and settled in St. Louis, Missouri.[9]

Of the four Colt brothers, James, the youngest, seemed the most concerned about maintaining close ties with his kin. Shortly after his move to Missouri, he sent Sam a letter expressing his dismay at the rifts that had developed among the siblings. With a mixture of anger and hurt, he complained that "John has not written me a friendly letter since heaven knows when—the same has been the case with Christopher." Sam himself came in for some chiding. "In this respect," wrote James, "you have done your duty better but not half so well as you should."

Invoking a story he had heard about a trio of lighthouse keepers who, out of some petty grievance, had lived together for more than seven months without ever exchanging a word, James made a heartfelt plea for familial harmony:

> I think it is unfortunate that four brothers should cease to keep up intercourse with each other when they can do so with so little trouble to themselves and when it can be productive of so much pleasure as well as good. This state of things is brought about among ourselves in consequence of each and all of us having too independent minds. We have too much self-sufficiency and vain pride. We all want to be independent of each other when it is certainly most wise for us to do away with such feeling. If there should be a misunderstanding among any of us, it should be the first object of those who are not parties to bring about reconciliation. If we adopt this as a rule, it will certainly be better for all of us.[10]

It was not long after James dispatched this letter that accounts of the Colt-Adams affair first appeared in the St. Louis papers, which reported (inaccurately) that the victim had been murdered in a dispute over two hundred dollars. James immediately composed a letter to Sam conveying his shock and incredulity, as well as a belief in John's blamelessness that would never waver:

> St. Louis, Oct. 6, 1841
>
> My Dear Brother:
>
> I cannot express to you the intense agony of my feelings at this moment. I have heard of the sad catastrophe which has befallen John. Our daily newspapers are full of circumstantial evidence against him, but I cannot for a moment believe he is guilty of the charge. The first intimation I got of it was through

yesterday's evening paper. I read it and threw it down—
and read it again. I cannot but conclude from what I have
seen in relation to the matter that he is in difficulty.

Suppose John did the act. Did he do it for the paltry
sum of two hundred dollars? No. For it would be against
all the impulses of our nature or any man to hazard his life
for two hundred dollars. Then if he did it, he must be
deranged. This may be so. For, mark you, has not John
been confined at his books for the last six months and do
you not know that Sarah's derangement was brought on
in the same way? I have thought that John would be
deranged, for you know that he has applied himself too
closely to books and to his work. His habit is and always
has been when he undertakes to do anything to do it with
all the intensity of a madman. If this is the foundation for
the charges against John or sufficient to name the
conclusion that he did the act, he was a madman at the
time he did it and this fact should be made to appear.

I cannot but hope that what I have seen in the papers
is all false. Not hearing from you leads me to think it
is so.[11]

James's desperate hope that the newspaper accounts were unfounded
was dashed the very next day when the mail brought a letter from Sam re-
laying the bad news. James immediately penned a reply, reiterating his belief that, if John had in fact committed the crime, he had done so in a state
of "derangement" induced by mental overexertion:

I have this moment received your letter of the 27th bearing confirmation of the newspaper intelligence. My mind
was prepared to receive it and I fear not the general result.
If it is possible I shall come and be with you in this hour of
trouble. Write me whether I had better do so or not.

The news of John's arrest and of his being a brother of
mine has spread like wild fire through the city and my
friends flock in to see me on the subject. But they see I am

calm upon the subject and therefore fear not the consequences. I have no doubt but that an alibi can be proven
and therefore no just suspicion can rest on John. But suppose this came to be done, was he not deranged? Has he
not labored too hard mentally and bodily? I say again this
brought on Sarah's derangement and John has when I have
been with him manifested derangement on this subject of
ambitions and notoriety. Let medical men examine him on
this subject. These things have undoubtedly suggested
themselves to you and you being present and knowing all
the circumstances can best judge as to what will be the best
course of action to pursue.

 Write to me every day and give me all the particulars.
I will write John and Father today. Would to God I could
at this moment be with you. God knows our family has had
afflictions enough. I did not think we were to suffer afflictions of such a nature. But do not give way under it. There
is a brighter sky ahead. If all the elements conspired together to crush me I would still war against them and nothing should conquer my energy but the grave.

Despite his seemingly heartfelt offer to hurry to Sam's side, James, for a
variety of reasons, would never make it back east during the ordeal. From
his law office in St. Louis, however, he did everything possible to assist
John's cause. Not long after the news of his brother's arrest reached him, a
story appeared in a St. Louis daily that was widely reprinted in papers
throughout the Northeast:

 The *St. Louis Pennant,* on the authority of a brother of
John C. Colt, residing in that city, advances the plea of insanity on behalf of the supposed murder of Mr. Adams. Mr.
Colt, who is a member of the St. Louis bar, informs the
Pennant that insanity is hereditary in their family and that
he has no doubt that his brother was insane when he committed the dreadful act with which he stands charged. He
further states that John had several times become suddenly

insane, generally after a period of intense application to study or to severe mental exercise. He further cites the case of a sister who committed suicide in 1827.[12]

James's willingness to trumpet such a painful personal matter as Sarah's suicide reflects the urgency of the situation. Clearly, he was ready to do whatever it took to save his brother from the gallows. However sincerely he believed his own theory, his very public proclamation that a streak of "hereditary insanity" ran in his immediate family was a calculated move—the sowing of a seed that would culminate, so he hoped, in John's acquittal.

While James Colt saw his brother's homicidal outburst as a consequence of excessive mental exertion, other observers traced the crime to different sources. For some, the Colt case demonstrated the inevitable outcome of youthful insubordination—the type of tragedy that resulted when parents spared the rod in dealing with refractory children. In papers throughout the country, John was accused of having been "a passionate, cunning, and revengeful boy," whose "whole course has been marked by self-will" and whose bitter fate "teaches a lesson that ought never to be forgotten: that parental disobedience and disregard to the laws of God in youth is most generally followed by a life of crime, ending in either a violent or disgraceful death."[1]

"Let the child who will not submit to be checked and guided tremble for the end of his own career," thundered one writer whose jeremiad was reprinted in papers throughout the country, "and let the parent tremble for the child who cannot be made to yield to just authority, and let him never dare to hope that the youth whom he cannot control will learn to control himself and curb his own wild passions!"[2]

In the *Tribune*, editor Horace Greeley used the Colt case to expound on his "most constant theme: the dangers that could destroy a young man alone in the city without a concerned family or a close-knit community to help mold his character." Despite his many advantages—"a respected and influential family, good talents and a winning address, liberal opportunities for mental culture"—John had "inevitably slid into a 'depth of horrid guilt and blasting infamy,' demonstrating afresh that Crime has a vital, growing power which thrusts downward deep into the heart its mighty roots and overshadows the whole inner being with its death-distilling shade."[3]

Another commentator, signing himself as "Junius," drew a different moral from the case. Denouncing Colt as a "literary pirate" whose accounting book had been copied with minor alterations from a competing text, this anonymous writer saw John's arrest for murder as the logical result of his ostensible penchant for plagiarism. "It is a most natural progress in crime from forgery to piracy to murder," Junius declared. "Men seldom break out into the commission of high crimes suddenly. Conscience, that inner monitor given by the Almighty to warn men against the violation of human and divine law, must first be blunted or deafened by the smaller class of crimes and misdemeanors before the soul becomes fit for the commission of the higher crimes of robbery, rape, and murder."[4]

The public's "excited curiosity" about the Adams murder—its hunger for every juicy detail—prompted another writer to editorialize on the perils of pandering to such impulses. Sounding much like modern critics who condemn today's tabloid entertainment for "glorifying" crime and inciting acts of copycat violence, this observer wondered

> how far public curiosity should be gratified in such a case. We are disposed to enquire whether this morbid taste for the details of crime may not help to provide material for its own gratification . . . We do not ask for apathy or indifference to crime; its frequent recurrence in such horrid forms calls for the most vigilant interest; but not for that fascinated interest, that shuddering admiration, with which we have suffered ourselves to be drawn into sympathy with vice until we have come to look upon great wickedness as great romance.[5]

Colt himself was deeply concerned about the public's "fascinated interest" in his case—though for the opposite reason. Far from inducing "shuddering admiration" and even sympathy, the intense news coverage, he felt, had so inflamed public sentiment that a fair trial might not be possible. Writing to a friend from his cell in the Tombs, he assailed the penny papers for "exciting the passions of the people to an alarming degree" and expressed his fear "that passion and not evidence will decide the case."[6]

On the very day this letter was composed, James Gordon Bennett published a lengthy editorial that confirmed John's darkest apprehensions about the press's prejudicial treatment of his case. Under the headline "Sympathy for Criminals," Bennett railed against the kind of people derided nowadays as "bleeding hearts," accusing them of mollycoddling "villains" while ignoring the rights of victims. In terms that any right-wing law-and-order advocate would applaud, he also denounced the judicial system for allowing criminals to go free on mere legal technicalities:

> It is called cruel nowadays to exercise a proper vigilance in the conviction of a scoundrel whether he exhibits himself in the capacity of a thief, an incendiary, or a murderer. No matter how much misery the crime may involve—no matter whether a man's house may have been burned down, or a woman's husband been foully murdered—the miscreant who has done the act is immediately taken into the keeping of the public mercy. "The humanity of the law" is invoked in his favor and the community is called upon to presume everything in his behalf.
>
> It is quite time for this false philanthropy—this misdirected and most absurd sympathy—to cease. It cannot be denied that it would be very much to be lamented if an individual should chance to be hanged for a crime he had not committed; but in our opinion, it is not the lesser to be regretted that fifty villains who have been guilty of palpable and undoubted enormities should be suffered to escape punishment through some pettifogging technicality of the common law forms or the still worse fanaticism of an ill-directed popular feeling. We have no participation in that false sympathy which, in displaying itself towards the criminal, has no feelings for the victims of his iniquity.

Presenting himself as a noble guardian of the public weal, Bennett concluded his piece with what amounted to a demand for John Colt's blood. Without mentioning either Colt or his victim by name, Bennett nevertheless made it plain that, in his considered opinion, the killing of Samuel

Adams was not a case of manslaughter—as the defense clearly intended to argue—but an act of cold-blooded murder deserving of the full penalty of the law:

> We refrain, as we have refrained in all similar cases, from saying aught that can prejudice public opinion upon cases still to be passed upon by Court and Jury; but we have a duty as well to the public as to individuals, and when we see that public likely to be poisoned by pernicious influences, it is proper for the press to guard the community from false opinions. As has been the case in similar instances, pains are being taken to impress upon the public a very false notion with respect to a case soon to be tried in our Courts. It is not true that the law presumes every case of killing to be a manslaughter unless an adequate motive for the commission of homicide be proved upon the accused. So far from this being the case, the law always presumes malice aforethought, express or implied in every case of homicide; and the prisoner is always bound to rebut that presumption by proof. The fact of the killing made out, the prisoner must prove the absence of malice if he would escape the penalty of murder.[7]

· · ·

The intense public excitement stirred up by Bennett and his competitors was very much in evidence on the morning of Monday, November 1, 1841, when—after a one-month delay—John's trial was scheduled to begin.[8] By 9:00 a.m., a throng of curiosity seekers, "anxious to catch a view of the noted individual," had gathered outside the courtroom. When the doors swung open promptly at 10:00, the crowd swarmed inside. Within two minutes, as one newspaper reported, "the large space allotted to the public was completely filled, and there was scarce standing room inside the railing."[9]

A few moments later, the star attraction was led inside and seated at the end of a long table at the front of the room. For the past week, reports had circulated that John had been reduced to a physically pitiable condition by extreme "mental agonies and terrors of conscience." Now, however, it became clear to observers that those stories, like so many others concerning John and his family, were mere rumor. Apart from his jailhouse pallor, he seemed hardly changed at all. "Certainly," one paper reported, "his appearance was not that of a haggard conscience-stricken man."[10]

In the articles that appeared the following day, most papers emphasized John's relaxed manner and refined appearance. He seemed "more calm, less agitated than on previous occasions," noted the *Morning Courier and New-York Enquirer,* and was "very genteelly dressed in black, with the air of a gentleman."

Seated not far from Colt, however, James Gordon Bennett saw things differently. To his eyes, Colt was "evidently laboring under great mental excitement, which he strongly endeavored to suppress. The skin over his cheek bones was suffused with blood, resembling a man of a strong nervous temperament after hard drinking; and his eye, which is peculiarly deep and penetrating, and has at times a wild, savage look, was incessantly in motion." It was only when he caught sight of his brother Samuel, who entered the courtroom a few minutes after it opened and positioned himself in the rear, that John's "savage" expression softened and a warm smile appeared on his face.[11]

As it happened, the day turned into a major disappointment for the spectators. No sooner had the proceedings gotten under way than Dudley Selden moved for a postponement. The trial, he argued, could not fairly be held "in the absence of a material witness"—namely, Colt's mistress Caroline Henshaw, who was on the brink of giving birth and had returned to Philadelphia to be with friends for "the period of her confinement."

District Attorney James Whiting countered by wondering why Caroline's testimony could not be submitted in writing. "Suppose this woman should die under her accouchement," he said. "If the gentlemen deem her testimony so important to them, why object to taking it by commission at once, so as not to be deprived of that evidence which they deem to them of so much value, in case of an event which is certainly within the range of possibility?" In the end, though, Whiting dropped his objection and agreed to a postponement.

Before he sat down, Selden directed a plea for journalistic restraint to the assembled newspapermen:

This case has been more commented upon by the press
than almost any other I have known, and I think very unfairly. And I would suggest whether the prisoner is not entitled to have a suspension of further remarks at least until
his trial. So much fiction has been blended with some little fact that it would be difficult for any—even unbiased
minds—to come to a fair and impartial opinion of the case
if this course be continued. And I say to those who have
done this that I trust they will see the propriety of a cessa-
tion.[12]

Among other "utterly untrue and unfair" stories that had been circulated by the press, Selden singled out the widespread accusation that "we
intend to raise insanity as a defense in this case. Most unjustly have we been
charged with getting up this fraudulent scheme of defense, as it has been
called, for the purpose of defeating the ends of justice. We have never said
so—and we never intended it. None of the counsel ever thought of such a
thing. Indeed, no plan of defense has been decided upon, other than what
the real merits of the case may justify."

A few minutes later, with Whiting's agreement, Judge William Kent
granted Selden's motion, and the proceedings were adjourned—much to
the audible disappointment of the spectators, who would now be forced to
wait another few months before the big show reopened.[13]

● ● ●

Despite Selden's plea for fairness, Bennett and his colleagues continued to
report on the case with no pretense of impartiality. In his article on the day's
events, for example, the writer for the *Brooklyn Daily Eagle* dispensed entirely with such standard modifiers as *alleged, accused,* and *suspected* in his
references to John. "The trial of Colt, the murderer of Adams," he declared,
as though the verdict had already been rendered, "has been postponed until
the next term of the Court of Oyer and Terminer, which will not be until
the first Monday in December."[14]

MR. COLT ARGUES WITH HIS PRINTER

Part Four

THE GARB OF JUSTICE

30

*N*ews of the postponement was slow to reach James Colt in St. Louis. Believing that the trial had proceeded as scheduled, he wrote to Sam on December 18, describing his state of "miserable suspense" as he awaited word of the outcome. "I never have doubted where the justice of this case lies," James declared, reaffirming his faith in John's innocence and referring to Samuel Adams's death as "the accident." "Of course," he urged, "you will write me immediately after the disposal of the case and then give me explicitly and fully your views in relation to the matter."

Receiving a prompt reply from Sam informing him of the delay, James immediately responded with a long and fervent letter, extolling Sam's fraternal devotion and contrasting it bitterly with the callous indifference of their brother Christopher:

> My Dear Brother
>
> I cannot express the feelings of gratitude which your letter awakens in my bosom. But why should I dwell upon it. "Time the only healer when the heart hath bled" will unfold to you many years of joy and happiness which your present magnanimity will bring about . . . I will pledge my life on the assertion that before many years flash over your head you will look back upon your present conduct in relation to our unfortunate brother John and myself as the proudest period of your life. Would to God I could be with you. I should then be able to share with you the labor and

affliction of this dark hour. But do not think that because I am two thousand miles off my thoughts do not dwell upon the heart-rending scenes which are passing around you. The distance only adds to my afflictions. I try to dissipate my thoughts but it is impossible.

But do not think either the world discovers in me this. It does not. I am perfectly calm, for I know that if there is a God in heaven we shall be rewarded for our present sufferings.

Before this reaches you, John's case will be disposed of but it will be a month nearly before I know the result. You will of course write me immediately and let me know everything. I think the jury will disagree but I merely guess at it from the exparte testimony. If they disagree, another trial will acquit him.

Whatever may be the result of John's trial do not, I entreat you, let it have any more effect upon your mind than possible. Your conduct during the trial and the exertions you have made and suffering you have passed through will sooner or later be made known to the public . . . While the public will thus sympathize with the misfortunes of John, thus will they commend the magnanimousness of your own conduct . . . I forbear all comment upon Christopher's comment. The end will prove which of the two brothers acted with most honor to themselves.[1]

• • •

With the trial still several weeks away and John's legal team absorbed in their preparations, Sam busied himself with his harbor defense scheme. Armed with a letter of introduction from an influential acquaintance, Major William Gibbs McNeill of the U.S. Topographical Engineers, he had traveled to Washington, DC, in early November and secured a private interview with the new secretary of the navy, Abel Upshur. After learning the specifics of the submarine battery and satisfying himself of its feasibility, Upshur agreed to advance Sam six thousand dollars for a preliminary test—

considerably less than the sum Sam had previously been promised but enough for him to proceed.[2]

Back in Manhattan, Sam took a room in the South Tower of the New York University building on the east side of Washington Square, a massive Gothic Revival structure that, in its early years, "served as both college and lodging house. Artists, inventors, and literary figures not on the University staff, moved into the upper floors, supplementing the young institution's slender financial resources." It was around this time, as he turned his energies to the "procurement, insulation, and testing of the several thousand feet of rolled copper wire" necessary for his device, that Sam began collaborating with his neighbor, Samuel F. B. Morse.[3]

One of America's finest painters, the fifty-year-old Morse was eking out a living as an instructor of arts and design at the nascent NYU (then known as the University of the City of New York), while working tirelessly to perfect and promote his recently patented invention, the electromagnetic telegraph. Still three years away from his triumphant demonstration in Washington, DC—when the coded message "What Hath God Wrought!" was carried across forty miles of wire strung between the old Supreme Court chamber in the U.S. Capitol and a train depot in Baltimore—Morse shared Sam Colt's interest in developing "insulated cable that was capable of transmitting electrical current relatively undiminished for substantial distances." In a note to his NYU neighbor, Colt offered to provide Morse with "some hints by which you may profit . . . before the materials for your Electro-Magnetic Telegraph are ordered." It was the beginning of a long and mutually beneficial association between the two "pioneers of American galvanic technology."[4]

On November 25, 1841, Congress approved the six-thousand-dollar appropriation for the development of Sam's underwater defense system. At that point, Sam "moved rapidly to acquire additional financing from the private sector."[5] Investors included a number of his powerful Washington friends—among them Major McNeill and Senator Samuel L. Southard—as well as the pioneering civil engineer Major George W. Whistler, who, thanks to his artist-son's celebrated painting, would come to be known by waggish historians as "Whistler's Father." There was another name, too, on the list of early investors: John C. Colt.

To defray some of the legal costs Sam had already incurred on his account, John had offered to pay his brother $125 to "be used for shares in the Submarine Battery Company." Besides a desire to ease Sam's financial burden, John might have had another motive for the investment. According to one well-known historian of the Colt family, John's gesture may have been intended to show the world that he was a man of means—not so hard up that he would murder a man in a petty argument over a "picayune" debt. Or perhaps, as the same writer speculates, the investment was meant to show that John possessed a serene faith in his own innocence—"that he was confident of the future and the justice of the court."[6]

31

Despite a lashing rain, an enormous crowd showed up at City Hall Park early on the morning of Monday, January 17, 1842, for the reopening of the Colt trial. "People of all classes and ages" thronged the pathways leading up to the building and packed every inch of the portico. When the doors opened at 9:00, the jostling horde swarmed inside. A few constables, armed with long staves, were on hand to maintain order. They made free use of their implements, "knocking about them right and left, and rapping people's heads and shoulders, sometimes quite outrageously." Their exertions, however, had little effect on the boisterous crowd, which shoved its way inside the courtroom, occupying every available space within two or three minutes. Shut out of the courtroom, "hundreds waited and clamored in the hallway; whilst in the park, there were also hundreds waiting to catch a sight of Colt or Mrs. Adams or any of the witnesses."[1]

Among those who made it inside was twenty-two-year-old Walt Whitman, then a writer for a new penny paper, the *Aurora*. Though Whitman would eventually compose soaring poetry celebrating the divinity inherent in even the most degraded individual, the frenzied excitement of the crowd afforded him a glimpse of the very worst side of human nature. Five years later, remembering "the struggle he had to get in the courtroom at the trial of John C. Colt," Whitman had still not gotten over his sense of outrage.

"There was a kind of ferocious interest felt in that case, which seemed quite disgusting," he recalled. "There existed a feverish jealousy lest he might be only sent to prison for life and not strangled. Public malignance was aroused; and cloaking itself in the convenient garb of justice, the most inhuman spirit of revenge pervaded the bosoms of the people."

"Wretched fellow!" wrote Whitman of Colt. "How he was hunted by an unrelenting public appetite for blood!"[2]

James Gordon Bennett was also in attendance, along with an artist named Forbes, who was there to sketch the prisoner for the *Herald*. That evening, the paper's front page was dominated by Forbes's portrait, rendered in woodcut. In it, John sits with an elbow on the arm of his chair, head resting on his closed hand. He is shown as a strikingly handsome man with a luxuriant head of dark, wavy hair, neatly trimmed side whiskers, finely molded features, and exceptionally large, penetrating eyes. His expression seems perfectly serene.

According to the accompanying story, John—who had been brought into the courtroom earlier that morning and sat in a corner, warming himself by the stove—was, in fact, "collected and calm." As he awaited the opening of the trial, he chatted freely with the person seated next to him: his brother Sam, who appeared to be far more agitated than the defendant. Another of John's supporters was present in the courtroom as well: Caroline Henshaw, who had returned from Philadelphia after giving birth to a boy and was invariably referred to in the papers as "the female who lived with Colt."[3]

Shortly before 10:00 a.m., John's counsel arrived. His cousin Dudley Selden was assisted by two other highly accomplished attorneys: Robert Emmett, son of New York State's former attorney general and a future justice of the superior court, and James A. Morrill. The latter had achieved recent celebrity as the lawyer for Mrs. Ann Lohman—alias "Madame Restell," the nation's most notorious abortionist—who had been brought to trial the previous July after the death of one of her customers.[4]

Opposing them was District Attorney James R. Whiting and his able young assistant, James M. Smith, Jr., in later years a justice of the Court of General Sessions. Whiting, whose own distinguished career would culminate with a seat on the state supreme court, had prosecuted the Restell trial. He'd prevailed over Morrill when "the mistress of abominations" (as she was dubbed in the press) was convicted of "unlawfully, wickedly, willfully, and maliciously" inducing an abortion by means of "a piece of wire, a pair of pliers, or some unknown instrument."[5]

At precisely 10:30 a.m., Judge William Kent entered the courtroom and took his place. An imposing figure, Kent was the son of the country's most eminent jurist, the former New York State chancellor James Kent, esteemed in legal circles as the author of the monumental *Commentaries on American Law*, a four-volume treatise credited with "disentangling a distinctively American practice from the inherited mass of British common law."[6]

After a brief delay while the judge awaited the arrival of two aldermen, the court was officially opened. By then, the other star attraction, Emeline Adams, widow of the slain victim, had arrived. A few months earlier, reporting on Mrs. Adams's allegedly premonitory dreams of her husband's murder, Bennett, in his most melodramatic style, had informed his readers that "her reason is a shattered wreck, and it is probable that she will soon lie peacefully beside her husband in the quiet grave."[7] Now, however—sounding somewhat piqued that she had not fulfilled his prophecy—he described her as "dressed in deep mourning" but otherwise looking "uncommonly well in health and appearance." In fact, far from hurrying to join her husband underground, Mrs. Adams would remarry in 1850 and live to a ripe old age, dying just eight years shy of the twentieth century.[8]

A ripple of anticipatory excitement ran through the crowd when John was summoned to the bar. Rising promptly at the calling of his name, he "walked to the end of the table where his counsel sat with a firm, steady step, an unblanched cheek, and an eye that did not quail," and took his place beside Selden. The audience, however, was in for a disappointment. Having braved the bad weather to be present at a dramatic spectacle, they witnessed instead a proceeding that was aborted almost as soon as it began. Ordered by the judge to call the roll of potential jurors who had been summoned to court, Clerk Henry Vandervoort rose and read out a list of forty-five names. Only nineteen men, however, had shown up.

Without bothering to conceal his displeasure at this turn of events, Judge Kent immediately announced his ruling. "The statute says that when twenty-four jurors do not answer to their names, the Court shall direct the Sheriff to summon a sufficient number from the city and county," he declared. "Considering the circumstances of the case, which render it likely that it will be difficult to form a jury, the Court therefore orders the Sheriff to summon three hundred persons from the county at large to be in attendance here at ten o'clock on Wednesday morning."

When Selden questioned "if that be time enough" to assemble such a large pool of potential jurors, Kent cited the precedent of Ezra White, a twenty-three-year-old hooligan tried in 1840 for stabbing a young man to death after crashing a party at a Lower East Side tavern. In that case, the sheriff had been directed to summon "two hundred jurors the next day." Kent acknowledged that there had been "some difficulty in getting them together" in such short order. As a result, he was now granting the sheriff an additional twenty-four hours for the task.

Before adjourning until Wednesday morning, Judge Kent issued one final ruling. In light of the clamorous scene outside the courtroom that morning, he directed the sheriff "to have ten additional constables to keep order."[9]

• • •

An unseasonable warmth enveloped the city on Wednesday, January 19, bringing out the curiosity seekers in even greater droves. "Very early in the day," the *Herald* reported, "thousands of persons were seen wending their way to the City Hall in the hopes of obtaining admission. Never was such intense excitement exhibited."[10]

A full two hours before the trial was scheduled to begin, the defendant, escorted by three police officers, arrived at court. Even at that early hour, so many people had assembled outside the chamber that Colt "had to press through the crowd gathered in the hall." Once inside, he seated himself, as before, near the stove in the far corner of the room and "amused himself reading a newspaper." When Sam appeared at 9:30, John—looking in "much better spirits" than "at any time since his arrest"—set aside the paper and began conversing cheerfully with his brother.

Promptly at 10:00, the proceedings got under way. With a sharp rap of his gavel, Judge Kent called for "perfect silence" in the courtroom and ordered the spectators—many of whom had risen for a better view of the defendant—to "take their seats at once." Clerk Vandervoort was then directed to call the roll of potential jurors. No sooner had he begun, however, than Dudley Selden rose with an objection.

Owing to the feverish attentions of the penny press, Selden argued, the case had received an unprecedented degree of publicity. "The subject matter of this trial has been more extensively published than any other that has ever occurred in this country," he claimed, "and it has entered every house and every room of the city." As a result, finding jurors with no preconceived opinions was a particularly challenging task.

"We want to distinguish between the man who can look with kindness on his fellow man and the one whose heart is hardened and knows not mercy," said Selden. Having been provided with the names of the three hundred potential jurors only the previous afternoon, he contended that the defendant had been deprived of a fundamental right.

"I call the attention of the court," said Selden, "to the statute which provides that every prisoner shall be informed as to the jurors so that he shall be enabled to meet them in challenge. Is it possible in twenty-four hours to ascertain whether or not the panel has been made up of men who are enemies to the prisoner, or who have made up their minds in regard to him?" Insisting that he had no desire to cause an unnecessary delay, Selden nevertheless asked for an additional "two days' time for scrutinizing" the list of jurors.

After hearing counterarguments from the district attorney—who again invoked the precedent of the Ezra White case and argued that the intense public excitement generated by the present crime was no "reason for the trial being thus deferred"—Judge Kent handed down his ruling. "The trial," he announced, "must proceed."

Vandervoort then proceeded to call the roll of names. Of the 300 men summoned, 228 answered. One by one, they came forward and were questioned: dentists and dry-goods dealers, cobblers and confectioners, booksellers and grocers, watchmakers and merchants, hardware clerks and housepainters. For twelve full hours, the examinations went on, interrupted only by a one-hour recess at 3:00. At 11:00 p.m., with 220 men having been called, just 11 jurors had been sworn. Directing them to be sequestered at the Knickerbocker Hotel on Park Row and "furnished with any refreshments they might require except spirituous liquors," Judge Kent then adjourned until 10:00 the next morning.

In all the monotony of that exhausting day, one moment stood out for James Gordon Bennett. It happened shortly before 8:00 p.m., when the City Hall bell began to toll, "pealing an alarm of fire in the Second District."

For Bennett, the ringing of the bell added a disturbing note to the proceedings. "This is at all times a mournful and unwelcome sound," he observed, "but it falls with a peculiar chill upon the ear when a murderer is present and the ministers of justice assemble to pass upon life and death. Such was the case here." Months would pass before that tolling of the fire bell took on an even more uncanny significance—not as a chilling accompaniment to the start of the trial but as a grim premonition of its terrible outcome.[11]

32

A great "rush of persons" tried to shove their way into the courtroom when the doors opened on Thursday morning. Thanks to the stave-wielding constables, however—who "put forth all their energies with a view to preserving order"—a degree of decorum was imposed, and "no more were admitted than could comfortably be seated."[1]

Dressed in his usual garb—black pantaloons, black satin vest, dark blue half overcoat, and a black silk handkerchief tied neatly around his neck—John was brought into the courtroom shortly before 9:00 a.m. With him were his brother Sam and, for the first time, their sixty-two-year-old father, Christopher, Sr.—"a venerable, fine, benevolent-looking man" who, according to James Gordon Bennett, "appeared as if he had been crying bitterly and long."[2]

The proceedings began promptly at 10:30 with the selection of the final member of the jury. No sooner had he been sworn in than several of his fellow jurors—anticipating a prolonged separation from home—asked permission to pay a visit to their families, "preparatory to the arduous and unceasing day and night work that was before them." Colt's counsel offering no objection, Judge Kent granted the request. The jurors departed, each accompanied by a constable who was ordered "not to lose sight" of his charge and "suffer no one to speak to him on the subject of the trial."[3]

After a ninety-minute delay, the jurors returned. At a few minutes past noon, Thursday, January 20, 1842, the trial of John C. Colt commenced in earnest.

Following the reading of the indictment—charging that Colt, at the "instigation of the devil," had made an assault with a hatchet on the person of Samuel Adams and inflicted a fatal wound on the side of his head—James Smith, the young assistant DA, rose to open the prosecution's case.

What rendered the jurors' job particularly difficult, Smith told them, was the intense public feeling aroused by the crime. Owing to the "unparalleled atrocity" of the murder, the case had excited an unprecedented degree of excitement in the community, as evinced by the "immense concourse which has here assembled to witness these proceedings." Everyone appeared to have formed an opinion on the case. The jurors, however, had been selected "after strict examination" because they had declared themselves as "being entirely free of bias." It was their responsibility to render a verdict based strictly on the facts. While they were obligated to give the prisoner the "full benefit" of any evidence that was "elicited in his favor," they must not allow their sympathies to affect their final verdict. "You may feel them," Smith declared, "but the jury box is not the place for their display."

After reviewing the details of the case, Smith concluded by anticipating—and taking a preemptive swipe at—the defense's strategy. "The prisoner's counsel will not, I believe, pretend to deny that Mr. Adams was killed by Mr. Colt but that this did not constitute murder. They will seek to reduce the crime to manslaughter by showing that there was no premeditation in the act, but that if Colt did kill Mr. Adams, it was done under the influence of a momentary passion, excited by a state of facts which perhaps justified such a feeling. Evidence will prove, however, that Mr. Adams was a man of such habits and disposition that he could not have done anything to excite feelings of animosity in any person. The violent character of the prisoner and the contrary one of the deceased leave but little doubt that the murder was willful and premeditated."[4]

• • •

Asa Wheeler was the first to take the stand. After providing a few basic personal facts—married, lived on Twentieth Street near Broadway, made his living as an instructor of bookkeeping and penmanship—he explained that he had first become acquainted with Colt in 1838, when the latter approached him about supplying an endorsement for his textbook. The two had not seen each other again until August 1841, when Colt appeared at the Granite Building to ask about renting Wheeler's vacant second room for six weeks.

Wheeler then provided a lengthy description of the layout and furnishings of the two rooms. District Attorney Whiting, who had brought along a diagram of the second floor of the Granite Building, passed it among the jurors to help them visualize the scene.

Most of Wheeler's testimony—which continued late into the afternoon, with a one-hour recess for dinner—consisted of a detailed account of the events of September 17, beginning with his arrival at his office at 2:30 p.m., when he had seated himself at his desk to work on a sample of "ornamental writing" to be used as an advertisement for his penmanship lessons. He described the entrance of his sixteen-year-old pupil Arzac Seignette a half hour later; the strange sound, like the "rattling or clashing of foils," that had startled them from their work at around 3:15; his attempts to peek into Colt's room to see what had caused the peculiar noise. Though Wheeler offered a few small, previously undisclosed details—mentioning, for example, that Sam Colt had evidently come by John's office on the morning after the murder, looking for his brother—the story was already familiar to everyone who had followed the unfolding of the case in the newspapers.[5]

Dudley Selden's cross-examination, which began in the late afternoon, seemed somewhat scattershot to most observers, though it did manage to establish one key fact. As James Smith had indicated, John's counsel clearly intended to argue that the killing of Adams had been an act of manslaughter, the tragic climax of an altercation that had grown increasingly violent and out of control. Wheeler had made it plain, however, that he had not heard any sort of commotion from Colt's room until the odd clashing sound that had interrupted his lesson with Seignette. Now, under questioning from Selden, he revealed that, despite the damp and chilly weather, his windows, which overlooked Broadway, had been "wide open."

"And is there much noise from Broadway at that time of day?"

Wheeler allowed that there was. Even with the windows tightly shut, the din from outside penetrated his room. When they were raised, the noise—particularly from the omnibuses rumbling over the cobblestones—often made it hard for him to communicate with his pupils: "much incommoded me in hearing them," as he put it.

"So it is possible that there might have been sounds coming from the room next door that you were unable to hear?" asked Selden.

Wheeler considered for a moment before replying. "Yes, persons might have talked quite loud in Colt's room at that time of day, and me in my room never hear it."[6]

•   •   •

Two more witnesses, Arzac Seignette and John Delnous, took the stand that day. Beyond a few minor details, they added little to Wheeler's testimony, though Delnous did provide a moment of levity during Selden's cross-examination. A few minutes after mentioning that he was "very nearsighted," the young bookkeeper described how "agitated" Mr. Wheeler looked when he, Delnous, first arrived.

"But you couldn't really see the expression on his face unless you were very close to him, isn't that true?" asked Selden, attempting to raise doubts about Delnous's credibility.

Delnous admitted that he had trouble "distinguishing persons" unless they were right beside him. Indeed, even at the distance Selden was standing—less than five feet away from the witness box—the bookkeeper could not "tell him from anyone else." Then, as though to prove that, despite his visual limitations, he was still a reliable eyewitness, he added: "But I can tell a white man from a black."

Selden did a double take. "Tell a white man from a black?"

"Yes, I can tell that you are white, not black," Delnous solemnly declared, as guffaws burst from the spectator section.[7]

•   •   •

Just a few hours after adjournment, a nearly verbatim account of the proceedings—transcribed by James Gordon Bennett with the speed and accuracy of a professional court reporter—appeared in the late edition of the *Herald*. Of course, there was nothing new or surprising in the testimony; the shocking bits were still to come. Even so, Bennett found a way to provide his readers with the kind of lurid thrills they expected from him.

At a time when "large woodcut illustrations were still an expensive and time-consuming rarity in a daily newspaper," Bennett splashed an exceptionally gruesome picture across the top of page one.[8] It showed a naked male corpse arranged on a table, knees raised, limp arms bent at the elbow, the upper half of the torso propped up against a pile of cloth. What made the image particularly ghastly, however, was the monstrously disfigured face—a hideous fright mask with a caved-in brow, crushed nose, shredded cheeks, exposed jawbone, and great gaping cavity where the right eye should have been. Even today, when graphic images of bloodshed and bodily mutilation are the stuff of daily entertainment, the picture retains the power to shock. To Bennett's contemporaries, unaccustomed to such sights, it must have seemed appallingly real.

The accompanying caption did perfect justice to the sheer horror of the image. "Samuel Adams, the Printer," it read, "Before He Was Cut Up and Salted."[9]

*B*ennett wasn't the only scandalmonger eager to cash in on the public's fascination with the Colt case. On the same day that the *Herald* published its picture of Samuel Adams's mutilated corpse, another penny paper—John Dillon and John M. Moore's *New York Tattler*—ran its own shocking illustration. In this one, an enraged, hatchet-wielding Colt looms over Adams, who has been thrown to the floor. With one hand, Colt clutches the front of Adams's shirt. With the other, he prepares to deliver a deathblow to the head of his terrified victim. Beside them stands the crate that will soon hold the printer's mutilated corpse.

Given such inflammatory publicity, it was no wonder that, as the *Herald* noted, "excitement over the trial" seemed to "increase with each passing day." On Friday, January 21, the crowds around City Hall "were greater than at any previous trial in this city."[1] Notwithstanding the heroic exertions of Deputy Sheriff J. C. Westervelt and "a strong body of officers," the hallway outside the courtroom turned into a mob scene as the crowd made a mad rush for spectator seats as soon as the doors opened.

The proceedings were delayed briefly so that the jurors, who had been sequestered for several days, could pay a short visit to their homes. A few minutes after 10:00 a.m., they returned to the courtroom "looking as refreshed as men who have enjoyed the toilet, the cheering touch of invigorating linen, and have parted in health and cheerfulness from those they love."[2]

Law Octon was the first witness scheduled to testify that morning. Before he could be summoned to the stand, however, Dudley Selden rose and, in a voice that rang with indignation, launched into a fierce denunciation of the *Herald* and the *Tattler* for running their lurid woodcuts. Describing each of the offending images in detail, Selden maintained that the titillating tactics of Bennett and his ilk—their "calculated efforts to inflame public passion"—threatened the very foundations of justice. "The ordinary representations are sufficiently bad," said Selden, "but when you come to that kind of publication that is intended to operate upon the prejudice and passion of the people, how is it possible to obtain witnesses capable of giving unbiased testimony or a jury that will fairly weigh the facts?"

Warming to his subject, Selden proceeded to make an argument that continues to be advanced to this day by critics of media violence: that continuous exposure to images of bloodshed and cruelty has a corrupting effect upon the audience, which demands progressively savage forms of entertainment to satisfy its atavistic cravings. If sensationalistic sheets like the *Herald* were permitted to operate unchecked, Selden warned, American civilization would inevitably revert to the barbarity of ancient Rome.

"The disease is rapidly growing," said Selden. "Your Honor, from his extensive reading, surely remembers the incidents in early history where slight and at first disgusting exhibitions of brutal combat finally became incorporated with public taste and sentiment and the Colosseum had to be raised to gratify public passion, where the gladiator displayed his power, and death and rapine became the food of an adulterated population. The same process is going on now. What yesterday would have struck the public with a sort of unwillingness to touch, today they approve of, and in a week they seek as food on which the human mind feeds."

Citing the statute dealing with those who "interfere with administration of justice," Selden concluded by calling on the court to "do what it ought to do and what I believe it will do"—namely, issue warrants of arrest for James Gordon Bennett and the *Tattler*'s John Dillon and John M. Moore.

Judge Kent, however, was unmoved by the argument. While sharing Selden's concern over the growing power of the penny press to shape popular opinion, he insisted that it was "not the duty of the court to grapple with such mighty questions" or to "undertake to reform the community." As for the pictures in the *Herald* and the *Tattler*, Kent was confident that the jury had been shielded from their pernicious influence.

"In the proceedings in this case," said the judge, "it has been the effort of the court, and I believe one which has been attended with perfect success, to keep the jury beyond the reach of all external effect. Since empanelled they have been strictly prohibited from conversing with others or of being placed in a situation where their minds could be likely to receive any outside bias."

Just the previous day, Kent continued, "one of the jurors asked permission to read a newspaper, but I thought it my duty to deny his request, and I have reason to believe, and do believe, that the jurors have been kept perfectly safe from everything that could operate from abroad in relation to the trial."

Concluding that "the jury has been kept pure and unaffected and can present a fair and impartial decision," Kent denied Selden's motion—a decision that drew effusive, if not sycophantic, praise from James Gordon Bennett. In an editorial that ran the following day, he extolled the judge for "surrounding the bench with that high-toned, moral, holy, and intellectual atmosphere that commands the admiration of society and advances the cause of civilization."[3]

• • •

Proceeding with his methodical reconstruction of the case, Whiting called Law Octon, superintendent of the Granite Building and the only witness whose racial characteristics—"light yellow skin colored man"—the newspapers found it necessary to specify. Substantiating Wheeler's account, Octon described the peculiar events of September 17 and his own firsthand observation, on the following day, of John Colt's struggles to move the heavy pine box downstairs.

Selden's cross-examination seemed designed to suggest that someone other than Colt might have committed the murder. He had Octon identify all the other tenants of the building, explain who had keys to the rear door, and describe the layout of the backyard. Since there was no doubt that Samuel Adams had died at Colt's hands, this line of questioning left some observers nonplussed, especially James Gordon Bennett, who—still smarting from Selden's attack on his integrity—derided it as "foolish and unnecessary."[4]

Richard Barstow, the cartman who conveyed the pine box to the *Kala-*

mazoo, was the next to take the stand. His testimony added nothing new to the already familiar tale, though he did lighten up the proceedings with some inadvertent humor when Whiting asked how much he had been paid for the job. "The gentleman gave me two shillings and sixpence in change," said Barstow, then added with a grumble: "I should have charged him three shillings, but I thought I'd have more trouble getting the other sixpence out of him than it was worth." Barstow's querulous tone—which suggested that he still felt aggrieved at having been underpaid—elicited chuckles from the spectator section and even a rare smile from Colt himself.

All traces of merriment vanished with the testimony of William Godfrey, the superintendent of carts, who had helped the authorities track down Barstow and assisted in removing the crate that contained Samuel Adams's moldering corpse. For the first time in the trial, the morbid curiosity seekers who had flocked to the courtroom in quest of ghoulish thrills had their expectations fully satisfied.

Under close questioning by Whiting—who clearly meant to horrify the jurors with the sheer ghastliness of the crime—Godfrey recounted his descent into the bowels of the *Kalamazoo*; the hoisting of the box between decks; and the removal of its lid by the ship's carpenter, who had pried it off with chisel and hammer, releasing a loathsome stench.

Inside the box, wrapped in some old awning, was "the dead body of a man," Godfrey explained. "The face was up towards the lid of the box. There was a rope around the neck and drawn round the legs so as to draw the head between the knees." The corpse was naked except for a shirt which was "torn halfway down" to the navel, leaving the breast exposed. There appeared to be a quantity of common table salt "scattered all over the breast," perhaps as much as "two quarts' worth." Maggots squirmed among the salt.

"The breast was green, mortified," Godfrey continued. "I've seen salt of beef when nearly dissolved, and this looked just like that. I could see the ribs. I've seen several bodies that had been mortified, and this looked like them, only a little more of a greenish cast."

By the time Godfrey was finished, a shocked silence had descended on the courtroom. In Selden's cross-examination, he did his best to impeach the character of the witness. Even Godfrey's admission, however, that he had wagered on the outcome of the trial with Malachi Fallon—deputy keeper of the Tombs and a notorious "sporting man who kept fighting cocks and bred pit dogs in the prison yard"—did nothing to mitigate the impact of his testimony.[5]

Assistant Coroner Abner Milligan, who followed Godfrey to the stand, described the other items found inside the crate. Stuffed beneath the trussed-up corpse were various articles of the victim's clothing: "a dress coat much cut to pieces and a black stock cut in front, smeared with blood and buckled behind."

Asked what had become of these garments, Milligan explained that, along with the crate, they had been taken to the Tombs and stored in an empty cell. A few days later, the clothing was disinfected by a young apothecary named E. D. Warner, who doused them with a solution of chloride of lime and vitriol water and allowed them to dry before returning them to the box. "After two or three days," said Milligan, "the smell became less offensive, but it's still pretty bad now."

Before Milligan was dismissed, District Attorney Whiting—intent on making the full horror of Colt's deed palpable to the jury—asked that the box be brought into the courtroom and admitted as evidence.

"If the whole box is brought in," Milligan responded, "it will make everybody sick."

Judge Kent reflected for a moment before making his ruling. Milligan was directed to bring only the lid of the box, along with the coat and the stock. "And as they are bound to be very offensive," Kent added, "we will have them examined the last thing. We will then adjourn immediately afterwards so the room can be ventilated."[6]

34

On Saturday, January 22, New Yorkers learned of another "horrid murder" that had occurred in their city. This one also involved a victim named Adams: Mrs. Ann Adams of 28 Amity Lane.

On the previous evening, at around 5:50 p.m., Mrs. Adams's husband, James, "a man of very intemperate habits and in the habit of beating and abusing his wife," returned home drunk and began berating the servant girl, Annie Gorman, "who was setting the table for tea." Seizing a plate and throwing it at her, Adams "said he would have her life, at the same time snatching up a large carving knife from the table."

Just then, Mrs. Adams, who had been out in the yard hanging laundry, rushed in and, seeing her husband brandishing the knife at the terrified girl, threatened to have him arrested. With an enraged roar,

> Adams sprang upon her, thrust the knife into her right breast some four inches, then gave her a second wound, driving the carving knife with great force through her corset board and the centre of her breast bone into the right ventricle of her heart. The murderer then pursued Annie Gorman, who sprang from the rear window into the yard, escaped, and ran to a neighbor's house in Wooster Street, followed by Mrs. Adams, screaming murder and covered with blood, who, after sitting down in a chair for a few minutes, expired soon after the arrival of the physicians. A constable having been sent for, came and, arrest-

ing Mr. Adams, conducted him to the upper police office where he was locked up and fully committed by the Coroner for trial.[1]

Savage as it was, the slaying of Mrs. Adams made little impact on the public. Within days, the story had vanished from the news, confirming James Gordon Bennett's observation that, when it came to selling papers, "such everyday matters" as mere wife murder could not hope to compete with a "sublime" horror like the Colt-Adams case.

• • •

As one commentator on the Colt affair has written, though the "trial began slowly and calmly," it "soon developed into one of the rowdiest, most startling, and most bizarre the city had yet seen."[2] The turning point in that transformation took place on Saturday the twenty-second.

Before the proceedings got under way, Abner Milligan arose with a surprising announcement about the box lid he had been ordered to bring in. While the crate itself was still in the empty jail cell where it had been stored for the past few months, the lid was nowhere to be found. "I have made a thorough search for it," said Milligan, "but it is lost."

Grilled by Whiting, Milligan explained that "almost everyone on the debtor's side of the prison had access to that cell." Though the door was padlocked, he had "no doubt that there are a great many keys that fit that padlock among the police officers and watch. It is a very common lock."

Furious over the loss of what he regarded as a key piece of evidence, Whiting summoned various employees of the Tombs, including Warden James Hyde, a turnkey named Swain, a "prison engineer" named Lummere, and Deputy Keeper Malachi Fallon. All denied knowing anything about the missing lid.

John David, a police officer, offered a possible clue as to what had become of it. While making the rounds of the Tombs several weeks earlier, David had detected "a powerful smell coming from one of the cells" and "was asked by the watchman, H. Patrick, if I'd like to see the box Mr. Adams was found in, the one that made the smell." David had declined the offer, but his testimony suggested that at least one man with access to the lid—Watchman Patrick—understood its potential value as a curio. David's tale lent credence to speculations that someone—if not Patrick, then an-other enterprising Tombs employee—had sold the lid, perhaps to the pro-prietor of one of the city's dime museums, where such grisly relics of notorious crimes always proved to be a big draw.

Since the cover was gone, Whiting—still determined to present the physical evidence of Colt's elaborate efforts at concealment—asked that the crate itself be shown to the jury. Milligan warned that even now, three months after its fetid contents had been removed, the box "was still very of-fensive." Nevertheless, bowing to Whiting's request, Judge Kent ordered the young assistant coroner to repair directly to the Tombs and "bring the item at once to court."[3]

• • •

For the first three days of the trial, John Colt had displayed little emotion, observing the proceedings with a kind of aloof interest. Apart from an oc-casional frown or a fleeting smile, his expression remained neutral. His brother Sam, seated beside him, seemed far more anxious than the defen-dant himself. As for their father, Christopher, the strain of the occasion had proved too much for the sixty-two-year-old gentleman, who had fallen ill and retreated to Hartford. To the spectators and newspapermen keeping a close eye on John's reactions, his impassive demeanor seemed the mark of a cold and even remorseless nature.

On Saturday morning, however, the court finally got to witness another side of John Colt. It occurred during the testimony of the first witness of the day, Mayor Robert Morris. Describing the visit he had paid to the boarding-house room that Colt shared with his mistress, Morris identified the items he had found in the small locked trunk that Caroline Henshaw had shown him. In addition to some printed advertisements for John's accounting text, a few letters and other personal documents, and the gold pocket watch owned by Samuel Adams, there was a folded piece of paper containing sev-eral locks of hair. The outside of the paper was inscribed: "Hair of Sarah Colt, my mother; Margaret Colt and Sarah Ann Colt, deceased."

At this point, John—who had grown visibly agitated as Morris de-scribed the cherished keepsakes—"burst into tears, covered his face and wept bitterly for some time."[4]

Colt's outburst was in marked contrast to the deportment of Emeline

Adams, widow of the victim. Though dressed, according to custom, in deep mourning, she evinced little emotion as she recalled her last meal with her husband, described the clothing he was wearing when he left home, and positively identified both his gold pocket watch and wedding ring. Even the sight of his "sadly torn and mutilated" coat, admitted as evidence and displayed to the jury, did nothing to shake her self-possession.

While some observers admired her calmness and composure under such trying circumstances, James Gordon Bennett remained irked by her refusal to become "a shattered wreck" and join her husband in the grave. Reporting on her testimony in the late edition of his paper, he made no effort to conceal his disapproval, deriding her performance as "cold, unfeeling and flippant."[5]

It was not until Dr. C. R. Gilman began to testify that Mrs. Adams appeared to grow unsettled. Gilman, who had performed the autopsy on Samuel Adams, offered the most detailed and graphic description to date of the flyblown thing that had once been Mrs. Adams's husband.

Along with a colleague, Dr. Richard Kissam, Gilman had been summoned to the Dead House, where he'd "found on the table the body of a man much decayed. Alongside the table was the box from which they told me the body had been taken. The body was excessively offensive and covered with worms."

It was clear at a glance that the victim had died of massive head injuries. "The whole of the upper part of his forehead was beaten in just about where the roots of the hair would be." Gilman judged that these wounds to the front of the skull could have "readily been made" by the implement that Whiting now displayed to the court: the hatchet-hammer found in Colt's office. He had, however, discovered a small but striking anomaly elsewhere. On the left side of the head "just behind the ear and a little above it," there was a "small, round, clean hole into which you could thrust a finger." Gilman was "at a loss to see how it could have been made. I never could account for it satisfactorily to myself. I suppose the hatchet might possibly have done it, but it would be a remarkable fact if it did."

A large nail or spike driven into the skull with a mallet might have produced it, said Gilman, but there was no evidence that anything of the sort had occurred. There was one other possibility, Gilman continued, raising an issue that would generate much controversy in the days and weeks ahead. The small, clean hole behind Adams's left ear could have been made by a bullet.

Of course, there were problems with this theory. The noise reported by both Asa Wheeler and Arzac Seignette—the "clashing of foils"—sounded nothing like the discharge of a pistol. Moreover, no bullet had been found inside Adams's skull, only some bone fragments floating among the putrefied mass of brain matter.

Still, considering John Colt's close relationship to the celebrated sibling seated beside him, it certainly seemed plausible to many observers that a handgun might have been involved in the murder.[6]

• • •

The jurors heard from two more medical experts that day, Drs. Kissam and Archer, who corroborated Gilman's findings and shared his belief that the finger-sized hole could not have been made by the hatchet-hammer. Whether it might have been caused by a gunshot, they were unable to say, since neither had ever seen "a skull that was pierced by a bullet." Other witnesses included Law Octon's wife, Mercy, who told of lending John a handsaw on the day before the murder, and the picture framer Charles J. Walker, who testified that when he had gone to Colt's office later that day to ask him for the saw, "he told me to go to hell."[7]

Before adjourning for the remainder of the weekend, Judge Kent issued his usual instructions to the jurors, reminding them that they were "to speak to no one about the trial" and go nowhere except "in the custody of officers." When one of the jurors, Charles Delvan, "enquired if they might be permitted to spend Sunday at home instead of remaining together during that day," Kent regretfully denied the request.

"If I were able," said Kent, "I would have the trial proceed without intermission but the law prohibits a court being held on Sunday." If the jurors so wished, he added, they could go to church, "but it was necessary that they do so as a body."

District Attorney Whiting worried that permitting the jurors to attend church could be grounds for a later appeal, since they might "hear a sermon about this matter that would influence their verdict." Kent considered this objection briefly before declaring that he would allow the jurors to attend church "if the prisoner consented." After a brief consultation with his attorneys, Colt agreed.

There was still one last order of business to be taken care of. As a "terrible commotion" broke out among the spectators, who jumped to their feet and began jostling for a better view, Abner Milligan entered with the lidless crate, carried it to the front of the courtroom, and set it down on the floor near the jury. A "middling sized packing box of the ordinary appearance," it consisted of two pieces of wood on each side and two on the bottom, all secured with nails whose ends protruded into the box. Inside was the bundle of canvas variously described as old sailcloth and window awning. The odor emanating from the box was, in the words of one reporter, "not gratifying to the olfactories," though it was the sight of the object even more than its smell that caused John Colt to wince and avert his face.[8]

As a number of jurors pressed handkerchiefs to their noses, Milligan testified that Adams's trussed-up body had been crammed into the center of the box. Holding up the piece of canvas, he explained that along with "some oakum," the cloth had been stuffed into either end of the box to keep the corpse from moving around.

By the time he was done with his testimony, a number of people at the front of the courtroom, including Dudley Selden, appeared visibly queasy. Even before Milligan had finished bundling the awning back into the box, "Mr. Selden and other gentlemen in the vicinity had fled the courtroom."[9]

35

It was no secret that John's attorneys intended to claim that the slaying of Samuel Adams was a case of manslaughter—not a cold-blooded, premeditated murder but a killing committed in the heat of passion and provoked by the victim. Anticipating this argument, District Attorney Whiting began Monday's session by summoning a parade of witnesses to attest to the printer's gentle and pacific nature.

David Downs, a cobbler who made boots and shoes for the printer and his wife, described Adams as a man of "very good temper." This impression was confirmed by several other witnesses. A bookbinder named James Fiora confessed that, though he had "blown up at" Adams on several occasions, the latter "never made any reply." John L. Blake, an elderly clergyman who had occupied rooms directly above Adams's shop for five or six years, described a time when he had spoken "harshly to him unintentionally. He made no reply, but I saw that his feelings were much affected and that he shed a tear." If anything, Blake claimed, Adams was "passive and mild" to a fault. Referring to the printer's juvenile apprentices, Blake declared that they "were frequently noisy, but he did not appear to have the necessary energy to keep them in proper discipline. He was always kind to them—perhaps too much so."

Some of the testimony, however, suggested that Samuel Adams was not quite the model of equanimity that his staunchest defenders claimed. Under cross-examination, several of the witnesses, including the Reverend Mr. Blake, were forced to concede that they could not say how Adams would react in circumstances that might "try his temper." Hugh Monahan,

Adams's foreman, had seen his employer "fly into a passion twice" during the preceding year, "once when a man threatened to sue him." Most relevant of all to Colt's situation was the testimony of a merchant named Charles Post, who suggested that, during the final months of his life when he felt under increasing financial pressure, Adams was prone to outbursts of extreme, irrational suspicion over matters of money—behavior that seemed to verge (in the terminology of a later era) on paranoia.

Post, called upon to identify Adams's gold pocket watch, had been present when the printer accepted the timepiece as partial payment for a debt owed him by the young merchant Lyman Ransom. During cross-examination, Dudley Selden asked Post how Adams had reacted when Ransom first explained that he did not have the money to make good on his note. Had Adams "displayed temper" or used "harsh language"?

When Whiting objected to this line of questioning, Selden appealed to Judge Kent. "I do not wish to lacerate the feelings of the friends of Mr. Adams by saying anything against his character or general conduct," Selden said in kindly tones. "I would not harrow the breasts of those attached to the unfortunate deceased whose bones have now been committed to the dust by even insinuating anything against him. Nevertheless, if we can show that he had exhibited a strong temper when endeavoring on another occasion to collect money, we have a right to do so."

After briefly considering the matter, Kent ruled in Selden's favor, declaring "that a man's temper could, under these circumstances, be shown." Selden then repeated his question to Post.

"Mr. Adams had a confab with Mr. Ransom," the merchant answered. "He seemed to be angry because Mr. Ransom didn't have the money to pay him. He told Mr. Ransom he believed he meant to swindle him out of his debt."

Had Adams said anything else? Selden asked.

Post allowed that he had, then repeated Adams's words: " 'Everybody is trying to cheat me.' "[1]

. . .

Before court was adjourned for the day, the mystery of the missing lid was finally solved, laying to rest the rumors that it had been sold to a dime museum, perhaps by the city watchman, H. Patrick. The answer was provided by another watchman, Benjamin Lewen, who revealed that a month or so earlier, he and a coworker named Ball had been on duty at the watchhouse during a particularly frigid evening. No coal had yet been laid up for the winter, so they went searching for "anything we could make a fire with." Seeing the lid inside the cell—and finding the door open—they had taken it, split it into kindling, and used it to build a fire.

Ball, who took the stand next, confirmed Lewen's story and added a detail that left no doubt that the wooden object the two men had incinerated was the lid of the infamous packing crate. "It smelled strong at first," said Ball, "but even stronger when we put it in the fire."[2]

36

*D*r. Gilman's testimony concerning the small, clean hole behind the corpse's left ear had raised a possibility that the prosecution was eager to explore: that the killing of Samuel Adams was a premeditated crime committed with a pistol. Colt, in this scenario, had "planned the encounter in advance and armed himself accordingly."[1] True, neither Asa Wheeler nor his student had heard a gunshot. But the district attorney felt he could account for that anomaly.

In the years before the development of self-contained cartridges, Colt's revolvers operated by cap and ball. Each chamber of the revolving cylinder was loaded with a charge of gunpowder and a lead ball. A small percussion cap containing a highly combustible compound was then affixed to a nipple on the back end of each chamber. When struck by the hammer, the cap would explode, igniting the powder inside the chamber, which propelled the bullet through the gun barrel.

It was, of course, the detonated gunpowder that produced the loudest bang. What Whiting proposed to show was that a man could be killed by a pistol loaded with a cap and ball, but no gunpowder: that the percussion cap alone could "explode with sufficient force to drive a ball into a man's head without making enough noise to be heard in the next room."[2]

Dudley Selden had objected on technical grounds to the introduction of any evidence concerning a firearm. The indictment, he argued, made no mention of any weapon except a hatchet. On Tuesday morning, however, Judge Kent began by ruling in favor of the district attorney—thus opening the way for some of the most remarkable scenes ever witnessed in an American courtroom.

· · ·

Recalled to the stand as the day's first witness, Asa Wheeler confirmed that John Colt did, in fact, keep a pistol on the premises. As Wheeler recollected, on the evening of September 13, just four days before Samuel Adams's disappearance,

> Colt came into my room after school was over, and in the course of our conversation he spoke of his brother. I asked him if his brother was the inventor of the patent pistol bearing his name. He replied that he was and asked me if I had ever seen any of his pistols. I said that I had not. He said he had one in his room and would let me see it. He went and got one and returned with it to my room. It was a very elegant weapon with a beautiful pearl handle and a very ingenious way of firing with a cylinder. It had his brother's name on it as the maker, I think. At any rate, he said it was his brother's.

Wheeler spent about fifteen minutes examining and handling the weapon. He never saw it again, though "after the discovery of the murder" he had immediately "thought of the pistol."

Grilled closely by Dudley Selden about the dimensions and workmanship of the gun, Wheeler acknowledged that he did "not know much about firearms—I know more about bookkeeping." He proceeded to prove the point with a comment that elicited a prolonged outburst of laughter from the spectators. Asked about the gun's cocking mechanism, Wheeler was at a loss to describe it. "But there was certainly a cock to that pistol," he declared, to the general merriment of the courtroom.[3]

The consul general of France, a gentleman named Charles de la Forest, was next on the stand. Monsieur de la Forest testified that he had purchased two particularly fine specimens of Colt's pocket pistols for the Prince de Joinville, who was then visiting the United States aboard the French navy frigate the *Belle Poule* (the ship that, sixteen months earlier, had transported Napoléon's remains from St. Helena back to France). Eager to try out his new acquisitions, the prince had fired one of the pistols on deck.

"When merely propelled by a cap," the consul testified, "the ball was sent one hundred fifty or one hundred sixty feet, struck a hard board, dented it, and rebounded ten or twelve feet. At a distance of twelve paces, again with a cap alone and no powder, the ball went through a book of about one hundred fifty pages and two thick covers. The noise was very trifling, like the cracking of a whip."

An assistant alderman named Charles A. Underwood agreed with de la Forest's characterization of the noise made by Colt's pistol when fired with a cap only. Though Underwood had never handled one of the revolvers himself, he had often visited the Patent Arms Manufacturing Company store on Broadway and had "seen there a ball sent from a Colt's pocket pistol, with a cap alone, the distance of twenty-five or thirty feet and half embedded in a board. I consider this Colt's pistol the very perfection in firearms."[4]

The prosecution's final witness was James Short, the "humble, broken-down son of Erin" from the city poorhouse who had been enlisted to wash Adams's decomposed body at the Dead House. "A miserable, nondescript-looking character, four feet high" (in the typically blunt words of James Gordon Bennett), Short recalled that there were "some bones laying loose" inside Adams's shattered skull. One of the pieces was "about the breadth of two fingers," the others slightly smaller. After removing and washing them, he had "given them to the doctors," who had laid them aside on a table. Later, after the autopsy was concluded and the body placed in a coffin and taken to the cemetery, Short discovered that the skull fragments were still there, so "I wrapped them in a piece of paper and ran down to the burying ground just in time to put them in the grave."

"That will be all, Mr. Short," said Dudley Selden at the end of his cross-examination. "You may step down."

"Yes, and I am glad of it," Short said as he rose from the chair, "for it's a very bad business, and that's a fact."[5]

• • •

A few minutes later, the prosecution having rested its case, John A. Morrill—by all accounts the most smooth-spoken of Colt's three attorneys—stepped to the front of the courtroom to make the opening argument for the defense.

"Gentlemen of the jury," he intoned, "it now becomes the duty of the counsel for the prisoner—their solemn duty—to enter more minutely into the examination of the evidence which has been produced against the unfortunate individual who stands before you, a young man just entering into life who has no friend around him but a brother—who is deprived by misfortune of the presence of his father. You know where his mother is, and also where are his beloved sisters.

"While you have sympathy for him, I must admit that you must also feel the loss sustained by the widow of Mr. Adams, one who has been bereaved by the loss of a tender and affectionate husband. The people ask that the laws shall be fairly administered, but while they do so, are sometimes carried away, and without thought will condemn an individual unheard. But the jury must lay aside these feelings—must lay aside feelings not only for the unfortunate prisoner but for Mrs. Adams and for public prejudice. You must take hold of the case with clear, dispassionate minds, remembering to blend with justice the attributes of mercy."

Following this prefatory plea for impartiality—laced with a heart-tugging allusion to the defendant's tragic family history—Morrill allowed a note of righteous indignation to enter his voice as he "complained of the new charge thrown upon them, of the life of the deceased having been taken by a pistol instead of by a hatchet, as mentioned in the indictment." He then went on to insist that if the jurors had "any doubt whether it was murder or manslaughter or justifiable homicide," they were legally bound to give the prisoner the benefit of the doubt.

He continued:

> Let us see if there is any evidence that Adams was murdered by John C. Colt. Has it been shown that there was an appointment, or even an allusion to an appointment on that day? Had Adams ever complained of Colt or has any bad feeling been shown between them? On the contrary, the best disposition existed between them, continued money transactions took place, and they were on the kindest and best of terms.

Had John C. Colt intended to murder Adams, would he do it in a room adjoining Wheeler's, when he knew his students and himself were engaged, where persons were continually? Would it be the felon's desire at such a time and under such circumstances, when detection was certain, to take a life? He must have been mad to do so. But thank God, we set up no insanity in this case, and the proposition shows the falsity on its face.

Having thus disposed of widespread rumors that the defense planned to mount an insanity plea, Morrill proceeded to sketch out the line of argument that he and his cocounsel intended to follow.

"In regard to the idea of premeditated murder, where is the motive? Where is the malice? Where is the bad intention of the prisoner? Some papers even went so far as to accuse the prisoner of purchasing articles for boxing up the deceased and salting him down," Morrill said, throwing a pointed glance at James Gordon Bennett, who was seated not far from him in the area reserved for the newspapermen. "We can show that, so far from having purchased those articles in advance, he already had them in his possession."

Indeed, said Morrill, despite the absence of an eyewitness, the defense was prepared to prove that the murder was not merely unpremeditated but justified. "No person saw Adams and Colt together except the Great God himself," he declared. "No person saw Colt and Adams together in that room. But there are providential circumstances which will show that there never was premeditation on his part but that he was acting in a way to protect himself according to the laws of the God of Nature. We will show that the blows were such as could only have been given in self-defense."

After addressing and dismissing several other points suggested by the prosecution—including the possibility that Colt had killed Adams for his gold pocket watch—Morrill turned to what he knew would be the critical issue for the jury: the chillingly methodical way that Colt had attempted to conceal his crime, and the ghastly treatment to which Adams's corpse had been subjected.

"Gentlemen," Morrill declared, looking each juror in the eye in turn. "In relation to the degrees of crime, you are to hold continually in your mind that you are bound to separate the actual homicide from the subsequent conduct of the prisoner. He might, overcome by excitement, have committed the deed and afterward found it necessary to conceal the body as Moses did the African when he had killed him—he thought it would be best to place him out of the way.

"No man under similar circumstances can tell how he would act. If he were as brave as Julius Caesar, he might say, 'I will put him in the box, I will use stratagem, I will conceal it.' But it is for you to weigh how the act itself was done. I will show you one act as to John C. Colt. They say in public prints that he was a hard-hearted man—everything bad and crude. But I will show that he was kind to the poor, always ready to do good, and has borne the character of one of the mildest and one of the best dispositioned men almost in this community."

After likening John to Moses and extolling him as a model of both Christian charity and civic virtue, Morrill closed with a humble assertion of faith in the jury's rectitude and fair-mindedness.

"Gentlemen, John C. Colt, poor and friendless, a fellow citizen, comes before you charged with a crime. He comes before you in defense of that life which is dear to all. He asks you to mete out to him justice. It is all he asks; it is all we ask. We seek but one thing—it is that he may have mercy according to law—and if he has such, we have no doubt that he will find a safe deliverance in your hand."

With that, Morrill reseated himself, while his cocounsel Dudley Selden rose and called the prisoner's first witness, whose testimony, in James Gordon Bennett's estimation, would "represent one of the most remarkable features of any trial ever known."[6]

37

Carrying a pair of slender wooden cases, the witness, Samuel Colt, stepped to the front of the courtroom. Asked to identify himself, he replied that, in addition to being the defendant's brother, he was "the inventor of Colt's patent firearms" and was "perfectly acquainted with their construction." At Selden's request, he then proceeded with what the papers described as "a series of experiments touching the power of pistols with caps alone."

Opening the larger of the two cases, he removed a five-shot revolver with an eight-inch barrel and began to load it. Holding it up for the jury to see, he drove a ball into each chamber, then put the percussion caps in place. As he performed this procedure, he explained that the bullets were standard musket balls of the kind "used for government service" and the caps were "the strongest that can be got." He used no gunpowder.

Holding the gun in his right hand, Sam placed his left by the end of the barrel and aimed at the wall near Judge Kent, "who moved his seat to be a little more out of range." Then, "as counsel, jury, spectators, and the bar all crowded to see the result," he snapped off the five rounds.[1] Though the caps exploded with a surprisingly loud report, they produced so little force that Sam was able to catch the balls in his bare hand as they emerged from the barrel.

Next, after reloading the gun, he took aim and fired at a book that Dudley Selden had propped up on a table about twelve paces away. The bullet "made but very little impression, penetrating only nine leaves and indenting twenty-four." Sam finished by repeating the experiments with the other gun, a short-barreled pocket pistol. The results were the same.

Before Sam was dismissed, Selden asked him if there was any validity to the theory advanced by the prosecution that a bullet from one of his revolvers, discharged only by a percussion cap, could have produced the small hole in Adams's skull.

Sam addressed his reply directly to the jurors. "It is impossible for a ball to penetrate the head from one of these pistols if a cap alone is used," he declared, "even if the pistol be held close to the head."[2]

Sam's testimony was corroborated by a physician named C. B. Zabriskie, who, in addition to his medical activities, worked as a sales agent for Colt's Patent Arms and ran the company store at 155 Broadway. Claiming that he had "fired off the pistols with a cap thousands of times in order to exhibit them," Zabriskie said that he did "not suppose, from my knowledge of the human skull, that it could be penetrated by a ball propelled only by a cap. It is impossible that the skull could have been more than bruised."[3]

• • •

The lucky spectators who managed to gain entrance that day had already been treated to a remarkable sight: a solemn courtroom "converted into a shooting-gallery" by Samuel Colt himself.[4] As it happened, another, even more dramatic display was still to come.

Recalled to the stand by Dudley Selden, Dr. C. R. Gilman—the witness who first suggested that the mysterious head wound was a bullet hole—made a surprising disclosure. Just hours before, on the order of the court, Samuel Adams's cadaver had been removed from its grave and carried to a "small building inside the burial grounds," where the head was "detached from the body" and reexamined by several of the medical experts who had already testified for the prosecution.

As Gilman explained, he and his colleagues began by inspecting "the cavity of the skull." They had found absolutely no evidence of a bullet— "no foreign substance there whatsoever," as Gilman put it. Next, Gilman had stuck the little finger of one hand into the disputed wound. His pinkie had "passed easily into the hole and rested at the second joint." He could feel that the wound had "ragged edges" and "was slightly oval—one part a very trifle larger than the other." His investigation had caused him to revise his earlier opinion. "My conclusion is changed from what it was," he declared. "I think it improbable that the hole was made by a ball of any description."

At the same time, he remained adamant that it was not caused by the murder weapon. "It is inconceivable to me how it is possible that such a hole could have been made by a hatchet." Perhaps, he ventured, when Adams's corpse was inside the crate, the skull had been punctured by a protruding nail. The shifting of the body as the box was "carried to Maiden Lane, put on board the vessel, and afterwards taken to the Dead House might have been sufficient to drive the nail through the head, and the hole might have been ground out larger and larger as the body moved around."[5]

To further refute the prosecution's theory that Adams was killed by a handgun, the defense had subpoenaed its own medical expert, the distinguished surgeon Dr. Valentine Mott, founder of the Rutgers Medical College and future president of the New York Academy of Medicine. Mott, however, had not been present either at the original autopsy or at the examination conducted earlier in the day by Dr. Gilman. The defense therefore wished "to have Mr. Adams's skull produced in court" so that Mott could examine it before testifying, said Selden.

District Attorney Whiting raised no objection to this startling request. Coroner Archibald Archer, however, pointed out that the "body had probably been re-interred by this time." Judge Kent immediately ordered him to repair to the cemetery, dig up the body for a second time if necessary, and return as quickly as possible with Samuel Adams's decapitated head.

• • •

While awaiting Archer's return, Selden called a half dozen witnesses to the stand, including several of John Colt's business associates, who attested to his "mild" and "gentlemanly" character. It was roughly two hours later when—in the oddly matter-of-fact words of an observer—"the head of Mr. Adams was brought into the court."[6]

Wrapped in newspaper, it was carried to the front of the chamber by Dr. Archer, while a great commotion arose in the spectator section and Judge Kent pounded his gavel for order. With the ghastly bundle in his lap, Archer seated himself beside the table reserved for the reporters, who were struck by the "thrillingly interesting" scene. "There Colt sat, within a few feet of it. The hand that struck the blow and the head that was still in death came nearly in contact. What must have been his feelings!"[7]

After a brief discussion among the lawyers, the medical experts, and Judge Kent, a decision was reached that "the head should be taken into an adjoining room and examined" by Dr. Mott and Dr. David L. Rogers, a prominent New York surgeon who had achieved earlier repute as an expert witness in the Helen Jewett affair. When the two physicians emerged less than an hour later, Rogers testified that he "was well satisfied from the examination and from comparing the hatchet with the wound that the hole was made with the sharp side of the hatchet. It fits the wound precisely."

Whatever sense of vindication the defense team might have felt at this moment was immediately quashed by District Attorney Whiting, who—in a stroke of "prosecutorial brilliance" that would have enormous repercussions on the outcome of the trial—"asked that the head and the hatchet be shown to the jury."[8]

Perceiving the potentially devastating effect of such a display, Selden instantly objected.

Judge Kent acknowledged that the proposed demonstration would undoubtedly be "painful." Nevertheless, he ruled that, in the interests of justice, the court "must yield" to the request.

In an apologetic tone—as if regretting the need for such a drastic measure—Whiting insisted that he and his cocounsel "were only seeking the truth." By "making desperate efforts to break down the testimony" of the prosecution's witnesses, the defense had left him no choice. "If it could be avoided," he said, "we would gladly agree not to have the head exhibited. But it is necessary that the jury see it."[9]

Before the demonstration could take place, all the women in attendance were ordered to leave the courtroom. More than a few, indignant at their forced exclusion from the ghoulish spectacle, protested loudly as they were ushered into the hallway.[10]

Once the doors were closed behind them, Dr. Archer, seated with the head in his lap, removed the paper wrapping and handed the blackened thing to Dr. Rogers, who held it up for the jury. "A thrill of horror passed through the crowded chamber," wrote one observer. "For the first time during the trial, the prisoner buried his face in his hands and groaned."[11]

With the head in one hand and the murder weapon in the other, Rogers demonstrated how the corner of the hatchet "precisely fitted" the small hole over the left ear. He then showed how the hammer part of the implement conformed to the indentation on the right sight of the skull, the two joining together "fairly as a mould." "It was," remarked the reporter for the *Sun*, "an interesting but dreadful sight."[12]

Dr. Mott, the last witness of the day, corroborated Rogers's findings in unequivocal terms. "I have no doubt," he declared, "that the hole was made with the hatchet."[13]

• • •

When the trial adjourned for the night, observers agreed that Selden had succeeded in utterly refuting the prosecution's theory. As Bennett put it, "all the humbug about the pistol wound was blown to the winds."[14] But Selden's victory had been purchased at a heavy price. Outmaneuvered by Whiting, he had been forced to expose the jurors to a sight that couldn't fail to appall them. For the twelve men who held John Colt's fate in their hands, "the awful impression made by the ghastly head," wrote one commentator, "would never be obliterated."[15]

38

It was lucky for John that the jurors were prevented from seeing the newspapers. On Wednesday, January 26, a story appeared that cast his character in a highly unflattering light.

Headlined "Civil Verdict Against John C. Colt," the article reported that, on the previous afternoon in the Philadelphia District Court, a judgment was rendered against him in a suit brought by the venerable Cincinnati publisher Ephraim Morgan, who was seeking to recover an unpaid debt of $576.68. Among legal experts, no one could think of a prior instance in which a defendant charged with homicide had been found liable in a separate civil lawsuit while his murder trial was in progress. As the newspapers put it, it was "a singular fact never before known."[1] It also raised serious questions about John's financial probity at the very moment when his lawyers were struggling to portray him as a victim of circumstance—a man unjustly assailed by a desperate creditor whose own belligerence was to blame for the tragedy.

• • •

Because of the crowds that continued to flock to the trial, many members of the bar found themselves unable to secure seats. On Wednesday morning, before the day's proceedings began, Judge Kent read aloud an anonymous letter from one of these aggrieved individuals, complaining that he and other "gentlemen of the legal profession were being excluded from the trial to make room for the common rabble."

Taking the writer to task for such high-handed sentiments, Kent declared that he "knew of no such persons as 'the common rabble'—the term is alien to our laws." Because of the large number of witnesses and "others necessary to the trial," space inside the courtroom was severely limited. Places also had to be reserved for the various reporters who were there to serve the public's right to "learn about the proceedings." Whatever seats remained, Kent affirmed, were available to anyone, regardless of profession or position. "The Court would be happy to accommodate the members of the bar," he said, "but it is not possible that control can be had over the spectators so far as to compel it."[2]

Of the nearly two dozen witnesses called to the stand that day, virtually all were there to testify either to Colt's easygoing nature or Adams's hot-tempered one. Among many others, John Howard Payne, beloved author of "Home, Sweet Home," declared that he had "the highest opinion of Mr. Colt in every way." By contrast, various individuals who had business dealings with Samuel Adams characterized him as "easily vexed" and "of an excitable disposition."[3]

The dramatic high point of the day, however, was the testimony of a witness whose appearance had been hotly anticipated since the trial began: John's mistress, Caroline Henshaw. If Tuesday's session had served up enough of the macabre to satisfy the morbid tastes of Edgar Allan Poe (who, as events would prove, was closely following the case in the papers), Wednesday's held out the prurient promise of sexual titillation. The women in attendance seemed particularly excited when Caroline's name was called, and as she "advanced to the stand," she "created quite a sensation among the audience."[4]

Taking her seat "directly opposite the prisoner," she threw back the veil of her bonnet, revealing a "remarkably handsome woman with dark blue eyes and round, fair, rosy cheeks."[5] Considering her highly compromised status as John's illicit bedmate, her strikingly poised and dignified demeanor won the admiration even of those most inclined to sniff at her morals.

Much of Dudley Selden's examination focused on John's actions and appearance in the days following the murder. He paid particular attention to the black-and-blue mark that Caroline had observed on the side of John's neck: clear proof, so Selden suggested, that Colt had been attacked.

Whiting countered with questions designed to raise a very different possibility: that the bruise had been caused not by an assailant but by the heavy wooden crate as John wrestled it downstairs. Mostly, however, the district attorney sought to stress John's unsavory character by reminding the jurors of his scandalous living arrangement with Caroline.

Under Whiting's cross, Caroline testified that she had "first become acquainted with Mr. Colt" eighteen months earlier, in August 1841, when both were residing in Philadelphia. At the time, she was boarding at the house of a widow named Stuart and met John when he came there to visit another lodger. Six months later, John "made arrangements to come to New York City." Caroline joined him there shortly afterward. It was then, she said, that they began living together, taking a furnished room at the boardinghouse of a couple named Hart, where she "passed by the name of Mrs. Colt." Later they moved to their present lodgings, a boardinghouse at 42 Monroe Street.

Their life together, as she described it, was one of simple domesticity. They shared a single room, so small that John's well-worn carpetbag had to be stored beneath the bed because "we had no other place to keep it." During the days, when John was at work, Caroline remained at home, sewing or reading or conversing in the parlor with other boarders. After supper, when John "went out of an evening," Caroline "generally went with him." On those rare occasions when he was out by himself, she "did not sit up for him" but went to bed around 10:00 p.m., though she "generally woke up when he came into the room."

Beyond her admission that she "was a mother by Mr. Colt," Caroline made no reference, of course, to their sexual relationship. Even so, her evocation of certain intimate details—of watching him undress when he returned to their room late on the evening of September 17, of seeing him slip into his nightshirt, of turning toward him "as he came into bed"—were startlingly frank in an age when such matters were rarely, if ever, discussed in public. The illicit nature of their relationship added a strong whiff of the forbidden to her account.

For all that, Caroline displayed no embarrassment as she testified. She remained dignified and unruffled, repeatedly casting a warm look at John, who "kept his eye steadily on her." Indeed, it was Whiting who ended up flustered. At one point, apparently meaning to ask *how* John was dressed on the morning after the murder, the district attorney mistakenly asked *if* he was dressed.

"Was he dressed?" exclaimed Caroline. "He was. Do you suppose a gentleman would go into the street without clothes?"

Her spirited answer brought an appreciative laugh from the audience and a flush of chagrin to Whiting's cheek.[6]

Immediately after her testimony, Selden called her former landlords, Isaac and Sarah Hart, to affirm her good character. When Whiting objected, Selden took the opportunity to insist that John would have made an honest woman of Caroline had he not suffered financial reversals during his sojourn in that city.

"The only ground why she and Mr. Colt did not form the relationship of man and wife," said Selden, "was owing to the breaking up of his business and inability to provide an establishment, but they both look forward to the day when they can be wed." Denying the prevailing perception of her as a fallen woman, Selden declared that "she was no prostitute except as regards him. He did wrong and she did, but adverse circumstances alone caused them to live together in the illegitimate manner they did. Still her character, in every other way, is good."

Accounts of the trial do not say whether John showed any reaction to Selden's backhanded defense of Caroline as a prostitute only "as regards him." As for Caroline herself, she was not around to hear it. By then she had already left the premises—escorted from the courtroom by Samuel Colt.[7]

39

With each passing day, the crowds clamoring for entrance to the Colt trial seemed to grow bigger and rowdier. Arriving at City Hall at 8:00 a.m. on Thursday, January 27, James Gordon Bennett marveled at the droves that had already gathered, and found it "impossible to compliment Deputy Sheriff Westervelt too highly for the excellent arrangements which he has made to preserve order." When the doors opened two hours later, the "courtroom immediately became crowded to excess."[1]

The morning session offered one "very singular scene"—nothing to compare to the thrillingly gruesome display of Samuel Adams's decomposed head but macabre enough to create a "considerable sensation" among the audience.[2] Shortly before noon—following the examination of several more witnesses called to describe Adams's peevish and short-tempered disposition—Dudley Selden produced a batch of badly stained and soiled items, including various articles of men's clothing. They been retrieved from the outhouse behind the Granite Building, where—said Selden—they had been dumped by John Colt on the night of the murder.

John P. Brinckerhoff, superintendent of a company in the business of cleaning out privies and converting the contents ("night soil," as it was euphemistically called) into a dried manure called "poudrette," was summoned to the stand to describe the recovery of the evidence. In the first week of October, acting on information provided by John Colt, one of Brinckerhoff's men, armed "with a light and a rake," had been lowered into the privy by rope. His search through the two-foot layer of stinking muck had turned up nothing. At Selden's insistence, however, another attempt was made on Tuesday, January 23. This time, instead of raking through the sewage by lamplight, Brinckerhoff's men had brought it out in tubs and examined it aboveground.

"Go on and state what you discovered there," said Selden.

Besides "some cloth and some pieces of towel," answered Brinckerhoff, they "found a bundle." This consisted of a large linen handkerchief with "diagonal corners" that were "tied in a hard knot." When the knot was undone and the bundle opened, it was found to contain a hat "cut lengthwise in two pieces"; a "folded-up vest," the color of which was difficult to determine, though "it might have been yellow"; a torn pair of gambroon pantaloons, also "neatly folded up"; a pair of suspenders that had been "taken off the pantaloons and wrapped up with them"; part of a badly torn shirt, "completely saturated with blood"; and a pair of shoes. A subsequent search through the thick mass of excrement had uncovered several other items, including "two keys, a silver pencil case, and half dollar piece."

"Is it your belief that the bundle was down there when you first examined that place?" asked Selden.

"From the state the bundle was in and the garments being rotted," replied Brinckerhoff, "I have no doubt that they have laid there for some months. I think the pencil case had also been there some time. Parts of it were very rusty. They must have been overlooked on the first examination."

Shown the pencil case and keys—which, like the other items brought into court, had been thoroughly scrubbed—several of Adams's associates identified them as articles "that he carried in his pocket." Selden then took the unusual step of calling his own cocounsel Robert Emmett, who testified that "a day or two after his arrest, Mr. Colt told me that he had thrown the bundle into the privy; that in pulling off the pantaloons of Mr. Adams, the keys, the pencil case, and half a dollar fell out; that he, Colt, afterwards put those things into his own hat, went downstairs, and threw them down into the privy."[3]

That John had disposed of evidence in the Chambers Street outhouse was the first new detail of the crime to emerge since his arrest four months earlier. But it was only a prelude to the revelations yet to come. Shortly after Emmett's testimony, both the district attorney and the defense announced that "they were through." Intent on wrapping up the trial before the weekend, Judge Kent directed that summations begin immediately after the afternoon recess. When the court reopened at 4:00, Emmett rose at once and delivered what would prove to be the trial's climactic surprise.

The case now before the twelve jurors, he declared, had no "parallel in the history of jurisprudence." Certainly, "there has never been a case in which public excitement has been so strongly directed against a prisoner." Unfortunately, the prosecution had made every effort to exploit those violent passions by casting the crime in the ugliest possible light. Why else, demanded Emmett, did the district attorney summon witnesses to testify "that the body of Mr. Adams had been salted down in the box?" Whiting knew very well that the defendant's "effort to conceal the body" made his offense seem particularly heinous. Surely the testimony concerning the salt "was only calculated to render Colt's actions still more disgusting." "The public officers," said Emmett in indignant tones, "have done their worst against Mr. Colt, and this was driving the last nail in his reputation."

To be sure, continued Emmett, the defense was in no way suggesting that the prisoner was an innocent man. "We do not contend anything other than that the death of Mr. Adams was caused by Mr. Colt." Nevertheless, he insisted, Colt's actions, "no matter how appalling in appearance," did not constitute a case of "deliberate murder" but rather of manslaughter. The "particulars of the crime," once fully known, "render that conclusion irresistible." Emmett now intended to present those particulars for the first time.

Reaching to the defense table, he took hold of a sheaf of papers, held it aloft, and revealed that it was the prisoner's handwritten confession.

"We have admitted that Colt took the life of Mr. Adams, and we now propose to tell you as far as possible how it was done," said Emmett, sending a ripple of excitement through the audience. "As none but the God above us saw the transaction, we have the right to show the manner in which the act was done. I shall speak in the first person, giving the facts as Mr. Colt would, were he to stand up and state them to you."[4]

Then, in the anticipatory hush of the courtroom, Emmett began to read the statement. His recitation would go on for several hours, and in that time, the world would learn virtually all that it would ever know about the murder of Samuel Adams by John C. Colt.

40

*S*amuel Adams called on my office, as near as I can recollect, between the hours of three and four o'clock. Whether he had any special object in view in coming at that time or not, I cannot say. When he entered my office, I was sitting at my table, as usual, and was at that time engaged in looking over a manuscript account book, as I had been engaged in this work for one or two days previous; that is, I was reading over the entries and reconsidering the arithmetical calculations belonging to the entries, etc.

"Mr. Adams seated himself in a chair near the table, and within an arm's length of myself, so near that if we both leaned our heads forward towards each other, I have no doubt that they would have touched. I spoke of my account, which he had at my request handed to me ten or twelve days before. I stated to him that his account was wrong, and read to him at the same time the account as I had made it out on another piece of paper, and requested him to alter his account as I had it. He objected to it at first, saying I did not understand printing. He, however, altered his figures as I read them from my account.

"After he had altered his figures, and on looking it over, he said that he was right at first, and made the remark that I meant to cheat him. Word followed word till it came to blows. The words 'you lie' were passed, and several slight blows, until I received a blow across my mouth, which caused my nose slightly to bleed. I believe I then struck him violently with my fist. We grappled with each other at the time, and I found myself shoved to the wall, with my side and hip to the table.

"At this time he had his hand in my neck handkerchief, twisting it so that I could scarcely breathe, and at the same time pressing me hard upon the wall and table. There was a hammer upon the table which I then immediately seized hold of, and instantly struck him over the head. At this time, I think, his hat was nearly in my face, and his face, I should think, was downwards. I do not think he saw me seize the hammer. The seizing of the hammer and the blow was instantaneous. I think this blow knocked his hat off, but will not be positive. At the time I only remember his twisting my neck handkerchief so tight that it seemed to me as though I lost all power of reason. Still I thought I was striking away with the hammer. Whether he attempted to get the hammer from me or not I cannot say. I do not think he did.

"The first sense of thought was, it seemed, that his hand or something brushed from my neck downwards. I cannot say that I had any sense or reflection till I heard a knock at the door. Yet there is a faint idea still remains that I shoved him off from me, so that he fell over; but of this I cannot say. When I heard the knock at the door, I was instantly startled, and am fully conscious of going and turning the key so as to lock it. I then sat down, for I felt very weak and sick.

"After sitting a few minutes and seeing so much blood, I think I went and looked at poor Adams, who breathed quite loud for several minutes, threw his arms out and was silent. I recollect at this time taking him by the hand, which seemed lifeless, and a horrid thrill came over me that I had killed him.

"About this time some noise startled me. I felt agitated or frightened, and I think I went to the door to see if I had fastened it, and took the key out and turned down the slide. I think I stood for a minute or two, listening to hear if the affray had caused any alarm. I believe I then took a seat near the window. It was a cold, damp day, and the window had been closed all day, except six or eight inches at the top, which I let down when I first went to the office and which remained down all the time I occupied it. I remained in the same seat, I should think, for at least half an hour without moving, unless it was to draw the curtains of the window close while they were within reach. My custom was to leave the curtains about one-third drawn from the side of the window towards Broadway.

"The blood, at the time, was spreading over the floor. There was a great quantity, and I felt alarmed lest it should leak through into the apothecary's store. I tried to stop it by tying my handkerchief round his neck tight. This appeared to do no good. I then looked about the room for a piece of twine, and found in a box which stood in the room, after partially pulling out some awning that was in it, a piece of cord which I tied tightly round his neck after taking the handkerchief off and his stock, too, I think. It was then I discovered so much blood, and the fear of it leaking through the floor caused me to take a towel and gather with it all I could and rinse it into the pail I had in the room. The pail was, I should think, at that time about one-third full of water, and the blood filled it at least another third full. Previous to doing this, I moved the body towards the box, and pulled out part of the awning to rest it on and covered it with the remainder. I never saw his face afterwards.

"After soaking up all the blood I could, which I did as still and hastily as possible, I took my seat again near the window and began to think what was best to do. About this time someone knocked at the door, to which, of course, I paid no attention. My horrid situation remained from this time till dark, a silent space of time of still more horrid reflection. At dusk of the evening, and at the same time some omnibuses were passing, I carefully opened the door and went out as still as possible and, I thought, unheard. I crossed into the park and went down from thence to the City Hotel, my purpose being to relate the circumstance to a brother who was stopping at that house. I saw him in the front reading-room, engaged in conversation with two gentlemen. I spoke to him, a few words passed between us, and seeing that he was engaged, I altered my purpose and returned as far as the park.

"I walked up and down the park, thinking of what was best to do. Many things I thought of—among others, was going to some magistrate and relating the facts to him. The horrors of the excitement, a trial, public censure, and false and foul reports that would be raised by the many who would stand ready to make the best appear worse than the worst for the sake of a paltry pittance gained to them in the publication of perverted truths and original, false, foul, calumniating lies. All this, added to my then feelings, was more than could be borne. Besides, at the time, in addition to the blows given, there would be the mark or evidence of a rope drawn tightly round the neck, which looked too deliberate for anything like death caused in an affray. Firing the building seemed at first a happy thought, and all would be enveloped in flame and wafted into air and ashes. Then the danger of caus-ing the death of others (as there were quite a number who slept in the build-ing), the destruction of property, etc., caused me at once to abandon the idea. I next thought of having a suitable box made and having it leaded in-side so that the blood would not run out, and moving it off somewhere and burying it. Then the delay of all this, and the great liability of being de-tected.

"After wandering in the park for an hour or more, I returned to my room and entered it as I had left it, as I supposed, unobserved. Wheeler's door was open and he was talking to someone quite audibly. I went into my room, entering undetermined and not knowing what to do. After I was seated in my room, I waited silently till Wheeler's school was out and his lights extinguished. During this suspense, it occurred to me that I might put the body in a cask or box and ship it off somewhere. I little thought at this time that the box in the room would answer; I supposed it too short and small and entirely unsafe as it was quite open.

"Wheeler's school being out, I still heard someone in his room, and as I then thought, laid down on some benches. The noise did not appear exactly like a person going to bed. I could hear the rustling of no bed-clothes. I felt somewhat alarmed, but then the idea occurred to me that it might be the person who Wheeler stated was going to occupy the room that I then occu-pied as a sleeping room as soon as I gave it up, which was to be in about ten days' time, was temporarily occupying his room for that purpose. Relieving myself by this thought, I soon lit a candle, knowing that no time was to be lost; something must be done. This was about nine o'clock, I should think.

"Having closed the shutters, I went and examined the box to see if I could not crowd the body into it. I soon saw that there was a possibility of doing so if I could bend the legs up, so that it would answer if I could keep some of the canvas around the body to absorb the blood and keep it from running out. This I was fearful of. It occurred to me, if I could bury or send this body off, the clothes which he had on would, from description, discover who it might be. It became necessary to strip and dispose of the clothes, which I speedily accomplished, by ripping up the coat-sleeve, vest, etc., which removing the clothes, the keys, money, etc., in his pockets caused a rattling, and I took them out and laid them on one side.

"I then pulled a part of the awning over the body to hide it. I then cut and tore a piece from that awning and laid it on the bottom of the box. I then cut several pieces from the awning for the purpose of lessening its bulk, supposing it was too much to crowd into the box with the body; i.e., it would not go in. I then tied as tight as I could a portion of awning about the head, having placed something like flax, which I found in the box, with the awning. I then drew a piece of this rope around the legs at the joint of the knees and tied them together. I then connected a rope to the one about the shoulder or neck and bent the knees towards the head of the body as much as I could. This brought it into a compact form.

"After several efforts, I succeeded in raising the body to a chair seat, then to the top of the box and, turning it around a little, let it into the box as easy as I could back downwards, with head raised. The head, knees, and feet were still a little out but, by reaching down to the bottom of the box and pulling the body a little toward me, I readily pushed the head in, and the feet. The knees still projected, and I had to stand upon them with all my weight before I could get them down. The awning was then all crowded in the box, excepting a piece or two which I reserved to wash the floor. There being a portion of the box, next to the feet, not quite full, I took his coat and, after pulling up a portion of that awning, crowded it partially under them and replaced the awning. The cover was at once put on the box and nailed down with four or five nails which were broken and of but little account. I then wrapped the remainder of his clothing up and carried it downstairs to the privy and threw it in, together with his keys, wallet, money, pencil case, etc. These latter things I took down in my hat and pockets, a part wrapped in paper and a part otherwise. In throwing them down, I think that must have rattled out of the paper.

"I then returned to my room, carried down the pail which contained the blood and threw it into the gutter of the street; pumped several pails of water and threw it in the same direction. The pump is nearly opposite the outer door of the building; then carried a pail of water upstairs and repeated said washing to a third pail; then rinsed the pail, returned it clean and two-thirds full of water to the room; opened the shutters as usual, drew a chair to the door, and leaned it against it on the inside as I closed it. Locked the door and went at once to the Washington Bath House in Pearl Street, near Broadway. On my way to the bath house, went by a hardware store for the purpose of getting some nails to further secure the box. The store was closed. When I got to the bath house, I think by the clock there it was eight minutes past ten. I washed out my shirt thoroughly in parts of the sleeve and bosom that were somewhat stained with blood from washing the floor. My pantaloons in the knees I also washed a little, and my neck handkerchief in spots. I then went home.

"It wanted, when I got home, about five minutes of eleven o'clock. I lit a light as usual. Caroline wished to know why I came in so late. I made no excuse, saying that I was with a friend from Philadelphia, I think, and that I should get up in the morning early to go and see him off. I went to the stand and pretended to write till she became quiet or went to sleep. I then put out the light and undressed myself, spread my shirt, etc., out to dry, and went to bed.

"In the morning, at about half past five o'clock, I got up, put my shirt and handkerchief, which was not yet quite dry, into the bottom of the clothes-basket under the bed. Always changed my shirt going to bed. In the morning put on a clean shirt and handkerchief and was nearly dressed when Caroline woke up. I said to her it was doubtful whether I should return to breakfast. Did not return.

"Went to the office, found all apparently as I had left it. Went after some nails. Got them at Wood's store; the store was just opening. Returned to the room, nailed the box on all sides. Went down to the East River to ascertain the first packet to New Orleans. Returned to my room—marked the box. Moved it myself—but with great difficulty—to the head of the stairs. Did not dare to let it down myself. Went to look for a cartman. Saw a man passing the door as I was going out. Requested him to help me down with the box. He got it down without any assistance—preferred doing so. Paid him ten or twelve cents. Went down Chambers Street for a cartman whom I saw coming towards Broadway. Hired him to take the box to the ship, foot of Maiden Lane—went with him.

"While he was loading the box, I went to my office for a piece of paper to write a receipt on—wrote a receipt to be signed by the captain on my way down the street—did not offer the receipt to be signed but requested one, which the receiver of the box gave me. A clerk was by at the time and objected to the form of the receipt and took it and altered it—wished to know if I wanted a bill of lading. I first remarked that as there was but one box, it was not very important; however, that I would call at the office for one. Did not go for a bill of lading. Tore up the receipt before I was two squares from the ship. Returned to my office by way of Lovejoy's Hotel in the park. Went to the eating room, called for a hot roll and coffee; could not eat. Drank two cups of coffee. Went to my office, locked the door and sat down for some time. Examined everything about the room. Wiped the wall in one hundred spots. Went home to bed."[1]

41

*H*aving reached the end of Colt's confession, Emmett replaced the document on the table. He then turned again to the jurors and, on behalf of the defense, set forth the legal crux of its argument.

"What is considered manslaughter under English law amounts to justifiable homicide under ours," he said, "and the present case comes within this class. The highest class of homicide known to our laws is premeditated design to take life." To convict Colt of murder, "the prosecuting officer must show 'premeditated design' "—prove that Colt had planned the crime in advance and lured Adams to his office with the express intent of killing him. "But there was no such thing," Emmett declared. Far from having "contrived the meeting," Colt had not even been "apprised of it."

The evidence clearly showed that Mr. Adams's death had resulted from an argument that raged out of control. "The passions of the men were aroused, and Mr. Colt, in his own defense, committed the act which took away that man's life," said Emmett. "From the testimony of Caroline Henshaw that she saw a mark on the neck of Mr. Colt, it is evident that a struggle took place. Mr. Adams, we have reason to believe, had his hands within Mr. Colt's neckcloth and was twisting it in such a manner as to cause suffocation. In such a situation, where self-defense only was exercised and death ensued, the case comes clearly under the class denominated by the statute as justifiable homicide."

Emmett went on for another ninety minutes, "reading the various laws and precedents governing the case, reviewing the evidence, and concluding with a most eloquent appeal to the jury." By the time he sat down, he had been speaking for nearly six hours. It was shortly after 10:00 p.m. when the court was adjourned until morning.[1]

. . .

With no more witnesses to be examined, extra places were available in the courtroom on Friday morning. When the crowd poured in at precisely 10:00 a.m., "about twenty ladies" immediately made for the witness chairs and "occupied them as spectators." John, looking "pale, very pale, wearied and haggard," was led inside a few moments later.[2] As soon as everyone was seated and the court called to order, Assistant DA Smith rose and addressed the jury.

He began by defending his chief against the attacks made by Emmett. "From his remarks, you would suppose that instead of being arraigned for a dreadful crime, the prisoner was a victim marked out for persecution—that the doer of one of the most brutal murders ever perpetrated was an angel of light!" The district attorney, however—that "talented and meritorious officer"—was merely doing his job "faithfully and correctly," as always. "When duty calls him, he is ever ready to perform the arduous and often painful duties of his office. Was it not his duty to present all the facts in the case?"

To be sure, Smith continued, presenting facts that might result in a sentence of death was a "thankless task," one that required a ruthless suppression of the "kind and benevolent emotions" with which all men are naturally endowed. "We are so constituted, such is our nature, that no matter how great may have been a man's offenses, the moment we see him suffering, the tide of sympathy flows for him.

"Towards the prisoner," he professed, "no one, except the brother who has stood by him throughout this case and the counsel who have so eloquently defended him, no one feels more for him than I do. My heart bleeds for him." And yet "there are cases where we have no right to allow our sympathies to control our judgment."

Sounding much like a modern-day law-and-order zealot—the type who decries the judicial system for mollycoddling criminals and blames the breakdown of society on "bleeding hearts"—he claimed that crime was running rampant in the city. "We scarcely take up a newspaper but we find two or three accounts of murder therein. And this grows out of that sickly sympathy manifested by courts and juries, and the almost certainty that the murderer will go clear. The jury must discard all prejudices and sympathies—the jury box is no place for such feelings. You have solely to deal with the testimony brought before you. With the *consequences* of your verdict upon this miserable, this wretched man, you have nothing to do. You are sworn to do justice, not mercy, and to see that justice prevails. The people expect it of you and demand it at your hands."

Smith used the remainder of his two-and-a-half-hour summation to argue that Colt's crime constituted willful and malicious murder, not manslaughter. While "the law makes allowance for any killing done in the heat of passion," he declared, "this is not one of them." Moreover, the sheer savagery of the crime, the "cruel and brutal manner in which it was done," proved that there was implied, if not express, malice.

As to motive, Smith proposed that, unlikely as it seemed, Colt intended to rob his victim—"to possess himself of the property which Samuel Adams had in his possession at the time," meager as it was. "I admit it is the most extraordinary case I ever heard of. But what is motive for one man would not be motive for another."

To judge whether "such a motive as I have suggested was strong enough to make him commit the act," it was necessary to examine "the character of Colt. If his character were extremely good, it would make a difference. Let us see the character he has displayed.

"Why, in all this trial," exclaimed Smith, "he has shown less feeling than any man here. When the box that once contained the dead body of Adams was exhibited before us and the bloody garments held up, the prisoner alone looked on calm and unmoved as if nothing had happened, while everyone else shuddered and stood back aghast. Therefore, I consider him of a cool, deliberate, and calculating disposition. The man that could sit here so calmly and listen to this trial could just as calmly plan and quietly execute the deed."

To be sure, Colt's eyes had watered at the sight of his family mementoes: the locks of his mother's and sisters' hair found inside the trunk along with Samuel Adams's pocket watch. Even there, however, Smith saw proof of Colt's implacable nature. "If I needed evidence to prove his coldness of purpose and hardness of heart," he asserted, "I would want nothing better than the course he has exhibited in relation to the hair of his mother. Who among you would throw such a relic in a box with his cast-off materials, placed side by side with the evidence of his guilt?

"Will the prisoner's counsel say that, because he exhibited feeling in this one solitary instance, we are to consider him mild, gentle, and humane?" cried Smith, warming to the subject. "Why, gentlemen, let me appeal to your feelings in this matter. Let me ask you what is the last thing a man forgets? What is that which lingers longest and sweetest upon our memory? Is it not the recollections of her who gave us being and who first taught us the lessons of virtue? The name of mother is the last uttered by the pirate under the yardarm and the murderer as he mounts the scaffold! She is the last the veriest wretch forgets! We often see the lights of genius go out one by one—vice makes inroads into the mind until almost the last traces of virtue become extinct—but while life still glimmers in the socket and a ray of reason lights the mind, man clings with fondness and reverence to the memory of his mother!"

How the jurors reacted to this sentimental appeal is unknown, though "several of the ladies in the audience seemed greatly affected."

According to Smith, the evidence left no doubt that the murder of Adams was "coolly and deliberately planned beforehand." Why had Colt brought the awning and the nails to his office in advance "if not for such a purpose as this? Why was the saw previously borrowed from the woman in the house? And why such agitation and concealment in his mode of using it? We were told by witnesses that when they knocked at the prisoner's door, the usual answer was 'come in.' But when Mr. Walker went to get the saw, Colt came to the door, opened it a short distance and said, 'Go to hell.' "

Colt had also been caught out in several obvious lies, most glaringly his insistence that he had hired a man to take the box downstairs—a statement flatly contradicted by eyewitness testimony. "Why, then, didn't the prisoner say in his 'confession' "—here Smith gave the word a conspicuously sarcastic inflection—"that he took it down himself?" Because, explained Smith, if someone else did the job, then the mark on Colt's neck could not have been caused by the crate, thus bolstering Colt's contention that the bruise was made by Adams. "If he did hire the man," asked Smith, "why not bring him forward as a witness?" The answer was clear: Colt had lied about the man because he was lying about the source of the bruise. He had never been attacked by Adams. The murder was an act of cold-blooded premeditation.

For every objection raised by the defense, Smith had an answer. Colt's counsel had argued, for example, that if their client "intended murder, he would never have chosen to commit it in such a public place as the Granite Building. But I would argue that Colt chose that place precisely because of its publicity and noise and because there he would be less likely to be detected or even suspected. Adams was such a businessman that Colt could not possibly lure him out of the city. Therefore he chose to kill him in a place where the noise would prevent any scuffle or cries being heard, and he chose the noisiest time of the day to do it."

Perhaps most damning of all was "the subsequent conduct of the prisoner. Would any of you have acted so?" asked Smith in an incredulous tone. "Would you have sat down coolly with the dead body at your feet and sit for hours deliberating how you could best conceal it, unless you had committed a cool and deliberate murder? He who could act so deliberately after the killing could as deliberately plan the murder.

"Again, on the Monday after the deed was done," he continued, "we find him in that very room where he had committed the murder merrier than ever, and even singing. He goes to the very room where he committed this horrible act and there in singing and smoking he passes his idle hours. This shows that this man's mind is singularly constituted—and therefore it is idle to say that because the motive for the deed is improbable, he could not have done it."

Smith also made sure to bring up Caroline Henshaw. "We do not wish to impugn a woman's virtue," he solemnly proclaimed. "But once she has lost that, when she comes upon the stand, we do not think it necessary to call evidence to impeach it."

Colt, Smith continued, represented "the only anchor that binds her to the world." If he were to be taken from her life, she would become a permanent outcast. "Testimony from such a source requires no impeachment. Such a witness has no incentive to tell the truth but is controlled solely by her own interest and feelings. She is the mother of the prisoner's child, and it would be strange indeed if the young mother would not come forward to testify strongly in favor of the father.

"Gentlemen," said Smith, approaching the end of his summation, "you must take the testimony, compare it, and weigh it perfectly. As to the murder, you have to pass upon the apparent intention. You must observe in regard to the prisoner whether he was the kind of man that would be likely to commit and premeditate the deed. It has been said that Colt is a remarkably mild and quiet man. If you believe that, is it not more conclusive that the murder was coolly done and intended for plunder?"

Smith ended by reminding the jurors that "the attribute of mercy does not belong to you, nor to the court, but to a higher tribunal." Then, with a final word of lawyerly false humility—"I will now leave the subject with those more capable than myself"—he returned to the prosecutor's table and took his seat beside District Attorney Whiting.[3]

42

No sooner had Smith reseated himself than John's cousin and lead attorney, Dudley Selden, rose to address the jurors. He began by promising them that his "remarks should not extend to a length unnecessarily to trespass upon their time."[1] Despite this assurance, he would end up speaking for more than five hours: two and a half before the recess and another three afterward. Long as it was, however, his performance would be widely applauded. Even James Gordon Bennett—still smarting over Selden's earlier call for his arrest—hailed it as a feat of "thrilling eloquence."[2]

Keenly aware that, for both the jury and the general public, John's cold-blooded efforts to dispose of the body seemed even more shocking than the murder itself, Selden wasted no time in addressing the issue. While conceding that Colt may have manhandled the corpse—standing on its knees, for example, to force them down into the crate—he insisted that John's actions "in relation to concealing the body" had "no bearing upon the decision as to the guilt or innocence of the defendant." However callous his behavior, John had been acting out of sheer desperation.

"He was in terror of his situation," exclaimed Selden. "There is no man but under such circumstances would have resorted to concealment rather than disclose what occurred. He determined upon the plan and set out to put it in execution. 'Poor Adams is dead,' said he, 'and I shall have to meet the consequences or conceal what has been done by means within my power.' "

The killing itself, insisted Selden, was clearly unpremeditated. That "a sudden quarrel" had sprung up between them was "borne out by the fact that Mr. Adams left Mr. Wells's store between two and three o'clock in an angry state of mind for the purpose of going to Colt's room." Once the struggle began, Colt had acted reflexively. "Adams had Colt by the throat," Selden declared, "and there was necessity of resorting to means of defending himself. The axe lay on the table, where it would necessarily be placed in that small room. Colt seized it, and in self-defense struck the blows. It was all done in an instant's time."

As for the question of why Colt struck Adams repeatedly and with such savage force, Selden argued that, while the first blow may have "deprived Adams of speech," it could actually have caused him to tighten his stranglehold—"to hold with even stronger grasp the neckcloth of Colt." To prove that even a mortally wounded man can muster a final burst of strength, Selden cited two well-known examples: Alexander Hamilton, who had supposedly "sprung from the ground" after being shot down by Aaron Burr, and Charles Austin, the young victim in a sensational 1806 manslaughter case, who, after being shot in the head by a lawyer named Thomas O. Selfridge, had "advanced upon Selfridge and struck him some violent blows before he fell dead."[3]

Selden next turned to the issue of motive. After asserting that Colt could not possibly have been seeking revenge since "he had none to gratify," he dismissed the charge that the murder was committed "for gain." For one thing, "had Colt been disposed to seek money in this way, he would have picked a more wealthy victim than poor Adams." Moreover, the fact that Colt had thrown most of Adams's possessions down the privy proved that he had not meant to rob him.

As for Adams's pocket watch, Colt "was aware that it was an elegant one, of peculiar workmanship, and must be discovered in case he afterwards attempted to wear it. Is it likely that he would have plundered another of such an article as this, and have committed murder in order to do it?" Besides, if the watch was so precious, why hadn't Colt gotten word to Caroline, following his arrest, "that the plunder was in his trunk and would be discovered by officers of the police, and bidden her to remove it"?

Caroline herself, Selden claimed, had been unfairly impugned by the prosecution. "The learned counsel said this morning that Caroline Henshaw's testimony was not entitled to confidence because she was living in a

state of adultery with Mr. Colt. If he means to apply that to her general conduct, he is much mistaken. I have seen those who pretended virtue guilty of
vice—have seen the wife whose word was no better than the mistress. She
may have been guilty on one point but is entitled to credit as regards every
other. Her testimony showed that she loved the prisoner but was determined to tell the truth."

In presenting the defense's view of the fatal quarrel—and specifically of
Samuel Adams's role in instigating it—Selden was required to marshal all
the tact at his disposal. "God forbid we should say anything against Mr.
Adams, his character or his conduct," he declared. To be sure, the prosecution had shown no such restraint in their treatment of John Colt. "He has
been represented as if he had been born for blood—has been persecuted and
maligned." Still, it was not for the defense to stoop to the same level. The
facts spoke for themselves.

"The present quarrel is immersed in darkness, and who commenced it
is not proved," said Selden, "but enough is shown to convey an idea of what
happened. We know that Adams went to Colt's room in a vexed mood,
having expressed surprise to Mr. Wells that Mr. Colt expected the proceeds
of the sale. Mr. Colt owed Samuel Adams only seventy-one dollars, but
Adams contended that he was owed more. Out of that disagreement, words
came up which produced blows and terminated in death. Mr. Adams had
hold of Mr. Colt in a manner to prevent him crying out and caused him to
use the hatchet in self-defense."

For each of the points raised by the prosecution to incriminate Colt,
Selden offered an alternative—and more convincing—explanation. Much
had been made, for example, of Colt's having borrowed the saw prior to the
murder, as if that proved he had planned the crime beforehand. But "Mr.
Colt was publishing a book," said Selden. "Is it too much to suppose that he
was building the box to send them off?" The prosecution had also maintained "that the mark on Colt's neck was caused by getting the box down
the stairs. But a man receives a weight on his shoulder, not on his neck—
and the mark seen by Caroline Henshaw was on the jugular vein."

In closing, Selden permitted himself a rare display of anger, upbraiding
the prosecution for actions that had no other purpose than to inflame the
prejudice of the jurors. "When Mr. Adams's wife was here," he exclaimed,
"one of the officers was directed to bring up the bloody garments and shake

them under her very nose. Even the grave was opened and the head severed from the trunk. The physicians said they could examine it in another room. But no—the prosecution found it necessary to place the head upon a table here in open court, so that you, gentlemen of the jury, might be influenced by the feelings observable among the spectators."

Selden knew he had more to worry about than the feelings exhibited by the spectators inside the courtroom. Community opinion was violently inflamed against his client, and—despite the jurors' seclusion—they were well aware of it. Every morning, as the twelve men entered City Hall, the mobs gathered outside the building had barraged them with cries for Colt's conviction. Afraid that they might bend to such pressure, Selden now reminded the jurors that their courage must not falter. "If there is a doubt, you are bound to present a verdict of acquittal. Indeed you must give a verdict of acquittal, even if you do so at the risk of your life in passing through the crowd.

"We leave his cause with you," concluded Selden, "requesting you to bear in mind that justice as well as mercy is a portion of the attributes of the criminal law."[4]

• • •

It was already a few minutes past 7:00 p.m. when Selden returned to his seat. District Attorney Whiting was on his feet at once. Initially, said Whiting, he "supposed that he could complete his remarks in two short hours." Selden's argument, however, had "ranged so widely that it is now impossible to say how long it will take. If the Court will hear me through in my argument, I will proceed now. Otherwise I would ask to have an adjournment until the morning."[5]

Although he had hoped to get through all three remaining summations, Kent had no choice. With a bang of the gavel, he adjourned until 10:00 the next morning, when the trial would enter its climactic day.

43

*T*outed from its opening day as the most riveting show in town—
a spectacle of "unsurpassed interest"—the Colt trial had more
than lived up to its billing. Now that it was nearing the end of its run, James
Gordon Bennett took the opportunity to offer an appreciative look back at
"this extraordinary drama."

In a lengthy editorial published on the morning of Saturday, January
29, he enumerated the features that had made it so special, beginning with
some raw statistics: three full days to "procure a jury from three hundred
persons"; six days "in hearing the evidence"; ninety witnesses examined,
seventy-nine for the prosecution and eleven for the defense; a day and a
half "consumed by three of the counsel to sum up." Still to come was the
closing of Mr. Whiting, expected to "occupy the whole of five hours this
morning till the recess. After that, Judge Kent will deliver his charge and
the case will go to the jury about dusk this evening."

What really made it memorable, however, were its many dramatic
highlights. "Altogether," gushed Bennett, "this has been one of the most
singular trials that ever took place in this or any other country." A year earlier, the city had been transfixed by another shocking murder, this one perpetrated by a New Jersey carpenter named Peter Robinson. On Thursday,
December 3, 1840, Robinson had lured a creditor, a banker named Abraham Suydam, to his house in New Brunswick. After knocking Suydam out
with a mallet, Robinson dragged the unconscious victim into the cellar,
bound him, gagged him, and left him lying there for three days. Early Satur-

day morning, Robinson "went to the house, dug a grave three feet deep before his still living victim, threw him into it alive, then struck him over the head with the spade, dashing in his skull." His trial in April 1841 had "excited a great sensation" and his subsequent hanging "was a gala event in New Brunswick."[1]

The Robinson-Suydam case certainly didn't lack for gruesome thrills. Judged purely as theater, however, Colt's trial easily eclipsed it—"threw the Peter Robinson affair far into the shade," as Bennett put it. "If this be not the strangest trial ever known, then we have yet to learn the fact."[2]

• • •

Bennett's main rival, Moses Beach's New York *Sun*, commemorated the imminent end of the Colt trial in its own exploitive way. Prominently displayed in its Saturday edition was the following advertisement:

> As soon as the Verdict of the Jury is rendered in the case of John C. Colt, we shall publish from this office the Trial Complete in pamphlet form. This pamphlet will comprise
>
> 1st—The evidence in detail as it has appeared from day to day in the *Sun*.
>
> 2nd—Faithful sketches and reports of the opening and summing up of Counsel on either side—which, from the well-known professional reputation of Messrs. Whiting and Selden, will doubtless present a greater forensic display than has been exhibited in this city for many years.
>
> 3rd—The charge of Judge Kent.
>
> 4th—Six Engravings, illustrative of scenes and characters which appear in the history of this dreadful tragedy.

"Bargain priced" at six cents, the sixteen-page souvenir pamphlet would make a handsome memento of the gruesome murder case and—as the advertisement noted—could "be sent to any part of the Union for newspaper postage only."[3]

• • •

With the denouement of the "dreadful tragedy" so near at hand, the crowds turned out in force. "There was a perfect mob around the City Hall from morning till night," Bennett wrote. "There were also about forty or fifty females in the court room all day," he added, marveling at a phenomenon that would become increasingly familiar in years to come: the high percentage of women spectators found at sensational murder trials, and their lively interest in the lurid.[4]

Bennett's estimate that the district attorney's summing up "would occupy the whole of five hours" was off the mark, though not by very much. Whiting ended up speaking from 10:00 until 2:15.

Whiting began by angrily rebutting the charges that the defense lawyers had leveled against him. Far from having "persecuted their client to death," Whiting insisted that he had been scrupulously fair to the defendant. "Would to God I could this day look into the testimony and ask you to pronounce the prisoner guiltless. But we live in a world where justice must be administered or society is dead."

If anyone were guilty of having "wrongfully conducted" themselves during the trial, said Whiting, it was counsel for the defense. From the very first, "they had the confession in their pocket, and yet they went through long and labored cross-examinations of witnesses who they knew from the bottom of their hearts told the truth—and then they abuse *me* for doing my duty in the case! Suppose they had said, when the trial commenced, 'We admit the killing of Samuel Adams and you need not labor to prove it'— how much time would have been saved!"

Knowing how hard it is for most people to send a fellow human being to his death, Whiting, like his assistant before him, reminded the jurors that they must not think about "the consequences" of their verdict but "simply to enquire into the circumstances of the case—to pronounce whether John C. Colt took the life of Adams, and if so, under what circumstances and in what temper. We allege that this act was committed with design, and if not this, that it comes under the provision of the statute that killing under circumstances which show a disregard for human life shall be accounted murder." Killing another human being did not in itself constitute murder, said Whiting. "It is killing with an evil mind, with a bloodthirsty heart." And for such a crime, not only the laws of man but the laws of God demanded blood retribution. " 'He that smiteth a man will surely die,' " quoted Whiting, " 'and he that comes upon his neighbor with guile to slay him shall be destroyed,' saith the Almighty."

Proceeding with a review of the case, Whiting raised a series of questions designed to dismantle the defense's version of events. If Adams had been so angry when he heard that Colt intended to keep the proceeds from the trade sale, why hadn't he proceeded straight to the Granite Building to confront Colt? Why had he taken such a roundabout way? Surely "his passion, assuming he had any, would have had time to cool, as the heat of the iron from the forge of the blacksmith when exposed to the air."

Why was the hatchet "laid carefully upon Colt's table," within easy reach? Even granting that "a quarrel had taken place as alleged," wouldn't Colt "have been more likely, unless bent upon murder, to strike with a chair?" Reviewing the fearsome injuries inflicted on Adams, Whiting insisted that—contrary to the representation of Colt as "everything mild, kind, and affectionate"—the sheer savagery of the wounds was proof of his "brutal temper." After all, "a blow upon the arm would have answered his purpose, for it would have released the grasp. He had no right to revenge an insult—even assuming that one was given—in this terrible way."

But in fact, Whiting declared, there was no proof at all that Colt had been assaulted. "Had the quarrel taken place as said, would the words 'you lie' have been made in a low voice?" asked Whiting. "Wouldn't they have been heard by Mr. Wheeler and his pupil?" If the prisoner had really sought out his brother at the City Hotel after the murder, why hadn't Sam Colt been called to the stand to corroborate that claim? If Adams had grabbed Colt's neckerchief and twisted it so hard that he could hardly breathe, "where was the neckcloth? Why wasn't it presented as evidence?" And what about the black-and-blue mark on Colt's neck? If Adams had really been strangling Colt, significant bruises "would have been left on his throat. We hear of a trifling mark, but nothing such as would have appeared there."

Under the pretense of sympathizing with Caroline for the harsh way that John had treated her on the night of the murder, Whiting managed once again to remind the jurors of Colt's debauched and unfeeling character:

We hear of Caroline Henshaw going to his bedside. She asked him, as Portia did Brutus when he came from the Senate House after committing a murder, what ailed him. He pushed her away, and she dared not, after that, ask this kind friend to see the marks on his neck—she dared not speak. She approached his bed, he threw her from it. She knew she was not his wife and dared not press it. But do not blame her, do not blame that slight girl. Blame the one whose heart was such that he could seduce her and keep her in abjection. The poor unfortunate girl must go down to the grave with the stain that is upon her. Let this be a warning to women—let them not put their earthly and eternal happiness in the keeping of such a man as that!

Turning to the issue of motive, Whiting stressed that the prosecution "was not bound to prove that Colt's motive was sufficient to induce him to kill. The law says that 'instigation of the devil' is a sufficient motive. It is impossible to assign definite and what we would call adequate motives for all deeds like this. If we prove there is premeditated design, that is sufficient."

He then defined precisely "what was meant by premeditated design." Contrary to common belief, it did not mean that the murder was planned far in advance. "All that is necessary is to show that there was time after the arm was raised to exercise reflection," explained Whiting. "Does the law require it shall have been a long time before? No—not even a single minute if the intention is to produce death and the blow is unnecessarily produced."

In concluding, Whiting allowed for the first time that the prisoner was stricken with remorse. His words brought tears to a number of people in the courtroom, including John himself, who leaned "on the back of his counsel's chair, hands over his eyes, and freely wept."

"I believe that life was taken by John C. Colt," said Whiting solemnly. "I believe that, if by laying down his own life, he could restore that man to his family, he would gladly do it. But does that excuse him for taking the life of Adams? You have a simple duty to perform. I have endeavored faithfully to do mine. There are in this city three hundred thousand souls committed to our care, and much rests upon us. Act in a manner that you can answer to your consciences hereafter. Deal justly—but deal firmly—between the people and the prisoner."[5]

•   •   •

Whiting's summation was followed by an abbreviated recess. When court readjourned at 3:30 p.m., Judge Kent—pronouncing it his duty "to close the last scene of this most interesting trial"—delivered his charge to the jury.

After offering the obligatory words of praise for the "patience and good feelings" displayed by the jurors "through the vicissitudes of this protracted trial," he turned at once to an issue raised by Dudley Selden: the possible effect that public outrage—"the excitement out of doors," as Kent called it—might have on the verdict. While acknowledging that "public sentiment" had undoubtedly "been aroused by the murder," he insisted that the court had "kept everything uninfluenced by contamination from without" and affirmed his faith that "perfect justice would be done" by the jurors, twelve men of "honest hearts and sound minds."

Since "it is admitted that Samuel Adams was killed by John C. Colt," continued Kent, "the only question is, was it murder, manslaughter, or excusable homicide?" Kent stressed, however, that a killing committed in a "cruel or brutal manner" can never be considered justifiable, whatever the provocation. Given the weapon Colt used and the nature of the injuries he inflicted, a "cruel and unusual manner may well have been attained in the case before you." It was therefore Kent's opinion that the jurors "could not acquit under this rule" and "must account this act either murder or manslaughter."

What defined a killing as murder was premeditation—"if it was effected, not in hot blood or in a fracas, but with design to take the life of Adams." As an example of malice aforethought, Kent cited the case of Edward Coleman, a "ragged Negro" who, on Saturday morning, July 28, 1838, "slipped up behind his wife as she was panhandling near Jolie's Music Shop on Broadway at Walker Street, squeezed her head to his chest, and all but cut it off with a razor"—a "horrible deed that result from his belief in her infidelity."[6]

Coleman, who became the first murderer ever executed in the Tombs yard, had plotted his killing days before committing it. As Whiting had already pointed out, however, a crime did not have to be planned long in advance to qualify as a premeditated act. "No definite time is fixed by the law," Kent explained. "Even if the design was formed after Adams came into the room," the jury was entitled to find Colt guilty of murder.

If, however, the jury felt that there was no premeditation involved, the crime fell under one of several classes of manslaughter. "If Colt intended only to beat Adams and ended up killing him, it is manslaughter in the first degree," Kent said. "If he killed him in the heat of passion, it is manslaughter in the second degree. Manslaughter in the third degree is killing a human being in the heat of passion with a dangerous weapon."

Turning to the trial, Kent maintained that there was no need to review "the great mass of evidence in regard to the killing," since Colt's confession had rendered so much of it moot. "The case really lies in a nutshell," he declared. To a significant extent, the jury's ultimate judgment would hinge on their estimation of Colt's character. As to that, said Kent, Colt's actions in the immediate aftermath of the killing showed him "to be an uncommon man," possessed of "the most wonderful coolness."

In emphasizing Colt's ostensibly cold-blooded temperament, Kent seemed to be siding with the prosecution. For the remainder of his speech, however, he went out of his way to offer John the benefit of every doubt.

Though "the District Attorney thinks the fact that Colt borrowed the saw is important," said Kent, he himself did not attach any great significance to it. Likewise the presence of the hatchet and the packing crate. Having been in Colt's possession months before his troubles with Adams, they could scarcely be regarded as proof of "preparatory design." The locale of the crime also "seemed to preclude the supposition of design." The Granite Building "is the most frequented house in the most populous city in the Union," Kent pointed out. "The time was near midday, and separated only by a folding door was a schoolroom filled with scholars." Under those circumstances, said Kent, "it is difficult to suppose that there had been a premeditated design to take life."

"In regard to the salt," Kent went on, "I do not consider it material." Beyond "inflaming the public mind," the notion that Colt "used salt to preserve Adams's body" had no bearing on the case. "It only shows Colt's foresight in guarding against discovery"—"a talent for concealment rarely equaled in the annals of death."

Indeed, continued Kent, the same could be said about every aspect of Colt's efforts to dispose of the corpse. To be sure, the "conduct evinced by Colt in packing up poor Adams's body" was shocking. But it hardly proved that he was guilty of murder.

Taking up each contested point in turn, Kent recapped the evidence in an eminently evenhanded way. As for Caroline Henshaw, Kent believed that the testimony of "that interesting young woman" was "worthy of confidence. Her manner was artless and childlike, unconscious of guile, and the impression on my mind was decidedly in her favor."

Looking at the question of motive, Kent conceded that cold-blooded murders were sometimes committed for the flimsiest reasons. "Savages" had been known "to shoot a man just to see how he would fall from his horse." Even so, said Kent, it was up to the jury to "think if there was any adequate motive" for the crime. Reviewing the possible causes—revenge, avarice, "the desire to protect reputation," a simmering grudge—Kent found that none of those motives "appeared probable."

As to "the character of the slayer and the slain," said Kent, "the evidence is favorable to both. Adams was shown to have been amiable. Nevertheless, he was capable, as attested by several witnesses, of using language of an insulting character. As to Colt, he has also been shown to be mild and pleasing in his manner. But there is evidence to show that he, too, had his times of excitable feelings." If the jurors were convinced that John's extraordinary "coolness of character" proved that he was "capable of premeditation," then they "must bring him in guilty of murder." On the other hand, the "certainty that Adams was capable of showing temper" lent credence to the "idea that he might have come upon Colt in a feverish state of mind and a fracas occurred between them." In that case, manslaughter was the appropriate verdict.

In bringing his charge to a close, Kent reminded the jurors that if "there is a reasonable doubt," they must find "in favor of the prisoner. Give the lowest degree of punishment to which you feel the case belongs," he instructed. "Consider the case fairly and mercifully, but do justice whatever may ensue. Resist everything like threats, and yield at the same time to nothing like morbid sympathy with anyone. Examine the subject and say what you believe and you will do your duty to the prisoner, your country, and your God."[7]

. . .

It was nearly 6:00 p.m. when Judge Kent finished. Moments later, the jurors retired to begin their deliberations. His face blanched of color, John watched them file from the room, while—seated beside him at the defense table—Sam Colt laid a fortifying hand on his brother's shoulder.

44

hroughout that frigid night, the crowd around City Hall grew larger by the hour. Knots of people huddled all about the park, debating every detail of the case and speculating on the possible outcome. Most of those gathered conversed in the solemn tones suitable to the occasion. Others, however—women as well as men—positioned themselves beneath the glowing windows of the courtroom and shouted their demand for Colt's conviction, their "loud and menacing voices penetrating even the jury room."[1]

Rumors swept through the crowd. Court officers stationed outside the jury room kept their ears to the keyhole and provided regular updates on the deliberations. After three hours, "the jury stood seven for murder, three for manslaughter, and two for excusable homicide." An hour later, "they stood seven for murder and five for manslaughter. By 11:00 p.m., "they stood ten to two." And there they appeared to be deadlocked.[2]

Judge Kent, who had gone out for dinner following the completion of his charge, returned to the courtroom around 8:00 p.m. and stayed until midnight, when he finally went home to bed. Shortly after his departure, John, overcome by exhaustion, stretched out on a bench, covered his face with his handkerchief, and fell into a fitful sleep. He was awakened around 3:00 a.m. with the news that—after nine hours of deliberation—the jurors had reached a verdict.

Kent was immediately sent for. He arrived about an hour later and immediately took his place on the bench. At approximately 4:00 a.m., Sunday, January 30, John was told to stand and face the jury.

"How say you, gentlemen?" asked the clerk.

The foreman, grim faced, replied without hesitation: "Guilty of murder."

Observers offered strikingly different accounts of John's reaction. According to James Gordon Bennett, he "appeared horror stricken." Another journalist, however, reported, "The prisoner did not seem to be much affected at the rendition of this verdict." On one point everyone agreed: that "his brother, Samuel Colt, appeared much affected, as though, upon hearing the verdict, his heart died within him."[3]

John's lawyer John Morrill ordered the jury polled, and as they gave their answers, several of the men burst into tears. Morrill, on behalf of the defense, then applied to the court for time to present their exceptions, and Judge Kent agreed to meet at 10:00 on Monday morning to hear them. After shaking hands with his lawyers and his stricken brother, John was led back to the Tombs.[4]

• • •

The trial was over, but for James Gordon Bennett, "the most exciting part of the drama" was still to come. "Will Colt be hung, or will a new trial be granted?" he asked breathlessly, as though the conviction were the latest chapter of a serialized cliffhanger. "Will the Governor dare to pardon him?"

Bennett was inclined to think that a pardon was unlikely. Within recent memory, the perpetrators of two of the city's most notorious murders had escaped the noose. Despite his manifest guilt, Richard Robinson, accused of the axe murder of the prostitute Helen Jewett, had been acquitted at his trial in June 1836. Four years later, after being sentenced to death for a brutal stabbing during a tavern brawl, the young Bowery tough Ezra White had his conviction overturned on a technicality. Retried, he got off with a four-year stint in Sing Sing Prison.[5]

Now, Bennett believed, Colt was doomed to serve as a scapegoat. "The public have been cheated so often that Colt has to suffer for the sins of Ezra White, Robinson, and all who have escaped for the last ten years," he editorialized on January 31. "Had the verdict not been 'murder' we don't know what would the consequences have been. It is a very unjust thing. But so it is."[6]

THE MARRIAGE IN THE CONDEMNED CELL.

Part Five

THE NEW YORK TRAGEDY

A s Bennett observed, Colt's conviction was a gratifying outcome to the public at large, whose hunger for retributive justice had been repeatedly thwarted in recent years. To John's
friends and supporters, however, the verdict came as a devastating blow.

The reaction of Lewis Gaylord Clark was typical. Coeditor with his
twin brother, Willis, of the *Knickerbocker Magazine*, the country's leading
literary periodical, Clark was a family friend of the Colts and, from the time
of John's arrest, had maintained "staunchly and publicly that the prisoner's
crime had simply been an unhappy accident." When the jury handed down
its decision, Clark was so distraught that—though he "adored Charles
Dickens above all other authors"—he could not bring himself "to attend an
important meeting that night to plan the great dinner in honor of Dickens,"
who was then visiting America.[1]

Word of the verdict quickly spread throughout the country in newspapers from Milwaukee to Maine; in religious publications from the *Catholic
Herald* to the *Evangelical Magazine and Gospel Advocate*; and in popular journals ranging from the *United States Magazine and Democratic Review* to *The
New World: A Weekly Compendium of Popular Literature and Knowledge*.[2]
While many of these publications merely reported the facts, others used the
verdict as an occasion to convey lessons tailored to their target audiences.

Indulging in "some reflections that are naturally suggested" by the case,
for example, the *Episcopal Recorder* asserted that John's "proficiency in iniq-
uity" was the result of his "defective religious education" at home, and offered some warning words to parents:

> We are told by those who know his history from childhood
> that Colt had no religious instruction around the family
> fireside, and that all those restraints which are the fruits of
> a pious father's counsels and a mother's tears were un-
> known by him. Let these facts sink into the hearts of par-
> ents! Your children are as depraved by nature as this
> miserable youth. Send them into the world with no ties
> that take hold on the family altar, and what security have
> you that they will not plunge into sin and ruin?[3]

The *Youth's Companion*, on the other hand, addressed its admonitions
directly to its juvenile readership, comparing John Colt to "the first murderer," Cain, and using both cases as examples of "how wrong it is, in anyone, to give way to bad and angry feelings."[4]

Even the *American Phrenological Journal* got in on the act. In an article
published not long after the conviction, an anonymous practitioner of that
then popular pseudoscience claimed that "in the spring of 1837, at the
Astor House, N.Y.," he had performed a phrenological examination of
Colt's head, the results of which had proved all too prophetic:

> His *temperament* was one of the most active and excitable
> that I ever witnessed, being *sanguine-nervous*. This, to-
> gether with the great size and sharpness of *Combativeness*,
> *Destructiveness*, and *Approbativeness*, led me to lay especial
> stress upon his irritability, the suddenness and ungovern-
> able fury of his anger, particularly when his honor was as-
> persed. I remember not only dwelling upon the excitability
> and power of his anger but also closing his examination by
> rising, taking a position nearly before him, and in a most
> emphatic manner and gesture, my finger pointing toward
> him and wishing to give force to the most important
> words, saying to him as follows: "Mr. Colt, I have one word
> of caution to give you. You are passionate and impulsive in
> the highest degree, which, with the great size and extreme
> activity of Combativeness and Destructiveness, will make
> you desperate in a moment of passion. I warn you to avoid

occasions calculated to excite it. When you find a dispute rising, turn on your heel and leave the scene of action; for when you become angry, your wrath is ungovernable and you are liable to do what you might be sorry for."[5]

Like other sensational homicides dating at least as far back as Shakespeare's time, the Colt-Adams case also inspired a crude broadside "murder ballad," composed and peddled by an anonymous hack eager to cash in on the unabating fascination with the crime. Titled "The New-York Tragedy"—"an account of a Horrid Murder, committed in a Room on the second story of the large granite building, corner of Broadway and Chambers street in the City of New-York"—it was priced at two cents and could be purchased wholesale or retail at the printer's shop, no. 71 Greenwich Avenue, Manhattan:

> Good people all, I pray give ear;
>   My words concern ye much;
> I will repeat a Tragedy:
>   You never heard of such!
>
> There was a man, an Author good
>   For making a BOOK you'll own;
> And for the KEEPING of the same
>   No better, than was known.
>
> Besides all this, I can you tell,
>   That he was well endow'd
> With many graces of the mind
>   Had they been well bestow'd.
>
> To print the BOOK and have it bound,
>   Colt, by agreement say,
> The printer should, the work when done,
>   Be first to have his pay.
>
> Upon the books, when they were sent,
>   Cash would advanced be;

Adams was to have his money,
   For so they did agree.

Wicked man, for the sake of gold;
   Which he would never pay,
He Murder did commit, and then
   The body put away! . . . [6]

Moses Beach, too, lost no time in cashing in. As soon as the verdict was handed down, the *Sun* rushed out its souvenir sixteen-page pamphlet, which sold so briskly that, within forty-eight hours, it was already in its third edition.

As promised, it featured a handful of woodcut engravings. Dominating page one was a picture labeled "Colt, the Murderer," showing John seated at a table and holding up a copy of his bookkeeping text. Below was an illustration of a comely young woman flashing a coquettish look while clutching a baby to her bosom. "Miss Henshaw (Colt's Mistress) and Their Child," read the caption. Two more portraits appeared inside: one of a grieving Emeline Adams raising a handkerchief to her eyes, and one purportedly of her husband. Seated at a writing desk, quill in hand, Adams was depicted as a nattily attired gentleman with dark curly hair, a bulbous nose, and a prominent, dimpled chin.

In truth, this last illustration bore little resemblance to the murder victim, for the very good reason that it was actually a picture of somebody else: Phineas T. Barnum.

The previous fall, Barnum—who had begun his show business career staging traveling exhibitions of a wizened African-American woman named Joice Heth, touted as the 161-year-old former nursemaid of George Washington—had purchased a run-down natural history museum on the corner of Ann Street and Broadway. Within weeks, he had set about converting it into the country's most spectacular showplace: Barnum's American Museum, home to such unparalleled wonders as a six-legged cow, Crowley the Man-Horse ("Nature's most astounding freak!"), the Feejee Mermaid, and a troupe of performing fleas. With his genius for self-promotion, Barnum had no trouble drumming up publicity in the city press. One early piece was an admiring profile of the showman that appeared in the New York *Evening Atlas* in the fall of 1841. Accompanying the article was an engraved portrait of the dark-haired, bulbous-nosed, dimple-chinned Barnum, handsomely attired and seated at a writing desk, quill in hand.[7]

Like thousands of other New Yorkers, Barnum—as he later recounted in his autobiography—was swept up in the excitement surrounding the Colt-Adams case. Eager to know what "poor murdered Adams" looked like, he "greedily purchased" a copy of the *Sun* pamphlet, opened to the picture labeled "Samuel Adams, Deceased," and was thunderstruck to find his own face staring out at him. Making inquiries, he discovered that "the stereotype of *my portrait* had been purchased from the *Atlas* and published as the por-trait of Adams!" The incident merely reinforced a lesson that Barnum had learned a long time before: when it came to exploiting public credulity by peddling outrageous hoaxes—"humbugs," as he called them—the news business was not so very different from show business.[8]

*O*wing to several unavoidable delays, John's lawyers were unable to present their bill of exceptions until the last day of February. The following morning, March 1, 1842, the bill was allowed and sent before the state supreme court for adjudication.[1] Months would pass before a decision was rendered. In the meantime, John remained ensconced in the Tombs.

• • •

"It scarcely seems credible to the present generation," writes a late-nineteenth-century historian of Manhattan, "that there was once a lovely and picturesque lake, bounded by Canal Street on the north, Pearl Street on the south, Mulberry Street on the east, and Centre Street on the west; and yet such was the case." Surrounded by "romantic hills" that "rose to a considerable height," the lake—so deep that it was "regarded by many as bottomless"—was known as Collect Pond, a name derived from its original Dutch designation, *Kalchook*, meaning "Shell Point," a reference to the "large deposit of decomposed shells that formed a point on the western shore."[2]

In the winter of 1808, when the city was hit with both unusually harsh weather and a severe slump in the maritime trade, a group of jobless seamen and other unemployed laborers, their families on the verge of starvation, marched on City Hall and demanded relief, "threatening to tear the Common Council members apart if they didn't get jobs." Appropriations were hastily voted and, "for want of something else to give them to do," the council had the men level the hills surrounding Collect Pond and fill it up with the displaced earth. Eventually "streets were cut through, Centre Street (formerly called Collect Street) running in a direct line north and south through what was the middle of the pond."[3]

Twenty years later, when the population of the city had grown to over two hundred thousand and "crime had increased in proportion," the Common Council—acting on the urgent need to replace the old Bridewell jail in City Hall Park—voted to erect a new prison and selected the old Collect Pond grounds as its site. Work on the project began in 1835. No sooner had the workmen begun digging than they hit the pond, forcing the contractor to sink piles of hemlock logs into the swampy ground to serve as a foundation.

Constructed at a cost of $430,000—the equivalent of more than $10 million in today's money—the building was designed by architect John Haviland, who modeled it after an engraving of an Egyptian temple found in a then popular volume, John Stevens's *Travels in Egypt, Arabia, and Palestine*. Distinguished by its gloomy granite portico with heavy columns adorned in Pharaonic style, the Halls of Justice (as it was formally known) had a deeply forbidding aspect. "A dismal-fronted pile of bastard Egyptian" was the way Charles Dickens described it on his visit to New York City in February 1842.[4] Resembling an immense mausoleum, the building was immediately nicknamed—and known forever after as—the Tombs. Within days of its opening in 1838, James Gordon Bennett decried it as "a loathsome and dreary charnel house" and demanded that it be immediately torn down.[5]

For a while, it seemed as if, like Poe's House of Usher, the edifice would collapse on its own. Constructed on the "sinking, marshy landfill" of the old Collect Pond, the building began to sag from the day it opened. Within five months, "it had sunk several inches, warping all the cells" and producing "four-inch cracks in some walls." As it continued to settle over the following years, the grinding, cracking noises convinced many nervous prisoners that the building was about to cave in, though it remained intact for more than sixty years until it was replaced with a Gothic-style building that opened in September 1902.[6]

The prison contained 173 cells arranged in four tiers, each reserved for a different class of criminal. Convicted prisoners occupied the ground floor cells prior to their transfer to state prison. The other three tiers were for individuals awaiting trial, the majority of them too poor to procure bail. Accused murderers were consigned to the second tier; those charged with burglary, larceny, and other "lower grade" felonies to the third; while the uppermost level housed an assortment of petty criminals.

The cells, measuring just six by eight feet and dimly lighted by a foot-high slit in the wall—were originally meant to accommodate a single occupant. For most of its existence, however, the Tombs was so overcrowded that two, three, and even four inmates were often crammed into one cell. Underheated, badly ventilated, pervaded by dampness from the muddy ground on which it was built, and reeking of sewage from its woefully inadequate drainage system, the prison was, as historian Timothy Gilfoyle writes, "a sanitary nightmare":

> When cells were doubled up, inmates usually slept on the narrow berth found in each cell, each one sharing his pillow with the other's feet. In periods of severe overcrowding, Tombs officials sometimes strung up hammocks for a third or even a fourth prisoner. Otherwise they slept on the floor . . . Drinking water came from a rooftop tank where water festered under the hot rays of the summer sun. Upon reaching the faucets in the cells, the water was "pretty near the boiling point and unfit to drink." Bathing facilities were worse. Since the Tombs was built with no such provision in mind, few were given the opportunity to bathe. Furthermore, bed sheets were changed every six or seven weeks, and inmate clothing was never washed unless prisoners paid for laundry service.[7]

As for food, the menu for the average prisoner was a "wretched and stinted fare" consisting "almost entirely of pallid stews and coffee made of burnt rye steeped in hot water. The only variant was an occasional ration of pale tea. The food was lugged from cell to cell in big buckets and ladled through the bars."[8]

Such were the conditions suffered by the majority of "poor and friendless" inmates. For the more affluent, however, the situation was radically different. "By paying the warden a proper sum," a man could not only secure a private cell in a special section reserved for wealthy prisoners but also adorn it with such "homey touches" as "singing canaries, a Kidderminster carpet, and fancy wallpaper." For the right price, the warden would even "have the Tombs carpenter put up a few hanging shelves, build in a clothes closet, or throw together some small tables to hold books, pipes, and tobacco." In contrast to the barely palatable stews dished out to the general population, the higher class of criminals could also pay to "have their meals brought in from the best hotels." Visitors came and went freely with little or no supervision. Altogether, as a writer for Horace Greeley's *Tribune* noted, "if a prisoner was rich or had political influence," he "lived like a gentleman, surrounded by every comfort."[9]

Thanks in part to the generosity of his brother Sam, John himself enjoyed a high degree of comfort during his extended stretch in the Tombs. "I have my meals brought in from an excellent restaurant," he wrote to one correspondent. "My cell is better furnished than half the rooms in the hotels, and in it there is as much spare room as in many of them."[10] In addition to Caroline, who "came to see him every day and remained for hours," he received frequent calls from John Howard Payne, Lewis Gaylord Clark, and other influential friends. On one occasion, he was also visited by the social reformer and journalist Charles A. Dana, who—incensed at the luxuries for sale to wealthy prisoners—produced a vivid and scathing portrait of John's life in the Tombs:

> The popular idea of a murderer in his cell is a grave one. The fancy paints with somber tints a cold, dark cell. A sickly shaft of light comes from the high, barred window and illuminates feebly the haggard face of the criminal as he sits upon his wretched pallet of straw. Whenever he moves or presses his trembling hands to his hot brow we hear the clanking of chains. The fires of despair burn luridly in his bloodshot eyes. At intervals the iron door creaks harshly open, and the rough keeper hands him his coarse fare. There is no furniture save a crazy chair or two, no carpet, nothing but the damp stone flags. And here he lies until he is led out to be hanged in chains or executed in whatever manner may be in vogue. Victor Hugo paints

this picture superbly. We shrink with horror from the con-
templation of the scene and wonder, since such is his fate,
how any man can commit murder.

They may do those things better in France, but how is
it in New York? Let us take a stroll through Murderer's
Row in the Tombs and glance in on homicide Colt. Coming in from the pure air and warm sunshine you say, as you
step upon the corridor, "Surely this is dismal enough!" And
so it is; but this is only the exterior of the parlors. As the
keeper swings open the door of Colt's cell the odor of sweet
flowers strikes you. It is no delusion, for there they are in a
delicate vase upon the center table. That handsomely
dressed little lady whom we passed on the stairs has just left
them. Tomorrow they will be replaced by fresh ones.

The table itself is a pretty one; there is nothing hand-
somer in Washington Square. It is of exquisite workmanship and is covered with a dainty cloth. In a gilt cage
hanging against a wall is a canary, whose dulcet strain
gushes out from his palpitating throat in a flood of melody.
A pretty set of swinging shelves suspended by silken cords
catches the eye. Here are to be found the latest novel, the
freshest magazine. Pictures here and there break up the dull
wall into gorgeous color. You tread on roses, for the cold
stones are concealed by rare Kidderminster.

And Colt; how is it with him? You see he is not sitting
on any pallet of straw. In a patent extension chair he lolls
smoking an aromatic Havana, while he reads the proceedings of his trial the day previous in the morning's papers.
He has on an elegant dressing-gown, faced with cherry colored silk, and his feet are encased in delicately worked slippers. His clothes are neat and up in style to the latest
fashion plate. He is cleanly shaven and has a general air of
elevation about him which is quite refreshing. To one side
of him is his bed, a miracle of comfort.

When he is tired of reading or smoking or sleeping he
takes a stroll in the yard. It is necessary to dress for this,

and his toilet takes considerable time. Finally he appears, booted and gloved. He may have his seal-skin coat on or he may appear in a light Autumn affair of exquisite cut and softest tint. In his hand is a gold-headed switch which he carelessly twirls during his promenade.

Then comes his lunch; not cooked in the Tombs but brought in from a hotel. It consists of a variety of dishes— quail on toast, game pâtés, reed birds, ortolans, fowl, veg- etables, coffee, cognac. Then it is back again to the easy chair with book and cigar. Such is life in Murderer's Row as lived by Colt, and a not unmerry life it is.[11]

• • •

Besides reading, smoking, and taking the occasional stroll around the yard, John passed the hours corresponding with friends and acquaintances in Cincinnati, Philadelphia, and New Orleans—the cities where he had spent the most time during his peripatetic life. Nineteen of his letters would eventu- ally find their way into print.[12] As to be expected, they are full of protestations of innocence. "I did but defend myself against a wanton, vile, and unpardon- able attack," he writes at one point. "This I would do again, at any time, when insulted and assaulted. No man would do less. His very nature compels him to this . . . I have nothing in this affair to reproach my conscience with."

He repeatedly denounces the "consummate scoundrels" of the penny press for stirring up public hysteria and accuses the jurors of either moral cowardice or active bias:

Twelve men, either from error or prejudice, trampled upon the evidence—they trampled upon the judge's charge— they trampled upon the law, for the law says that when there is a doubt, it should be given in favor of the prisoner. They were out nine hours wrangling about a decision; there was much doubt, and strange to say they threw the doubt against the prisoner. There will be no difficulty, if justice be done, in setting aside their opinion, as it is now well known that several of them either willfully or un- guardedly expressed hostile opinions before the trial.

Not without justification, he insists that he was convicted "for endeavoring to conceal a misfortune, not for killing a man."

He devotes considerable space to setting the record straight about his victim. Contrary to depictions of Adams "as one of the mildest and meekest men the world has ever seen," the printer was "a most aggravating fellow in his language. I had always before attributed his manner to ignorance, not to ill will. However, I was mistaken. I was cherishing a viper that was ready at any time to sting me."

In one particularly dramatic letter, John provides an account of the "fatal quarrel" far more graphic than the one contained in his original confession. Adams, he claims, not only tried to choke him but grabbed him "by the privates" ("*per prives parties*," as John latinizes it): a charge that, if true, goes a long way toward explaining the frenzied violence of Colt's reaction.

> Adams's assault on me was entirely wanton. I never was cooler and calmer than when he came into my office, and his entrance was abrupt and quite unexpected. He accused me at once with an intent of cheating him, to which I calmly replied that I was astonished that he should say so, and requested him to give some reasons for warranting such a charge. Word followed word, and in the meantime I drew out his account from my portfolio, and so far as there was cheating on foot, I showed him the evidence of it on his part, in his account. As he would not hear to reason, and feeling alarmed at his manner and language, I applied to him unavoidably, in answer to his abuse, in perfect justice, his own unmeasured terms. At this he became more exasperated and gave me a slap with the back of his hand across the mouth which, you may be assured, was returned in due justice, as I sprang to my feet in self-defense. He almost instantly seized hold of my neckcloth, which placed me in his power—pressing me to the table and wall, he struck me three or four times in the breast and seized me *per prives parties*. Everything seemed to turn black. I was in agony and exerting myself for relief, how I know not.
>
> The last distinct recollection I have, before I was re-

lieved by his fall, was that of trying to press him off with my left hand, as I held to his collar, endeavoring with my right hand, at the same time, to raise myself from the table, as he had me pressed over backwards upon it. It was in this painful position that I seized that cursed hatchet and gave him the unfortunate blows that I did. When relieved from his horrid grasp, I beheld for the first time my awful defense. Heaven knows the number of blows I struck him. There may have been four or five. And when I reflect upon the instrument most unfortunately seized and instantaneously used, it is only to be wondered at that his head was not dashed into a thousand pieces.

About the future, John expresses serene confidence. He is convinced that the bill of exceptions will be "carried up" to the Supreme Court and that he will "get a new trial and be justly dealt with." But even if the final decision should go against him, he is resigned to his fate. "Death," he assures a friend, "hath no terrors for me":

I have ever had hopes of beyond this world. Did I believe that this existence was the beginning and the end, I should curse the giver. No—impossible—it cannot be. The universal world—the mighty heavens above—speak in signs more conclusive than argument, more appealing than parables, that there is a God above—just, mighty, all-powerful. No man should fear to shake off this mortal coil—this dying, sickening, painful body—this incarcerating prison-house to the mind—this incubus to the heart—this chain of disease and corruption to the soul.

Imbued with the conviction that "there is a world above this, and a more just one," he is, so he claims, prepared for any eventuality. "Let come the worst," he declares, "I shall die as calm as any man died."

*I*n preparation for their appeal, John's lawyers enlisted the aid of Dr. David L. Rogers, the eminent surgeon whose display of Samuel Adams's decapitated head had been one of the dramatic highlights of the trial. Rogers was requested "to investigate the probable relative position and actions of John C. Colt and Samuel Adams during the recontre which ended with the death of the latter." After conducting a series of experiments, he prepared a lengthy report detailing his findings and "the reasonings by which he has arrived at such conclusions."[1] The report, eventually submitted to Governor William Seward, stands as a remarkable piece of early forensic science.

Rogers notes, for example, that "blood was found on the wall [of Colt's office] in larger spots and greater abundance at the height of a man's head than elsewhere." In addition, the testimony of Asa Wheeler and his pupil Arzac Seignette clearly indicated that "after the fall of Adams no blow was inflicted." Taken together, these facts lead Rogers to conclude that "Adams was in an erect position at the time the fatal blows were inflicted."

Based on a highly sophisticated analysis of the number, shape, and position of the wounds, Rogers is further able to deduce that Colt and Adams were standing "face to face within a foot-and-a-half of each other during the whole of the fatal encounter." He then asserts that "one of the parties at least must have firmly grappled with the other while the blows were inflicted." His proof is compelling in its simplicity: "Several blows were received by Adams, any one of which would have felled him if unsupported, yet he did not fall till after the infliction of all the blows."

Rogers, however, goes one step further. In the most ingeniously argued section of his report, he demonstrates that "Adams was grappling with Colt at the time the first blow with the hatchet was given and was the first to close and grapple." Rogers bases his conclusion on four main points.

To begin with, if Colt "had been the assailing party," he would logically have "approached Adams from behind, which he evidently did not." More-over, the testimony of Asa Wheeler indicated that Adams had not cried out in alarm, which he doubtlessly would have done if attacked from the front by Colt. Third, if Colt had "commenced the attack, he would have selected a distance which would have given him the full sweep and force of his right arm." The first blow inflicted on Adams, however, proved that this was not the case. Finally, the absence of defensive wounds on Adams's arms strongly suggested that his "arms were engaged during the recontre."

In short, it was Rogers's belief that the quarrel turned deadly when Adams leapt to his feet, lunged at Colt, and violently grabbed him, forcing him into a "lower position." To be sure—as Robert Emmett had observed in his closing statement—no one but God knew precisely what truly tran-spired. Insofar as 1840s forensic science was able to reconstruct the crime, however, all the evidence suggested that John had been telling the truth.

48

For a while, Sam Colt shared his brother's hopeful outlook. In early February—at the very time that John was telling friends that he expected to get a new trial—Sam went out and purchased a ten-dollar flute for himself: a sign, according to the speculations of his most authoritative biographer, that he was in a sufficiently optimistic frame of mind to indulge in some lighthearted diversion.[1]

From the evidence of his diary, he was still in an upbeat mood one month later during a brief trip to Connecticut. By then, with Dudley Selden and his associates concentrating on John's appeal, Sam had refocused his own attentions on his submarine battery project. During the first week of March, he traveled to New London, Stonington, and Mystic to "investigate several intriguing leads on the attempts of an obscure Connecticut inventor, Silas Clowden Halsey, to conduct a torpedo attack" during the War of 1812.[2]

Halsey's efforts had been undertaken in response to emergency legislation enacted by Congress offering private citizens a hefty reward for the destruction of British warships. He had tinkered together an ingenious "submarine boat"—a tiny, one-man affair with a hand-cranked propeller and an air tube poking out of the water. Attached to the front was a small, corkscrewed spear with an explosive charge attached. The plan was to sneak beneath the hull of one of the British vessels blockading New London Harbor, drive the spear into the hull, then retreat before the explosion went off. On the night of June 30, 1813, he had set off on his mission and was never heard of again.[3]

For several days, Sam traveled around the various Connecticut towns, interviewing veterans of the war, including Captain Jeremiah Holmes of Mystic, who had participated in the efforts to attack the British fleet with submarine explosives and provided Sam with a detailed description of Halsey's ship and torpedoes.[4] Though engaged in serious business, Sam appears to have been in a relaxed, even carefree mood, as his comically misspelled journal entries make clear. On Sunday, March 7, for example, he records that, after attending "piscopal chirch" in Norwich, he "rambled through the town & over the hils," then "called on Mrs. Chappell was introduced to her husband (fine fellow) & to of her brothers, took tea & spent the evening very pleasantly to say nothing of the whiskey." The following morning, he took a "stemebote" back to New London, admiring the beautiful "senery on the river." The rest of the day was "spent very pleasantly at the residence of Captain Bassett in company of Miss Bassitt & Miss Church."[5]

Back in New York City, he continued his experiments. Just a few days after returning from Connecticut, he reported to Naval Secretary Abel Upshur that he had succeeded in setting off an underwater charge "at a distance of ten miles." In the same letter, he assured Upshur that he would be ready to make a public test of his harbor defense system "about the first of May."[6]

Delays in the delivery of zinc plates and other vital components forced Sam to postpone his demonstration ("all progress in my experiments must wate," as he put it to one correspondent).[7] He was finally ready in midsummer. Ever the showman, he decided to stage the event in the harbor off Castle Garden, the popular amusement spot on the southern tip of Manhattan where he had held a demonstration of his repeating rifles five years earlier. The date he chose was the Fourth of July—thirteen years to the day after his first, boyhood experiment with underwater explosives on Ware Pond.

Ballyhooed by the city press, the event drew thousands of spectators who crowded the wharves on both the Lower Manhattan and Jersey City waterfronts. Among those in attendance were Mayor Morris and the entire city council, along with reporters from a dozen newspapers. At precisely noon, the firing of a twenty-gun national salute signaled the start of the demonstration.

A derelict hundred-ton naval "vessil" (as Sam spelled it) had been provided for the occasion. "Fitted with temporary masts from which were displayed various flags with piratical devices," the "old hulk" was towed through the water until it reached a speed of roughly three knots. Two hundred yards way, on the deck of the seventy-four-gun warship *North Carolina*, Sam—surrounded by naval officers and other official observers—activated his galvanic detonating device. The "effect of the explosion was tremendous," wrote the reporter for the *New York Evening Post*. "The vessel was shattered into fragments, some of which were thrown two or three hundred feet in the air, and there was not a single piece left longer than a man could have carried in one hand."[8]

The response of the spectators was captured by a gentleman named John Mount, who witnessed the demonstration from the Jersey side. Two days later, on July 6, he sat down and composed an effusive letter to Sam, congratulating him on "the entire success of your recent submarine explosion."

"As the dense volume of smoke rose heavenwards," Mount enthused, "its terrific grandeur could only be exceeded by the amazement and wonder of all the multitude around me at the means by which it was accomplished . . . I trust, my dear sir, that the government will properly appreciate the vast importance of this mode of defense and that you may reap the honors and emoluments to which you are justly entitled."[9]

Sam himself was justifiably pleased with the results of his experiment. He had no time to savor his triumph, however. On the very day that he received Mount's admiring letter, word arrived of a long-awaited decision in his brother's case. And for Sam and the other supporters of John Colt, the news couldn't have been worse.

*E*ven before the New York Supreme Court took up John's case in its July term, his lawyers had made a separate bid to have the conviction overturned. On Friday, May 6, 1842, John Morrill and James Emmett appeared before Judge Kent at the Court of Oyer and Terminer to make a motion for a new trial. Word having spread that Colt himself would be present, "all the world assembled to see him." The rumor proved unfounded, however. Colt never appeared, "and all the world was disappointed."[1]

The principal ground for the motion was that one of the jurors, a boardinghouse owner named Nathan R. Husted, "had expressed strong and unqualified sentiments as to the guilt of the prisoner" before being sworn in. Specifically, a lodger at Husted's hostelry had heard him remark that if it were up to him, "Colt would be hanged first and tried afterward."

District Attorney Whiting countered that "Colt had received a fair and impartial trial" and that the motion constituted "an impeachment of the juror, an honorable and honest man" who had performed "a most unpleasant and unthankful duty," only to find himself "arraigned for having expressed an opinion relative to the prisoner."

A week later, Judge Kent handed down his ruling. This time, John was brought into court. The spectators who filled the room to capacity watched him intently as Kent read his decision.

"The remarks of Mr. Husted," said the judge, "were made at his own house in October last. They were casual and unpremeditated and unaccompanied by discussions." After careful consideration, Judge Kent therefore ruled, "This court, under the affidavits produced, cannot disturb this verdict, and they deny the motion under the firm conviction that granting it would impair, if it did not vitally weaken, the administration of justice in criminal cases of magnitude and importance."

John, who had kept his gaze steadily fixed on the judge, showed no trace of emotion as the decision was rendered. It was as if, wrote James Gordon Bennett, "he had expected it as a matter of course."[2]

• • •

Two months to the day after John's lawyers made their unsuccessful motion before Judge Kent, Dudley Selden appeared before the state supreme court at Utica to argue for a new trial.

There were two major grounds for his plea. The first had to do with jury selection. After the fiasco of the first day of the trial—when only nineteen out of forty-five potential jurors had shown up—Judge Kent had directed the sheriff to summon "three hundred persons duly qualified to serve as jurors." He had, moreover, demanded that all three hundred appear in two days' time and refused Selden's request for a lengthier postponement. Selden now insisted that, by ordering so large a number in so short a time, Kent had deprived the defendant "of a fair opportunity for scrutinizing the panel and preparing for a proper exercise of his right to challenge."

Selden further argued that since "the only instrument specified in the indictment as the means of committing the offense was a *hatchet*," Judge Kent had "erred in allowing proof tending to show that the death of the deceased might have been caused by the discharge of a pistol."

Following Selden's presentation, District Attorney Whiting arose to argue on behalf of the people. Even before he could speak, however, the court announced its decision.

The judges were "unable to see any ground for interfering with the proceedings." To begin with, "The statute in respect to summoning jurors prescribes no precise limit as to numbers but says that the sheriff shall be directed to summon so many as are necessary to make at least twenty-four jurors from whom a jury may be selected . . . As to the refusal of the court to postpone, this was also a matter resting in discretion and therefore not the subject of review in the present case."

The judges further ruled that Kent was correct in allowing evidence regarding the pistol, since the indictment also contained a count charging that the killing had been done "with a certain instrument to the jurors unknown."

The defense's motion having been denied, the court ordered that "the proceedings be remitted to the Oyer and Terminer with directions to proceed and pass sentence."[3] Eight months after his conviction, John Colt would finally receive his dread judgment.

50

At 10:10 on Tuesday morning, September 27, 1842—a year, almost to the day, since his arrest—John Colt was led into the packed courtroom by officers James Colvin and Frank F. Smith. Apart from his jailhouse pallor, his appearance had changed "very little from what it presented at the trial" and his "manner and demeanor" struck most observers as "perfectly calm and collected." Making his way to the front of the room, he took his usual seat beside the stove and—with his back to the gawking spectators—occupied himself in perusing the morning newspapers, looking up occasionally to exchange a word with his lawyers and his brother Sam, seated directly beside him.[1]

Twenty minutes later, Judge Kent entered and took his seat. Following some preliminary business, John, clutching a sheet of paper in one hand, was asked to rise. The clerk, Henry Vandervoort, then faced him and intoned the ritual formula: "Prisoner, you may remember that you have heretofore been indicted for a certain murder; upon that indictment you were arraigned; upon your arraignment you pleaded not guilty and put yourself upon the country for trial, which country has found you guilty. What have you now to say why judgment should not be pronounced against you, according to law?"

"I have prepared a few remarks that I wish to go to the court," John said with his usual composure.

"Do you wish it read aloud?" asked Kent.

"Certainly, sir," John said, reaching out the paper to Kent. He then reseated himself while Kent briefly scanned the document.

A moment later, Kent—whose expression had darkened noticeably—launched into Colt's statement in a voice that carried to the furthest corner of the courtroom:

> The position I now hold is to a sentient being the most agonizing possible. It is more painful than the struggle of death itself. But it is a form of procedure that I am obliged to pass through before my case reaches the last tribunal of the state to which it will be carried in accordance with that justice which cannot be denied to the meanest of mankind. Most cheerfully will I submit my case to final examination by the Court of Errors. I fully believe that it will set aside the judgment of the jury, who were so far led aside by prejudice and error as to trample on the evidence—to trample on the law—to trample on the judge's charge. Amid the thousand false rumors in circulation at the time of and before my trial, it may not, however, be considered surprising that the jury were misled from coming to a right conclusion. All that, unfortunately situated as I am, I can expect is an impartial trial by jury. This is all I desire, and this the meanest vagrant in the streets has a right to demand. Misfortune, not crime, has placed me in this position, and although as low down as possible without being annihilated, still, rest assured, I have not so lost my self-respect, nor regard for the credit of the peoples, as to submit calmly to this injustice. As this consequently is not to be the end of this business, I desire that the Court will spare me the pain of all unnecessary powers of sentence, especially the accompanying comments."

By the time Kent reached the end of this statement, his voice was taut with suppressed anger. Throwing the paper onto his desk, he glared down at John and proceeded to upbraid him in a tone of "high dudgeon."[2]

"The court has no desire, I can assure you, to make unnecessary comments," he said icily. "The scene is as painful to the court as it is distressing to you. I only refuse to accede to your request by making a few remarks on the conduct of the jury. It is due to justice and it is due to one of the most intelligent juries that ever sat in a court of justice that I should not allow them, in this their appropriate tribunal, to be traduced."

In the same affronted tone, Kent went on to defend the jury as a select group, drawn from "three hundred of our most respectable citizens"—men who had borne "with the most exemplary patience and dignity even unnecessary delays in the progress of the trial, earnest only to discover the truth from the appalling evidence spread before them.

"Insofar, therefore, as this paper expresses dissatisfaction with and contempt of the court and the jury, it is the conclusion of him who now addresses you that it is entirely incorrect and unsupported," said Kent, still glowering at John. "If that court erred at all, I believe it did in too lenient a construction of the circumstances of your offense, and happy will it be for innocence in all future time to be brought before a tribunal as willing to hear, as ready to believe, as humane to forgive."

As he spoke, Kent's voice had risen with indignation. He now paused, as though to get hold of his emotions.

"I do not wish to prolong this distressing scene," he continued after a moment, speaking more softly, though in a no less caustic tone. "You are a man of education—a man of talent. We have had the most striking and impressive evidence that you can calmly contemplate and coolly meet the most alarming crisis in human life. I will not therefore address to you any of the commonplace, ordinary topics addressed to criminals on the approach of death. I leave that to your reflections, simply adding that so far as the court is concerned, they are now about to appoint the ultimate hour of your existence, and I trust you will meet that hour relying not on human means, and that when earth is disappearing from your view, your thoughts will not be placed on earthly things. It is my duty to say in addition that it appears to me that you evince the most total insensibility regarding the crime whose commission has brought you to the bar. For it should be remembered that, though lawyers and juries debated what degree of offense it came to— whether it was technical murder or technical manslaughter—no man ever doubted that it was a crime of the greatest magnitude and enormity, and one which has left the stain of blood-guiltiness on your soul!"

Taken aback by Kent's tirade ("the judge came down on me like a hurricane," he lamented afterward), John leapt to his feet.[3] "I did not mean to convey the idea that the jury acted willfully wrong but that they were misled," he protested. "The judge's charge is the best argument to prove that. I do not impugn the motives of the jury—I only speak of them as having been in error, which is, I believe, now the opinion of nine-tenths of the community.

"As far as regarding my own conscience in this affair," John continued, adopting a lofty tone that, to the ears of many listeners, bordered on the supercilious, "I assure you, sir, that I would rather trust the whole affair to God than to man. I never committed an act in my life that I would not have done again under the same circumstances. Depend upon it, I am not the man who could receive an insult without making some retaliation. The retaliation was not made with any idea of killing the man, but he made the assault and was responsible for the consequences. I think, sir, you have misapprehended entirely the sentiment I meant to convey on that bit of paper."

Drawing himself up to his full height, he then calmly declared, "I am ready for the sentence, as I know it cannot be avoided."

Whether John's concluding words to Kent were a display of manful pride or blind insolence would be a matter of much debate in the coming days. To Kent, however, the matter was clear. Fixing John with a withering look, the judge said: "The sentence will now be pronounced, with an expression of regret with which the court have marked such morbid insensibility which you exhibited in your last speech and which convinces me that any further remarks would be lost on you. The sentence of the court is that you, John C. Colt, on the eighteenth of November next, be hanged until you be dead, and may God have mercy on your soul. Remove the prisoner."

At the bang of Kent's gavel, John swiveled on his heels and strode toward the doorway, head high, without the least apparent trace of emotion. It was his brother, Sam, whose face wore a stricken expression as he followed his brother from the courtroom.[4]

51

ednesday's newspaper accounts of John's sentencing marveled at the man's contradictions, expressing equal measures of awe at both his audacious spirit and his apparent lack of any sense of remorse. In his written statement and particularly in his last, defiant speech to Judge Kent, John, all agreed, had "exhibited as much boldness and as little feeling as could be imagined"—a stout heart coupled with "a mind dead to all moral feeling."[1]

This ambivalent attitude toward John's "reckless hardihood and effrontery" was particularly pronounced in the *New York Herald*, where James Gordon Bennett devoted a lengthy editorial to the subject. Commenting on Colt's "remarkable behavior throughout the scene," Bennett could hardly restrain his admiration. "His confidence, his assurance, his courage, his coolness, all rolled so together, and rising to the sublime of impudence, as we may call it—surpass anything on record. He is truly *sui generis*, and under other aspects, and with a different education, and another destiny, might have served for a hero—or a chieftain of the highest order—for a master spirit to revolutionize the age."

Unfortunately, continued Bennett, John's limitless potential had been undermined by "a want of moral and religious culture." Whereas other commentators attributed Colt's downfall to everything from his supposedly permissive upbringing to the corrupting influences of the city, Bennett—riding his own hobbyhorse—blamed it on "the great error in the education of the youth of the present age of the world," who were inculcated with "the vain principle of personal honor": an insidious ideal that led them to take offense at the smallest perceived slight and demand violent satisfaction for any in-sult.

"Instead of being taught the precepts of Jesus Christ as he delivered them on the mount," Bennett complained, "our young men have their minds filled with personal pride—personal consequence—the false theories of moral honor with its machinery of insults, satisfaction, resentment, pas-sion, duels, and death."

Colt's closing statement to Judge Kent—his brazen assertion that, under the same circumstances, he would do the deed again because "I was insulted"—reflected the "ridiculous code of honor" that prevailed among America's young men."[2] For Bennett, the "false and bloody code of honor" that led to such "wretched quarrels" was nothing short of sacrilege. Bereft of Christian principles, Colt's boldness was mere sinful pride: "a degree of hardihood," concluded Bennett, "that Satan himself could not surpass."[3]

52

To counter the negative portrayals of John in the press, his friends embarked on their own public relations campaign (a "venture in spin control," as one historian describes it),[1] subsidizing the publication of a biographical pamphlet that cast the subject in a highly sympathetic light. Titled *An Authentic Life of John C. Colt*, the seventy-page work was authored by Charles F. Powell, a popular writer of historical romances whose fiction—"Nahwista; a Story of the Colonies," "Zeulia of Madrid," "Kit the Orphan," "The Painted Rock"—appeared regularly in journals like the *Knickerbocker* and the *Boston Miscellany of Literature and Fashion*.

Shortly after the trial ended, Powell paid a visit to the Tombs, accompanied by two of John's close friends. They found him seated at his writing table, "a one-volume octavo edition of Goldsmith's works by his side." As they entered the cell, John, wearing "slippers and a dressing-gown," rose to greet them. In glaring contrast to the public at large—who "look on him as a monster"—Powell was struck by John's "gentle" expression, his "courteous and manly bearing." Only once during the visit, when the subject turned to the penny papers, did his "sweet and mild" voice turn bitter.

"The newspapers!" he exclaimed. "*They* are the true mischief breeders! *They* are really the unprincipled and remorseless murderers! By the pen there is more slaughter—and that of the most heartless and ferocious character—than either by lead or steel!"

Immediately following the visit, Powell dashed off the biography, basing it on information gathered from John's friends as well as on his prison-house interview with the subject himself. Powell's favorable impression of Colt is reflected throughout the work, where the subject is described as a young man of "extreme bravery," "great generosity of disposition," "ardent and ambitious spirit," "moral and temperate habits," "excellent conduct and remarkable talents." Every episode recounted by Powell illustrates John's sterling qualities: the keen sense of justice that, during his boyhood, "inclined him to take sides with the weaker party in all juvenile quarrels"; the "kind-hearted" impulses that led him to nurse a half-frozen lamb back to health during his time on his uncle's farm; the "zeal and fidelity" he displayed while apprenticing at the Union Manufacturing Company; his "Herculean labors" as a young supervisor on the North Branch of the Susquehanna Canal; his "studious and industrious" habits while clerking for his cousin, Dudley Selden; and more.

How an individual of such "frank, open, and manly character" has come to be "in prison under sentence of death" is, Powell writes, "a mystery." He can only assume that Colt "possesses two characters, one inherent, the other superinduced by circumstances." Endowed from birth with many "attractive qualities," John had developed a moody, distrustful side, largely—Powell posits—because of the faulty guidance of those "intrusted with management of his early years," especially his hardhearted stepmother, who was constantly "at work against him." In the end, Powell concludes, John possessed a naturally benevolent, affectionate, and amiable temperament that had been "warped" and "imbittered" by excessively critical "relations and teachers" who failed to appreciate or encourage his particular talents and ambitions.[2]

• • •

Several months later, not long after the fiasco of John's sentencing, a second pamphlet appeared, combining a three-page biographical sketch—cribbed from Powell's work—with a compilation of John's jailhouse letters. This one, titled *Life and Letters of John Caldwell Colt,* was even more unabashed in its advocacy. In it, John is portrayed not only as a paragon of Franklin-esque virtues—frugality, industry, self-reliance, temperance—but as a man who, through some perverse "sport of destiny," has been cruelly misunderstood throughout his life, most recently by Judge Kent. In a passage that might have been dictated by John himself, the anonymous pamphleteer—seeking to clarify the comments that had so infuriated Kent—explains that the judge "mistook the feeling of the remark he was handed to read. The prisoner meant to say that his disposition led him to resent an insult, and that the same causes operating upon his mind would produce the same effect— unknown and beyond control. There are thousands of men who, upon being called liar—scoundrel—or swindler, would strike the man who said it—a blow might lead to a scuffle—in a scuffle men become maddened, the mildest are infuriated, and consequences are no longer in their control."[3]

The pamphlet concludes with a direct appeal to the public, entreating them to rally to John's defense: "A few days and it will be too late to repair the wrong. A few days, and unless there be some merciful—some just— interposition, thousands of hearts will be wrung with agony and horror for the untimely death of a young, amiable, gentle, and, as all who know him believe, innocent man!"[4]

There was good cause for the urgency of this plea. On the day the pamphlet went on sale—October 21, 1842—exactly one month remained before John was scheduled to be hanged.

53

heir bid for a new trial having been refused by both Judge Kent and the New York State Supreme Court, John's attorneys made a last-ditch effort to obtain a writ of error by applying to the only person left who could allow it: Reuben Hyde Walworth, the last man to hold the soon-to-be-abolished position of chancellor of New York, the highest judicial office in the state.

In future years, Walworth's own family would be at the center of a highly publicized homicide, arguably the most sensational case of parricide in the annals of New York crime. In June 1873, Walworth's forty-three-year-old son, a prolific popular novelist named Mansfield Tracy Walworth, was shot to death by *his* own son, nineteen-year-old Frank Hardin Walworth, who lured his father to a Broadway hotel room and gunned him down with cold deliberation. The murder weapon was a five-shot Colt revolver.[1]

That tragedy, however, was still several decades away when the chancellor was asked to intervene in John's case. His ruling came on November 3, two weeks and a day before the scheduled execution. After reviewing each of the points raised by John's lawyers in their earlier appeals, Walworth found that there was no "reason to doubt that the prisoner has been properly convicted."

In explaining his ruling, Walworth offered a highly unusual aside. "No one not immediately connected with the condemned individual whose case I have been considering can more deeply regret than I do the situation in which he is placed, or sympathize more sincerely with his numerous connections," he wrote. "It has been my great fortune to be acquainted with many of them, and I know them to be among the most respectable in any community. With one of them, a lady who is his very near relative, I have been in terms of intimacy and friendship for more than thirty years."

After making this remarkable confession, Walworth stressed that he was not the sort to allow such personal matters to influence his decisions. "In the administration of justice, upon which not only the safety of the community but all that is dear in life depends, the calls of private friendship must, or at least, should always give way to the stern demands of public duty," he proclaimed. "Having therefore arrived at the conclusion that there is no probable cause for supposing that there is any error in the judgment in this case . . . I must refuse to allow this writ of error."

To more than one observer, it appeared that Walworth's "friendship and intimacy" with one "very near relative" of the condemned man had actually worked against John—that the chancellor, precisely because of his close connection to the Colt family, felt the need to prove that he was operating without bias. As one legal analyst remarked, there was "something like an ostentation of deciding according to strict law" in Walworth's written opinion, as though he feared that a less stern judgment would be read as a sign of favoritism.[2]

• • •

Only one recourse now remained to John's supporters. On November 4, 1842, the day after Chancellor Walworth handed down his ruling, a small party of them boarded an Albany-bound stagecoach to embark on the last desperate battle for John Colt's life.[3]

54

For William Henry Seward, the power to grant pardons was a particularly onerous burden of office. During his two terms as governor of New York State, he was constantly besieged by petitioners. On one morning alone—as he records in his journals—he was approached by no fewer than five female supplicants: the widow of an old acquaintance, imploring him "to release her son from the county jail"; a woman, eight months' pregnant, begging "for the pardon of her young husband, a watchman, who had committed burglary"; a "maiden lady" whose brother was "in the state prison at Auburn for forgery"; a "poor brokenhearted creature whose honeymoon was scarcely passed before her husband was dispatched to Sing Sing"; and a "grocer's wife whose husband was consigned to the penitentiary for larceny." Later that same day, he was presented with yet another appeal, this "one for a pardon to Thomas Topping, convicted of the murder of his wife."[1]

Determining whether to dispense executive clemency was not only a trying task for the governor, it was, more often than not, a thankless one. Seward commonly found himself under fire for his decisions, accused of either playing political favorites or ignoring the will of the people. His pardon of his friend and fellow Whig, James Watson Webb, for example—who had been sentenced to two years at hard labor for violating the law against dueling—drew widespread criticism and ridicule from Seward's Democratic foes. On the other hand, he incurred the outrage of thousands of his own constituents for refusing to pardon Benjamin B. Rathbun, a prominent Buffalo businessman who—despite his imprisonment for forgeries amounting to several million dollars—was one of upstate New York's most admired citizens.[2]

Of the countless cases he'd been faced with during his four years in office, however, none, by Seward's own admission, was as agonizing as that of John Colt. In the days following Chancellor Walworth's decision, Seward found himself under assault by partisans of the condemned man. "Each docking of a steamboat from New York brought the influential. His own political supporters, big Whigs, arrived hourly and breathed the words, 'Pardon Colt.' " As the campaign for clemency mounted, it "eclipsed all other state business."[3]

"You have no idea of the fatiguing weariness of the week spent in hearing every form of application for pardon to Colt," Seward wrote to his wife, Frances, describing the parade of supporters who had come to plead on the prisoner's behalf. Among them were Seward's "friend and former counselor," Willis Hall, until recently the New York State attorney general; David Graham, Jr., a prominent New York City attorney and author of *A Treatise on the Law of New Trials in Cases Civil and Criminal*; Judge Ambrose Spencer, former chief justice of the state supreme court; and Lewis Gaylord Clark—all of whom, wrote Seward, came "to inform me that Colt was unjustly condemned."[4]

Besides these personal callers, Seward was inundated with written pleas for executive intervention. "My table groans with letters from gentlemen and ladies of acknowledged respectability and influence," Seward wrote to his wife. "Among the former are gentlemen of the press and of every profession, urging and soliciting the pardon of Colt."[5]

Many of these letters based their appeals on legal grounds, arguing that the "evidence of premeditated crime was insufficient to warrant" the verdict, that Colt was clearly "the helpless victim of uncontrolled passion," and that the outcome had less to do with the crime itself than with communal revulsion at the "attempt at concealment." Others made their case on moral grounds. For example, Dr. Blanchard Fosgate—physician to the New York State Prison at Auburn and the author of such works as *Sleep Psychologically Considered, Dream-Thoughts of Waking Circumstances,* and *On the Influence of Coffee over the Narcotic Effect of Morphia*—maintained that a commutation of Colt's sentence would be in the "best interests of society." However disguised under the name of justice, Blanchard argued, the infliction of the death penalty was nothing more than revenge—a "direct stimu-lus" to a brutal appetite rooted in the "early history of our race." By com-muting John's sentence to life imprisonment, Seward would be fostering "the higher qualities of our nature—repentance, benevolence, and sympa-thy for our fellow men in adversity"—and thus assisting in "the progress of mankind toward a more lofty and just comprehension of the value of human life."[6]

Not all of the communications received by Seward presented their ar-guments in such measured tones. There were crank letters too, including at least one direct death threat:

> You have time to grant a pardon to him whom your preju-dices are about to deprive of a life as dear to him as yours is to you. Yes, you have *full* time, but not the *disposition*; you thirst for the blood of a fellow-being, and you *may drink* it to the last drop; but by the Almighty God, into whose presence you usher a poor soul with a load of sin upon his head, by the hopes I entertain of immortality hereafter, I *swear* that one who has *lived* for him, and will at any time *die* for him, holds you responsible to the very tittle for what may happen to him! Should he suffer an ignominious death, his corpse shall not be interred before *your* life pays the forfeit, and you follow him to an *eternal hell*!
>
> You may disbelieve me *now*, but too soon, perhaps, will death cause you to regret the past. As for Kent, his fate is sealed, provided John C. Colt is hanged. I say BE-WARE![7]

• • •

After days of "consuming anxiety," Seward reached his decision on Friday, November 11—one week before the scheduled execution. It would be pub-lished in its entirety in Saturday's *Albany Evening Journal* and, in succeeding days, reprinted in newspapers throughout the country.

Those friends and supporters of John who hoped for—even expected—a pardon would have been heartened by Seward's preliminary remarks, since he began his review of the case by acknowledging that the crime had not been premeditated. At the same time, Seward noted, the victim "was a meek and inoffensive man. He was unarmed, and visited the prisoner, although under excitement, yet without any hostile purpose; and when the remains of the deceased were found, the head, fractured with certainly five and probably more wounds, no longer retained the human form."

For Seward, the inordinate savagery of Colt's attack ruled out the argument that it was made in self-defense. "Such a homicide could not have been accidental or necessary for self-defense," he noted. "It was committed with a deadly weapon in a cruel and inhuman manner upon a defenseless and powerless man."

For the accused to be convicted of the "milder" charge of manslaughter, the defense would have to show that he "was in imminent danger, and in the heat of passion, suddenly excited, intense, uncontrollable, and allowing no time for reflection, and that he did not design to produce death, and was unconscious that such a consequence might follow his violence." The evidence, however, spoke loudly against such an assumption.

For Seward, as for virtually everyone else, it was John's actions following the killing—his "almost superhuman" efforts to "remove the evidence of the fatal transaction"—that spoke most damningly against him. In the governor's view, those actions could have been performed only by a man "guilty of deliberate and willful murder":

> Guilt seeks concealment . . . If the blood which had been spilled did not accuse the prisoner, he would not have endeavored to remove the stains it left. Much less would the accused have mutilated those remains and disposed of them in a manner, the very account of which produces a revolt of all the sympathies of the human heart.

As for John's argument that his attempts at concealment were prompted by fear of public disgrace, Seward was having none of it:

> Manslaughter, although declared to be a felony and punished as such, is regarded by the offender, as well as by society, as a misfortune rather than a crime. He who has committed it, if he possesses the common tendencies of

our nature, deplores the injury he has done, but conscience vindicates him and sustains him against accusations of a higher crime. Society exacts his punishment with reluctance and he suffers no ignominy.

As much as anything else, it was John's complete lack of contrition—the cool, unrepentant demeanor he had exhibited during his final courtroom appearance—that hardened Seward against him.

His conduct in relation to the crime and its consequences has been insincere, inhuman, relentless, and remorseless. He is vain, self-confident, and irreverent; imbued with false sentiments of honor, morality, justice, and virtue; and seems incapable of compunction for crime committed or sorrow for injuries inflicted. Penitence and resolutions to amend are indispensable, among other conditions, of pardon. No such conditions are offered in the present case. The prisoner has forgotten his victim, heaped insult upon his humble and bereaved family, defied the court, denounced the jury, and presented himself before the executive as an injured, not as a penitent man.

In the end, Seward could find no cause to "interpose his executive power between the sentence of the law and its execution." For John C. Colt, "the expectation of pardon, the last hope of life, must be relinquished."[8]

. . .

In making known his final determination—that all the impassioned pleas for clemency had failed and "the hopes entertained by many can no longer be cherished"—Seward expressed his "earnest wish that the few days which yet remain to the prisoner may be spent in preparing to appear before that dread tribunal appointed for all men." Similar sentiments were conveyed in various newspaper accounts of Seward's decision. In Monday's New York Sun, for example, Moses Beach declared, "All hope for a melioration of the dread fate which the law has pronounced against the unfortunate John C.

Colt has vanished, and he has now no alternative left him but to resign himself composedly to the embrace of death, to which on Friday next he must inevitably yield."[9]

But Beach was wrong in one crucial regard. For John Colt, death might indeed be inevitable on "Friday next." But as he would prove, there were other alternatives left him besides resigning himself composedly to its embrace.

55

espite the evident finality of Seward's decision, three dozen members of the New York State Bar Association met on Tuesday morning, November 15, to draw up a petition demanding a reprieve. That afternoon, the group set out for Albany to present its case to the governor in person. At the same time, John's lawyers notified Sheriff Monmouth Hart that, because of a legal technicality, the warrant for Colt's execution was invalid and "should not be carried into effect." Hart—who had developed strong sympathies for Colt and had sent Seward his own letter protesting the sentence "on the ground of the injustice of the verdict"— seemed more than willing to refuse "the painful and disgraceful task."[1]

Even so, preparations for the execution proceeded apace. A wagon was dispatched to New Jersey to bring back the gallows and rope used to hang Peter Robinson, the New Brunswick carpenter who had perpetrated the shockingly sadistic murder of banker Abraham Suydam two years earlier. According to the abolitionist and moral reformer Lydia Maria Child, this measure was taken for no other reason than to add one more "bitter drop" to "the dreadful cup of vengeance." "As the memory of Robinson was execrated more than other criminals," wrote Child, "they sent for his gallows to add to the degradation"—to "give an additional pang" of humiliation to the proud Colt by treating him no differently from the most reviled murderer in recent memory.[2]

As the day of the execution approached, it seemed as if New Yorkers could talk of nothing else. "Colt is the all-engrossing topic," wrote the noted attorney and indefatigable diarist George Templeton Strong.[3] To those, like Lydia Child, who regarded the death penalty as a holdover from a barbaric past—"legalized murder in cold blood"—and believed Colt to have been unjustly condemned, the city appeared to be in the grip of a primitive bloodlust. "The very spirit of murder was rife" among the populace, Child lamented. "They were swelling with revenge, and eager for blood."[4] With space for no more than three hundred witnesses in the courtyard of the Tombs, printed invitations to the hanging—"You are respectfully invited to witness the execution of John C. Colt"—became the most coveted items in town.[5]

To the very end, John's defenders refused to give up. When Seward refused the request of the thirty-six lawyers who had traveled to Albany—dismissing them as "seditious"—John's counsel made another desperate appeal to Chancellor Walworth, "praying that the Chancellor will reconsider his refusal to allow a writ of error." "His friends are still moving heaven and earth to save him," wrote George Templeton Strong, who, as late as Thursday, felt that there was "still an even chance" of a reprieve.[6]

For a moment, it seemed as if the "persevering pleaders" on John's behalf had succeeded. Late Thursday afternoon, a rumor swept through the city that Colt had been reprieved until January. Though "confidently repeated and believed by everyone," it was quickly proved to be unfounded. "Colt's second application to the Chancellor was met by a peremptory refusal," Strong recorded in his journal that evening, "and as there was no hope of success with the Governor, his last chance is gone." By then, even Sheriff Hart had announced that he would, after all, go through with the hanging. Given the prevailing sentiment among the citizenry, Hart feared that he himself might be lynched if he refused to carry out his duty.[7]

It was the Reverend Dr. Henry Anthon who delivered the devastating news to John. Rector of St. Mark's Church in the Bowery, Anthon—who was "firmly convinced of John's innocence"—had been approached by Sam to "attend to the spiritual welfare" of his brother.[8] He was with John in his cell when Sheriff Hart called him aside. Hart—who could not bring himself to tell John—begged Anthon to perform the awful task and "to ask John at what hour tomorrow he wished to be executed."

Though John professed to be unafraid of death—"Let come the worst, I

shall die as calm as any man died," he had boldly declared in one of his published letters—his reaction belied his bravado. At the news, he "flung himself on the bed and rocked there in agony for a moment or two."

At length, John regained his composure, sat upright, and—in a ragged
voice—said: "Sunset."[9]

The temperature never rose above twenty-eight degrees on Friday, November 18. There was, of course, no such measurement as "windchill factor" back then, but the stiff wind from the west must have made it feel considerably colder. Throughout much of the day, dark, lowering clouds hung over the city like a pall.[1]

None of this deterred the eager crowd that began gathering outside the city prison at daybreak. By 8:00 a.m., according to one contemporary, "the Tombs was literally besieged by a mob, blocking every street around it, all assembled . . . to gaze eagerly at the walls that contained the miserable prisoners and to catch what rumors they could of what was going on within them." Eventually, their number would swell to the thousands—men, women, and children—some having traveled from as far away as New Hampshire.[2]

A group of police officers under the charge of A.M.C. Smith was stationed at the prison entrance "to prevent the ingress of any except those who had tickets of admission." No women were to be allowed inside, and a few could be heard complaining loudly of their exclusion. As the hour of the execution approached, the rooftops of all the surrounding buildings would be packed with spectators of both sexes and all ages, straining for a view of the courtyard. Despite the bitter weather, a holiday air prevailed.[3]

• • •

John had not slept that night. Seated at his table, he had passed the hours writing letters to friends and family members. He had just set down his quill and was blotting the last of these missives when his brother appeared at his cell door. The time was approximately 6:30 a.m. After a few minutes of intense discussion, Sam left again on an errand.

Roughly an hour later, William Dolson, a barber who operated a shop on Centre Street and was commonly known as "Deaf Bill," arrived by prearrangement to give John a final shave under the watchful eye of Deputy Sheriff Frederic L. Vultee. No sooner had Dolson departed than a young man brought in a basket containing John's breakfast, prepared at a local eatery called Cowder's Victualling Cellar. John was finishing up his last meal when the Reverend Dr. Anthon arrived at precisely 9:00.[4]

Though the two men had known each other only for a few days, their hours together spent in prayer, spiritual conversation, and discourse over doctrines like original sin and predestination had forged a close bond between them. Rising from his breakfast to greet Anthon warmly, John offered the minister his chair, then seated himself at the foot of his bed. Reaching over to take a small package from the table, he handed it to Anthon and asked him to open it. Inside were a bunch of gold coins and bank notes, amounting to five hundred dollars.

Explaining that he had received the money that morning from his brother, John asked Anthon to deposit it in a savings bank and see that it was doled out to Caroline at the rate of twenty dollars per month to help support her and their newborn child. He spoke fervently of "how anxious he was that the mother and child should lead a virtuous life and the child be duly educated." Anthon, deeply moved by John's solicitude for the welfare of Caroline and the baby, gave way to tears and vowed to assume responsibility for the child's religious upbringing.

The longest of the letters John had written that night was addressed to his son. After reading it aloud to Anthon—who found himself "overpowered with emotions"—John sealed it in an envelope and passed it to the minister, explaining that it was "to be kept for his small child until it shall be old enough to understand its contents." He then told Anthon that he had one final favor to ask. He and Caroline wished to be married. Would Anthon perform the ceremony?

Anthon, without hesitation, assented.[5]

• • •

During each of his preceding visits with John, Anthon had "pressed upon him the indispensable necessity as one mark of true penitence of a confession of the sin for which he had been condemned." He now exhorted him again to make a clean breast. As he had done on every previous occasion, John "solemnly declared that he committed the act in self-defense."

"I have said so again and again," he exclaimed with a catch in his voice. "But what is the use? They will not believe it, they will not believe it."

"Will you carry this as your confession to the bar of God?" asked Anthon, reaching over to clasp John by the hand.

"I am full prepared to do so," John replied. "I would not die with a lie upon my lips."

Satisfied, Anthon suggested that they "spend the time profitably in prayer" and asked John "if there was any passage in the Bible in particular he wished to read."

"I will leave the selection to you," said John.

Taking up his Bible, Anthon proceeded to recite passages from Luke 15:7 ("I say unto you, that likewise joy shall be in heaven over one sinner that repenteth, more than over ninety and nine just persons, which need no repentance"), 2 Corinthians 5:1 ("For we know that if our earthly house of this tabernacle were dissolved, we have a building of God, an house not made with hands, eternal in the heavens"), and Luke 18:35–43 (in which Jesus restores sight to the blind man at Jericho).

Anthon read until 10:00, then—assuring John that he would be nearby—retreated to a vacant cell two doors down the corridor, "leaving the prisoner alone to his own reflections."[6]

• • •

Even as John communed with his spiritual counselor, he could hear the activity in the prison yard, where the gallows was being erected directly outside his window.

This gallows did not operate by conventional means. There was no elevated scaffold upon which the condemned man stood, nor a trap through which he plunged to his death. Instead, as one contemporary described the apparatus, "The culprit stands on the ground and is lifted up by means of pulleys and a rope to which is attached about 250 pounds. This weight is held at the top of the cross piece by a small cord which is cut by a hatchet,

when the weight descends and the doomed man is suspended with a sud-
denness that is supposed to destroy at once all consciousness."[7]

Though the hanging was not scheduled until late afternoon, invited
witnesses began arriving early in the morning so that they could get the
most advantageous views of the gallows. By noon, the courtyard was so
packed that late arrivals could be heard complaining that Colt "was not to
be hung high enough for those in the back of the crowd to see him."[8]

• • •

John's lawyers Dudley Selden and Robert Emmett showed up at his cell at
around 11:00 in the company of their colleague David Graham, Jr., who had
just returned from his futile visit to Governor Seward in Albany. Informed of
their arrival, Anthon returned to John's cell to prepare for the ceremony.

Roughly fifty minutes later, Caroline was escorted into the cell by Sam
and John Howard Payne. She was "attired in a straw bonnet, green shawl,
claret colored cloak trimmed with red cord, and a muff." Though she managed a brave smile, "her appearance denoted much anxiety, and she was
much thinner than when a witness at the trial."[9] At precisely noon—in the
presence of Sam, Payne, the three attorneys, Justice Gilbert Merritt, and
Sheriff Monmouth Hart—John and Caroline were wed by the Reverend Dr.
Anthon. "The mistress became by law a wife," as one historian put it, "and
the same law decreed that in four short hours she would become a widow."[10]

The strange, somber nuptials would, in coming days, inspire the penny papers to new extremes of overwrought wonder. "What a bridal scene!" marveled
one reporter. "The marriage hall a prison cell! The prospect from the bridal
window the bridegroom's gallows on which he was sentenced to die a felon's
death in a few short hours. What an anticipation for a bride! Ere the setting of
the sun to mourn over the ignominious grave of him with whom her reputation and fortunes were just linked by the sacred ties of love and matrimony!"[11]

At John's request, he and Caroline were left alone to bid each other
farewell. While Anthon retired to the nearby vacant cell, Sam, John
Howard Payne, and the three attorneys waited in the corridor, where Sheriff Hart paced ceaselessly up and down, "evidently deeply affected by the
shocking duty he was about to perform."[12]

Shortly afterward, Anthon called Sam into his cell and gently asked if
"he had made arrangements to provide for the internment." At the ques-

tion, Sam "was completely overcome." "Oh," he cried, "I did not think it would come to this!"

Seeing his anguish, Anthon "felt no hesitation in offering temporary use of a vault in St. Mark's and the services of the sexton." Sam, in a voice quaking with emotion, offered a fervent thanks before stepping back into the hallway.[13]

At one o'clock—"the honeymoon of an hour" having ended—Sam reentered the cell "where John was still engaged in conversation with his wife, who was sitting at the foot of his bed, convulsed with tears."[14] By then the Colts' friend Lewis Gaylord Clark had arrived at the prison. At John's request, Clark and Payne, along with the three lawyers, were admitted into his cell, where tearful good-byes were exchanged.

A few minutes later, the five visitors, all weeping openly, stepped back out into the corridor, leaving Sam and Caroline alone with John for another ten minutes. When Sam finally emerged, he looked, according to one observer, "even more ghastly than the condemned man." For her part, Caroline "could scarcely support herself, so violent were her feelings and acute her sufferings. She stood at the door of the cell for a minute—Colt kissed her passionately—strained her to his bosom—and watched as her receding form passed into the corridor. Here she stood and sobbed convulsively as though her heart would break for five minutes. At last she was led away by Colt's brother, and his friends followed."[15]

• • •

Once his loved ones were gone, John asked to speak privately with Sheriff Hart. Making a last desperate appeal, John proclaimed once again that he had not meant to kill Adams, and "begged the sheriff to postpone the execution." Hart, steeling himself against his own sympathies, replied that "it was impossible to delay any longer than 4 o'clock, and John must now prepare himself to die."

John appeared to submit. Extracting his watch from his vest pocket, he synchronized it with Hart's, then asked to see Dr. Anthon. The moment Anthon entered the cell, John took him by the arm and said, "Now, let us pray."

"O my God, I come to thee," John began, as the two men knelt side by side. He then "poured out his soul in prayer, supplicating for his wife, his child, friends and enemies," while Anthon "exhorted him to die with Christian fortitude."[16]

After ten minutes, Anthon got to his feet and retreated to the vacant cell "to count the minutes until four o'clock."[17] John then asked his keeper, Mr. Green, "to let him be alone until the last moment." His cell door was closed, Green remaining just outside.

About an hour later, at around 2:40 p.m., a deputy sheriff named John Hillyer came by to bid John farewell. He was admitted into the cell, where John—who had been walking back and forth—shook him warmly by the hand and said, "God bless you, and may you prosper in this life, which is soon to close on me." Hillyer, deeply moved, then took his leave—the cell door was locked—and John was left all alone.[18]

• • •

As the execution hour approached, the mob outside the prison walls—which had been "horribly boisterous throughout the day"—grew even more raucous, sending up, in the words of one reporter, "a continuous and dissonant shout as of ten thousand voices. It seemed like the hungry cry of an army of wild beasts, eager for their prey."[19]

Within the packed prison yard, there were also some who seemed giddy with excitement—"buoyant with the ecstasy of anticipation." On the whole, however, the prevailing mood was solemn. Among the witnesses were judges and aldermen, legislators and lawyers, police magistrates and other civil functionaries. There were also "several members of the theatrical profession, anxious to catch a glimpse of a real death scene, which they have so often mimicked on the stage," as well as various "members of the press, shuddering at the painful duty they were required to perform."[20]

At 3:50 p.m., a group of police officers armed with long wooden staves came out into the yard and cleared a path in the crowd for the condemned man to pass through on his way to the gallows. By then the strong west wind that had been gusting all day had cleared the sky of clouds. Overhead, "the planet Venus was distinctly visible in the broad glare of the day, notwithstanding the brilliancy of the sun's rays." Within the prison yard, out on the surrounding streets, and throughout the city, people turned their eyes heavenward to marvel at the sight. In the days to come, many would "regard it as a portent."[21]

• • •

Sheriff Hart had given John as much time as possible. At 3:50 he went to the cell to escort the doomed man to the gallows. With him were his deputy, J. C. Westervelt, and the Reverend Dr. Anthon, who was clutching his prayer book.

Keeper Green unlocked the door. Anthon, who was in the lead, stepped inside the cell. Immediately he let out a cry, threw up his hands as if to shield his eyes, and backed out into the corridor, "pale as death." As he staggered back to the vacant cell, Sheriff Hart hurried to John's cot.

Mouth agape, sightless eyes halfway open, John was stretched out at full length, "as if laid out for a funeral by others." His bloody hands lay crossed on his belly. Jutting from the center of his shirt was the handle of a clasp knife, its blade buried deep in his chest.

For a moment, Hart merely stared down at the corpse. Then, removing the glove from one hand, he touched John's cheek. The skin, he testified afterward, was "still warm."[22]

• • •

A tense, expectant silence had descended on the crowd within the prison yard. All eyes were turned toward the doorway from which the condemned man was to emerge at any moment. All at once, an officer of the police court, Andrew J. Campbell, burst through the doorway and ran toward the gallows.

"He's committed suicide!" shouted Campbell. "Colt is dead in his cell!"[23]

At that very instant, a cry rang out from somewhere in the crowd. "The prison is on fire! The prison is on fire!"

Overhead, a great stream of flame and smoke billowed from the prison roof. As the witnesses gazed upward in shock and confusion, the Franklin Street gate burst open, and the mob that had waited outside all day began to pour through.[24]

• • •

At the sight of poor Colt's blood-soaked body, the Reverend Dr. Anthon felt he might faint. He had just managed to make his way back to the vacant cell and sink onto the cot. It took a full five minutes before he recovered his senses. Now, seated upright on the edge of the bed, he became aware of a great commotion outside the window: shouts, screams, cries of alarm. His first thought was "that the mob had risen and was storming the Tombs." Only gradually did he become aware of another sound: the clanging of the City Hall bell, signaling a fire.[25]

•　•　•

Fanned by the strong westerly wind, the blaze was quickly out of control. By the time the volunteer members of Southwark Engine Company 38 arrived on the scene from Nassau Street, the seventy-foot-high wooden cupola on the rooftop of the Tombs was totally engulfed in flames.

Unhitching their engine from the four-horse team, the firemen—attired in their distinctive fitted jackets and leather helmets with long black brims—dragged it through the packed crowd into proximity with the blaze. Newly purchased from a company in Philadelphia, the engine—a handsome apparatus proudly maintained in spit-and-polish condition and operated by foldout "pumping brakes"—was capable of throwing water a horizontal distance of 180 feet from its central tank. Even with the most vigorous efforts of the forty-eight men required to operate the pump, however, the water could not shoot high enough to reach the conflagration. The fire was finally extinguished—but not before the entire cupola had burned down to the roof.[26]

•　•　•

By then, Coroner Archibald Archer had arrived at John's cell, where he found Sheriff Hart keeping watch over the body. Despite his suitably solemn mien, Hart—according to the testimony of one contemporary—could "ill conceal his relief" that he would not have to carry out the hanging.

Outside the prison walls, the prevailing mood was very different. Cheated of the hanging, the disappointed mob—in the words of the same observer—reacted "with fierce mutterings of frustrated rage."[27] There were mutterings of another kind, too. Even before the ashes of the prison tower had cooled, wild rumors about John Colt's suicide—conspiracy theories, as a later age would call them—had begun to circulate.

*I*n the days leading up to the execution, reports that John's friends were plotting elaborate, last-minute rescues had already appeared in the press. On Thursday afternoon, for example, the *Herald* claimed that "the sum of $1000 had been offered to each of three of the deputy keepers of the City Prison, provided they would connive at the escape of Colt by allowing him to dress in the clothes of Caroline Henshaw, who would be sent into his cell for that purpose."[1] Even more improbable was a widely disseminated rumor that "employees of the Tombs had been bribed to cut down Colt's body from the gallows while it was still warm and smuggle it quickly to the Shakespeare hotel at the corner of Fulton and Nassau Streets, where two doctors would restore it to life by the use of a galvanic battery."[2]

However far-fetched, these stories reflected the widespread opinion that a man with as many wealthy and influential connections as John C. Colt would never be allowed to die on the gallows—that his powerful supporters would somehow contrive to save his life. In the minds of countless New Yorkers, the mysterious blaze that had broken out at the very moment of the scheduled hanging seemed a clear confirmation of this belief. By Friday evening, a story had "swept through the city that Samuel Colt had been arrested on suspicion of setting fire to the prison with a view to divert the attention of spectators and thus attempt a rescue."[3]

• • •

Like every other rumor relating to the bizarre events of that day, this one was completely unfounded. Even as the city buzzed with false reports of his arrest, Sam was sitting in the Court of Sessions chamber, attending the coroner's inquest.

Shortly after arriving at John's cell that afternoon, Coroner Archer had summoned and sworn in a jury of twenty-two men. After viewing the body, they had repaired to the Halls of Justice to hear testimony from a dozen witnesses.

Dr. Alexander Hosack, who, along with the prison physician, John R. McComb, conducted the postmortem examination, "found that the suicide had been premeditated and arranged with mathematical accuracy. A hole two inches square had been cut out of the prisoner's vest and shirt with the knife, so that nothing might interfere with the knife. Through this hole and into the body about a half an inch below the left nipple between the fourth and fifth ribs, the knife had been lodged. The left ventricle of the heart was pierced, to a depth of about an inch and a half with the four-inch blade." It was a mark of John's steely resolution that, with his last bit of strength, he had managed to "work and twist the knife round and round in his heart to puncture it as thoroughly as possible."[4]

From McComb's testimony, it was clear that John had been contemplating suicide for some time. A week before the execution date, he had asked the doctor "for a book on anatomy." When McComb refused, John "then made a number of serious inquiries as to the location of the large veins and arteries of the body, evincing a disposition to ascertain at which particular point death would be the most easily and effectually produced."[5]

Sheriff Hart, informed by McComb of these highly suspicious queries, had confiscated the buckhorn-handled penknife that John used to sharpen his writing quills. John had subsequently sneered at this measure, remarking "that such precautions were useless, inasmuch as if he wished to kill himself, he could open his veins with his teeth."[6]

In the event, of course, John had not been compelled to rely on his incisors. Someone had smuggled the suicide weapon into his cell. Questioned by the coroner, the various witnesses—Hart, deputies Westervelt, Vultee, and Green, Keeper William Jones, the Reverend Dr. Anthon, Sam, and Caroline (referred to in the papers for the first time as "Caroline Colt")—all testified that they "had no knowledge of how the deceased came into possession of the knife."

Once the last witness was examined, Coroner Archer charged the jury "that if any evidence had been furnished of any person having given the knife to Colt, he could be indicted for manslaughter; but as no such evidence was furnished, the jury would simply find what was the cause and manner of the death of the deceased."

The jury then retired and, after a brief absence, returned with a verdict "that John C. Colt came to his death by a wound inflicted by himself but the jury are unable to say in what manner he came to be possessed of said knife."

Immediately following the inquest, John's body, which had been placed in a coffin, was transported to the Dead House. Early the next morning, in keeping with the Reverend Dr. Anthon's offer, it was conveyed to St. Mark's Church and, in the presence of Sam, Caroline, John Howard Payne, and several other of John's friends, interred in a vault.[7]

• • •

As for the mysterious conflagration, it took another day or two for the cause to be determined. Suspicious as it seemed, there turned out to be a perfectly straightforward explanation. Because of the wintry weather, the watchman stationed in the tower, who habitually warmed himself by a potbellied stove installed for that purpose, had made a particularly large fire that afternoon. At a few minutes before four o'clock, he had left his post to view the execution. No sooner had he gone than "the stove-pipe became red-hot and set fire to the cupola roof."[8]

Precisely because it was so simple, this explanation failed to convince many people. In the view of countless conspiracy-minded observers, the blaze was just too coincidental to be anything other than a diversionary tactic. Despite all evidence to the contrary, there were those who did not and never would believe that John Caldwell Colt had died on November 18, 1842.

Caroline M. Henshaw. (now Colt's Wife,)

Conclusion

⁕

LEGENDS

58

On Sunday, November 20, the Reverend Dr. Samuel Hanson Cox of the First Presbyterian Church in Brooklyn preached what the *Herald* described as "an able and eloquent sermon on murder." Inspired by the tragic denouement of the Colt affair, he "dwelt at some length upon the crime of self-murder, regarding it as little less heinous than the murder of a fellow being."

In Cox's view, suicide was symptomatic of social and moral decline, being especially prevalent—so he claimed—in such decadent foreign capitals as London and Paris. Alarmingly, said Cox, "the cities of the United States, if they had not actually overtaken their trans-Atlantic sisters in this respect, were close upon their heels." This national surge in suicide was a deeply worrisome development—"one which," he argued, "demanded the solemn considerations of every right-minded and patriotic citizen."[1]

Cox was hardly the only one to draw large, portentous lessons from John's suicide. In the days and weeks following the "bloody close" of the Colt affair, magazines and newspapers were full of editorials that turned the tragedy into a cautionary tale. In the evangelical press, John was widely portrayed as an unbeliever, a man who—despite his professions of faith— "seems to have been under the influence of a false system of morals—a perverted sense of honor—and a sentiment that is at utter variance with the mysterious revelations of Christianity."[2] As such, his fate was foreordained. As one midwestern journal put it, "An educated man without religion is like a ship without ballast, the sport of every breeze, a mere toy and whim-wham with no mastery over himself or power of resisting the evil influences of others."[3]

For others in the evangelical community, the problem wasn't John's wholesale rejection of religion but rather the particular brand of Christianity he purportedly embraced. In one of his published letters, as well as in his reported final conversation with the Reverend Dr. Anthon, John had expressed scorn for the orthodox Calvinist beliefs in original sin and eternal damnation for all but the elect. "God is one of infinite goodness," he had asserted. "Agreeably to my views, it is as absurd to suppose that the Creator would inflict an infinite punishment upon one of his creatures as it is to suppose in the first place that he created man as sin. Man is doubtless punished according to deeds done in the body."[4]

In thus affirming "the cherishing hope he entertained of a happy hereafter, his trust in the efficacy of the divine atonement, and his disbelief in endless punishment," John—in the view of many observers—had aligned himself with the movement known as Universalism. This small but increasingly popular sect held to the highly controversial doctrine of eternal salvation for all humankind: the concept that punishment for earthly sins ends at death and that every departed soul ascends to heaven.[5] In the view of its many critics, this heretical notion was little more than a license to sin. "Without the threat of retribution, human beings were left morally adrift, fell victim to the baser passions, and doomed society," went the argument.[6] They also contended that, among its other "bad moral effects," Universalism led logically to suicide:

> For if our existence, in this world, be uncomfortable, why may we not put an end at once to misery and enter into blessedness? Indeed, according to the clearest dictates of universalist reason, if a man finds himself sunk into degradation and misery, self-destruction becomes an imperious duty; for by it "we ascend instantly from the condition of a downtrodden, suffering sinful mortal to that of a glorious, exalted, immortal spirit." Many have acted on these principles.[7]

In "the manner of his life and death"—committing both murder and suicide while serenely espousing a faith in his ultimate salvation—Colt, in the opinion of the enemies of Universalism, served as a striking illustration "of the nefarious influence of that doctrine which denies the future eternal punishment of the wicked."[8]

There was, of course, one major problem with this argument, as defenders of Universalism were quick to point out: namely, that Colt had at no time ever been affiliated with the denomination. "Colt a Universalist!" scoffed a writer for the *Trumpet and Universalist Magazine*. "Was he ever known as a Universalist? Did he ever attend a Universalist church? Was he ever connected with Universalism in any way?"

Even assuming for the sake of argument that Colt *was* a Universalist, read the article, "what then?" Did that prove "that Universalism leads to murder and suicide?" Turning the tables on his orthodox foes, he quite reasonably pointed out "that probably nineteen-twentieths of those who have died on the gallows have believed unhesitatingly in the doctrine of endless misery. What will this fact prove? It will prove with a force equal to nineteen to one that the doctrine of endless misery leads to murder and other capital offenses."[9]

• • •

If the Colt tragedy became instant fodder for the enemies of Universalism, it also fed into other raging controversies of the time. One remarkable editorial, echoing the arguments of early feminists like Margaret Fuller, used the Colt case to attack the lack of intellectual opportunities for women. Deploring the prevailing philosophy of female education—which held that too much schooling rendered a woman unfit for her proper household duties—this writer maintained that John's downfall was the result not of his faulty religious training but of his mother's deficient education:

> The idea appears to be entertained that an educated woman is unfitted for the exercise of those domestic qualities which render the fireside and the home happy and attractive. But how sadly erroneous is it! It is an educated, an intellectual woman alone who can render the fireside permanently attractive—it is she alone who can properly contribute to domestic enjoyment—she alone who can understand and discharge the important duties and re-

sponsibilities devolving upon a mother . . . Had not the
mind of Washington received its impulse and taken its
course from an intelligent and virtuous mother's influence, can it be presumed that he would ever have been
saluted with the proud title of "His country's deliverer," or
have been a model for all that is great and noble in morals
and politics? And had the naturally wayward propensities
of Colt been checked and restrained in infancy and youth
by a mother's head, and his moral qualities sufficiently
cultivated, far different doubtless would have been his
fate.[10]

Other reformers invoked the Colt case in their assault on capital punishment, a battle that grew into a sweeping nationwide campaign during
the early 1840s.[11] In her best-selling essay collection *Letters from New-York*,
activist Lydia Maria Child—a powerful voice in the anti-gallows
movement—described with bitter woe the "convulsive excitement" that
pervaded her supposedly "Christian community" in the tense days leading
up to John's planned execution:

> The effect of executions on *all* brought within their influence
> is evil and nothing but evil. For a fortnight past, this whole
> city has been kept in a state of corroding excitement . . .
> Each day, hope and fear alternated; the natural effect of all
> this was to have the whole thing regarded as a game, in
> which the criminal might or might not become the win-
> ner. Worse than all this was the horrible amount of diabol-
> ical passions excited. The hearts of men were filled with
> murder; they gloated over the thoughts of vengeance, and
> were rabid to witness a fellow-creature's agony.[12]

In a similar vein, Horace Greeley—though agreeing with the jury's
verdict—deplored the ugly passions incited by Colt's death sentence. "We
hope that this tragedy in all its proportions has done much to hasten the
abolition of the Punishment of Death," he editorialized in the *Tribune*:

What has been the influence of the Punishment of Death in this case? What moral effects have been produced by its existence? Have we not seen the community divided with regard to the justice of the sentence? . . . Not from compassion to criminals but from regard to the community—whose sympathies and whose feelings are so unhealthily excited by public executions—whose abhorrence of crime and reverence for laws are confused and disturbed by these deeds of legal butchery—we demand the abolition of the Punishment of Death.[13]

Perhaps the most intriguing of all the editorials to appear in the wake of John's suicide was a piece in the November 24 issue of the New York *Sun*. Headlined "The Moral of the Recent Tragedy," the essay is remarkable for its psychological sophistication and acuity: its recognition of the extent to which our actions are motivated by what a later age would call unconscious impulses.

The "fearful drama" of the Colt affair, the author writes, teaches "how little we know ourselves—what strangers we are to our evil propensities . . . and how terrible and uncontrollable is the wild tempest of human passions when once they obtain the mastery over the reason and the conscience":

But a few short summers since, John C. Colt was sporting round the hearth of fond parents in all the gaiety and glee of child-like innocence. And but a few months since, he was threading the devious path of life with all the pride and ambition of self-confident youth. Who that might have seen him at either period of life would not have been appalled at the thought that his career was to be in crime—in blood—in double murder? Had he been told as he walked abroad erect among his gay companions that such would be his fate, how would his eye have kindled and his bosom swelled with deep and irrepressible indignation? And yet, young men of New York, he did it all. He knew not himself, and was not master of his fierce and desolating passions.

"Let us be admonished by this terrible example," the writer concludes. "Let us ask—Do we know ourselves any better than he knew himself? Do we comprehend, and have we the fixed moral principle, the high moral energy, to control the fearful volcano of human passions whose maddened fires roar and blaze within our bosoms?"[14]

In its avoidance of pat moralizing—its acknowledgment that, operating beneath our awareness, there are dark, destructive drives that can only be neutralized through a process of deep and ruthless introspection—this article strikes a singularly contemporary note. Though it was published anonymously, scholars have since identified its author as the twenty-three-year-old journalist Walt Whitman.[15]

*W*hile preachers, pundits, and crusaders of various stripes put the Colt case to their own particular uses, the public continued to traffic in rumor and gossip. "The fever of excitement into which our city was lashed on Friday has subsided but little and continues to rage in all circles," reported the *Sun* on Monday, November 21. New Yorkers, the paper continued, were in the grip of "a perfect Colt mania."[1]

The most persistent story had it that the dead body found in John's cell was that of a "pauper convict" and that, during the tumult of the fire, John himself had been smuggled out of the prison and put on a ship bound for France.[2] Among those who accepted that John had in fact committed suicide, speculation swirled around the source of the suicide weapon. With the exception of the Reverend Dr. Anthon, virtually everyone who had visited John during his final hours was suspected of having supplied him with the fatal pocketknife, though the consensus seemed to be that it had been "concealed in the long clothes of the baby that Caroline Henshaw carried with her into the cell when she went there to be married."[3] That the infant, according to every newspaper account, had not been present at the ceremony did nothing to dampen the rumor.

One particularly disturbing story quickly made the rounds. It was recorded by George Templeton Strong, who heard it from George Anthon, son of the clergyman. In his diary entry of November 22, Strong notes that John had been "reluctantly persuaded into" suicide in order "to spare his family" the ignominy of the gallows. Exactly who did the persuading was left unsaid; though as the world knew, only one member of John's family had been at his side throughout the ordeal and had much to lose by having the Colt name besmirched with the permanent taint of dishonor.[4]

At the same time that this rumor reached Strong's ears, James Gordon Bennett was publicizing another, unsubstantiated story. In addition to the suicide, John's last-minute marriage to Caroline—"the strange and somber bridal," as one penny paper called it—had been a subject of intense speculation.[5] Most people assumed that John had wed his mistress for noble motives: to "redeem the character of the unfortunate woman" and to legitimize their out-of-wedlock son.[6] Bennett, however, claimed that there was another and far less admirable reason.

"Circumstances that have recently come into our possession," wrote Bennett, had persuaded him that Colt and Caroline were actually married "in Philadelphia before the murder of Adams took place in this city. After this deed was committed, it became necessary that she should be used as a witness, and knowing that her testimony could not be received as the wife of Colt, she was introduced as plain Caroline Henshaw, and for the purpose of carrying out the deception as originally practiced, the marriage ceremony was again performed, in order to blind the eyes of the world to the previous transaction."

To Bennett, this somewhat tortured story offered the only plausible rationale "for the commission of an act that, under any other circumstances, appears perfectly inexplicable."[7] There was, however, another explanation for John and Caroline's marriage, one so shocking that many years would pass before it was brought to light.

The infant son born to Caroline Henshaw had been named Samuel Colt, Jr.—a tribute, so the world assumed, to Sam's steadfast devotion to his brother. For the rest of his life, Sam would look after the boy and his mother. His efforts on their behalf began shortly after John's death, when he sought help from a woman who had long proven herself a friend to the outcast and oppressed: Lydia Maria Child.

Born outside of Boston in 1802, Child taught for a time at a girls' school before achieving prominence as the author of the historical novel *Hobomok*, published when she was just twenty-two. A few years later, she founded the pioneering children's magazine the *Juvenile Miscellany*, then turned out a series of popular domestic advice books, beginning with *The American Frugal Housewife*. By the mid-1830s, Child had taken up the radical causes of abolitionism and women's rights. After moving to Manhattan in 1841, she became editor of the abolitionist newspaper the *National Anti-Slavery Standard*, to which she contributed a regular column, "Letters from New-York," later collected into the best-selling volume of the same name.

As Child's chief biographer notes, these city sketches were remarkable, among other reasons, for their haunting, deeply sympathetic "vignettes that encapsulated the daily lives of the poor":

> a "ragged urchin" staggering under a load of newspapers, his face "blue, cold, and disconsolate," his childish voice "prematurely cracked into shrillness by screaming street cries at the top of his lungs"; a woman "with garments all

draggled in New-York gutters," lying in the street where she had "fallen in intoxication"; two small girls with "scanty garments fluttering in the wind" and "blue hands . . . locked in each other" as they struggled through snow drifts and stopped every now and then to exchange the single "pair of broken shoes," bound with rags, that they shared.[1]

Child's widely read piece on John Colt, originally published in the November 24, 1842, issue of the *National Anti-Slavery Standard*, not only dealt with another of her causes—the crusade against capital punishment—but went out of its way to stress the estimable traits of John's character. "I mean no extenuation of the awful crime of John C. Colt when I say that, through the whole course of this terrible tragedy, he has shown the self-same qualities which men admire under the name of military greatness," Child wrote. "The stern silence with which he shut up in his own breast his secrets and plans; his cool self-possession under circumstances that would have crazed a common brain; his bold defiance of the law, which he regarded as a powerful enemy; the strong pride which bore him up under a long imprisonment and prompted him to suicide; all these indicate such elements of character as military heroes are made of." Mrs. Child also praised Sam, who "never forsook his disgraced and suffering brother; but sustained him throughout by his presence and sympathy; and made almost superhuman efforts to save him from his untimely end."[2]

Whether Sam and Mrs. Child were already friends when this essay was written is unclear, though the two shared a mutual acquaintance in Lydia Huntley Sigourney.[3] In any event, within two weeks of John's suicide, Sam had approached Mrs. Child to solicit her aid in finding suitable living arrangements for his brother's widow and the infant boy he was determined to "treat as if he were his own son." We know of Sam's visit from a letter that Child addressed to her friend John Sullivan Dwight on December 1, 1842. A former Unitarian minister and key figure in the Transcendentalism movement, Dwight was at the time a teacher of Latin and music at Brook Farm, the Utopian commune established at West Roxbury, Massachusetts—the founding members of which included Nathaniel Hawthorne.[4] Referring to Caroline, Mrs. Child wrote:

Mr. Colt's brother has been to see me and consult with me about her. He says he believes her to be a modest, worthy girl; that she never formed any other connection than that with his unfortunate brother . . . He says he feels it a duty to do more for her than feed and clothe her; that he ought, as far as possible, to throw a protecting influence around her and the child whom he shall in all respects treat as if he were his own son. "I want to educate her," says he; "to put her under influences that will make her a judicious mother for my brother's son. But where shall I find a suitable place? I have thought of a country clergyman's family; but she would be pointed at in a country village, and she would have little chance to improve intellectually; and in most cases there would not be that entire forgetfulness of her peculiar situation, which is desirable." I at once thought of the West Roxbury Community, and mentioned it; at the same time telling him that you were so much crowded that I thought it not very likely you could take her. I had *other* fears than those of your being crowded. I thought you might perhaps fear the "speech of people." But, my dear friend, this is a real case of a fellow creature fallen among thieves, wounded and bleeding by the wayside. If she were a loose woman, I would be the last to propose such a thing. But I think she is not. She is, as I believe, an honest confiding young creature, the victim of a false state of society. She is almost heart-broken, and longs for seclusion, soothing influences, and instruction how to do her duty. If you, with your large and liberal views, and your clear perception of human brotherhood, if *you*, at West Roxbury, reject her, where, in the name of our common Father, *can* I find a shelter for her poor storm-pelted heart? . . . My soul is on its knees before you, to receive this poor shorn lamb of our Father's flock. I am in agony, lest you should not listen to my supplications, for somehow or other, though a stranger to me, God has laid her upon my heart.

Mr. Colt seemed to leave the arrangements to *me*; but

I thought his idea was to have her board with you for a
year, doing what conveniently she could, consistently with
the care of her child; and you to make such deductions
from the price of board as her labors were worth; and if you
found her a useful and pleasant inmate, to make such after
arrangements about the education of the child, &c as
should seem proper.[5]

• • •

Even as he coped with his grief and sought a haven for Caroline and his infant namesake, Sam pressed on with his submarine battery project. Two
more public demonstrations of his remote-controlled underwater mine had
followed the first. In August 1842, before an audience that included President John Tyler and members of his Cabinet, he had blown up a sixty-ton
schooner moored 150 yards offshore in the Potomac River. Another spectacular display took place on October 18—just a month before John's execution date—when Sam's destruction of a 260-ton target vessel in New
York Harbor was witnessed by an estimated forty thousand spectators.[6]

To be sure, there were powerful politicians who opposed Sam's undertaking. Notable among them was Representative John Quincy Adams, the
former U.S. president. Ignoring the old adage about love and war, Adams
believed that the use of submarine mines was unsporting, and that if enemy
ships were to be blown up "at all, it should be done by fair and honest"
means. Despite Adams's objections, however, Congress voted to appropriate a substantial sum to Sam's ongoing experiments.[7]

• • •

Historical records do not indicate whether Mrs. Child succeeded in securing a yearlong residency at Brook Farm for Caroline and baby Sam. What *is*
certain is that by early 1844—while continuing his experiments and ar-
ranging for a fourth and final demonstration of his invention—Sam was
casting about for another suitable position for Caroline.

The evidence is contained in several letters from his brother James. By
then, the twenty-eight-year-old James had been admitted to the bar and
fought a pistol duel over an "amorous relationship" with the wife of a fellow

lawyer—a scandal that did nothing to impede his rapid advancement to judge of the St. Louis Criminal Court.[8]

Though Sam's own letters do not survive, it is clear from James's responses that by early 1844, Caroline had received enough education to teach school out west. That, at any rate, was the life Sam now imagined for her. James, however, consistently discouraged this plan.

"In relation to Caroline's coming out to this city for the purpose of teaching school," he wrote from St. Louis on February 23, 1844, "I cannot, now, recommend it for several reasons . . . The west is full of surplus teachers and every day do I see instances of both males and females who are entirely destitute of a means of living . . . This city is full of teachers and all of them are distressed for the want of patronage."[9]

Eight months later, the ever-persistent Sam was still pressing James to find a teaching job for Caroline. James, however, continued to resist, adding a new argument to his original objection: that, besides being "literally filled with teachers and governesses," the West, with its relatively loose and lawless moral atmosphere, was no place for a vulnerable young woman like Caroline.

"I have made repeated suggestions to some of my female acquaintances, to such persons who would be most likely to aid me with their counsel, and have invariably met with no encouragement whatsoever," he wrote to Sam on October 11, 1844. "Their answer is if you want to save her character, do not permit her to come here . . . The waywardness of the western people would lead her to be very much exposed and this in no way could be prevented. She would be almost as much so here as she would be if she were 'at large' in NY . . . The whole west is made up of new settlers, adventurers, and speculators, and among such people what could she expect?"

In the same letter, James offered an alternative proposal:

> My plan for Caroline is this. Next winter if it is
> possible one of us goes into Virginia or North or South
> Carolina and to some of the old and worthy families
> there, represent her situation, and if possible—to secure
> her a home among some of them. In Virginia among the
> old families the feeling of true chivalry is of much higher

standards than in comparative new countries, and it is so
in North and South Carolina. In these states they have
private teachers. Here we have none nor governesses. A
situation could be found where her feelings would be
respected and she could enjoy herself in a little
society . . . The family should be of high moral tone and
there are many such as I am informed by Virginians and
North and South Carolinians who are here. She could
make herself useful and become, there, an ornament to
her sex. Besides, the noble little boy would come under
the best influences. The New England influences would
be too bigoted or rather too severe, the western too
careless, but the Virginian, &c would be of that character
that would lead him to feel that all he may hope for in
the future would alone depend upon himself (I mean so
far as character is concerned), which he would meet with
noble examples of success and would receive
encouragement the most liberal in his early travel of life.

Nothing in the historical record, however, suggests that either Sam or
James followed through on this plan. Caroline and her "noble little boy," so
far as is known, never found refuge among the chivalrous slave-holding
families of the South.

• • •

Just five days before the first of these letters was written, Sam's hope of securing a big military contract was dealt a serious blow. On February 18,
1844, he lost his main government advocate, Abel Upshur—recently appointed secretary of state—who was killed on board the newly commis-
sioned warship USS *Princeton* when one of her massive guns exploded
during a demonstration.

Despite this setback, Sam forged ahead with preparations for his fourth
and final demonstration, acquiring the 500-ton schooner *Brunette* for use as
a target vessel. On April 13, 1844, as the ship—renamed the *Styx* "for its
death cruise"—moved under full sail down the Potomac River, Sam set off
his mines before a massive crowd of onshore spectators that included the

president, his Cabinet, and members of Congress, who had adjourned for the occasion. In a great eruption of water, smoke, and timber, the ship was "instantly shattered to atoms."[10]

As a pure pyrotechnical display, the destruction of the *Styx*, like Sam's three preceding demonstrations, was a spectacular success. Military professionals, however, remained deeply skeptical of Sam's system. "As experiments," wrote one influential observer, "these, as many others, were very beautiful and striking, but in the practical application of this apparatus to purposes of war, we have no confidence."[11] By then, moreover, the United States and Great Britain had reached an agreement over several disputed border issues, eliminating the threat of Anglo-American hostilities and the need for a costly harbor defense system.

In the end, nothing would come of Sam's invention. Though he was compensated for "personal expenses incurred during his experiments," Congress refused to commit additional funds to the project. After devoting more than three years to its development and promotion, Sam was forced to abandon the venture. Its failure was "one of his greatest personal disappointments."[12]

For a while, he channeled his unquenchable energies into a collaboration with his friend Samuel Morse, setting up a business called the New York and Offing Electro-Magnetic Telegraph Association, a subscription service for stock traders, commodity speculators, newspaper editors, and other professionals who stood to profit from receiving overseas news ahead of their competitors. Stationed at the westernmost tip of Coney Island, a fleet of fast sloops maintained by the company would sail out to meet incoming vessels and gather the latest information from abroad, which was then flashed via telegraph to Manhattan. Like every other enterprise he had thrown himself into, however, Sam's wire service failed to live up to his hopes. By 1846, the thirty-two-year-old inventor was permanently done with telegraphy and as financially hard pressed as ever.[1]

• • •

It was the bloodshed on the Texas frontier that finally made Samuel Colt's fortune.

In June 1844—in a real-life version of a scenario that would become a cliché of countless Western movies—a band of fifteen Texas Rangers under the leadership of the legendary Major John Coffee Hays encountered a war party of eighty Comanches along the Pedernales River. The Comanches were renowned as "the finest light cavalry in the world," each warrior capable of letting fly a half dozen lethally aimed arrows in a matter of seconds while riding bareback at full gallop. Expecting an easy victory over the badly outnumbered Rangers—armed, so the Indians assumed, with their usual single-shot muzzle loaders—the Comanches were thrown into confusion when Hays and his men came charging at them while firing their pistols at a furious rate. Within minutes, half the Comanches lay dead on the ground, while the rest of the war party fled.[2]

Exactly how Hays and his men came into possession of their handguns—early model Colt repeaters—remains unclear. What *is* certain is that "Hays's Big Fight," as it came to be known, not only foreshadowed the fate of the Plains Indians but also altered the destiny of Samuel Colt.

One of the Rangers involved in that skirmish was Captain Samuel Hamilton Walker. When war broke out with Mexico in 1846, Walker was sent east to procure weapons for the U.S. Army. Within days of his arrival in New York City, he and Sam had met, forged an instant alliance, and concocted a new, heavier caliber, six-shot revolver designed to Walker's specifications. A prototype of this imposing "hand cannon" was submitted to Secretary of War William L. Marcy, who—with Walker's enthusiastic endorsement—placed an order for one thousand of the pistols to be delivered in three months' time.[3]

Sam's elation at achieving his long-sought goal of a military contract was only slightly tempered by the fact that, with his Paterson factory gone, he had no evident means to fulfill it. Colt, however, wasn't the sort of man to be deterred by such a trifle. Deploying his considerable powers of persuasion, he prevailed on some of the nation's finest gunsmiths—among them Edwin Wesson and Eliphalet Remington—to drop whatever else they were doing and supply him with parts, which were then assembled in the armory of Eli Whitney, Jr., son of the famed cotton gin inventor. Their cylinders engraved with an image of "Hays's Big Fight," the full complement of Colt Whitneyville-Walker holster pistols (so named by firearms aficionados) was delivered on schedule. Walker himself was brandishing a pair when he was killed on October 11, 1847, while leading a company of 250 Rangers against more than 1,600 Mexican lancers in the Battle of Huamantla.[4]

Another governmental order of one thousand pistols quickly followed. From that point on, nothing would stand in the way of Sam Colt's "ascent to the top of the pyramid of American industry."[5] Within a few years, he owned his own state-of-the-art factory in Hartford, superintended by his old friend, the mechanical genius Elisha K. Root, who devised a system of steam-powered mass production that put Colt in the forefront of America's industrial revolution. With the great westward migration—spurred by the discovery of gold in California—demand for Colt's six-shooters boomed, while the outbreak of war and revolution throughout Europe opened up rich new markets for his weapons. As sales of his revolvers continued to soar—from twenty thousand per year in 1851 to fifty thousand per year by 1854—Colt kept expanding his facilities, which culminated in the construction of his vast armory on the banks of the Connecticut River. By the time this technological showcase began operation in 1855, Colonel Colt— as he now styled himself—had become an international celebrity and one of the country's richest men.[6]

• • •

Sam had first met Elizabeth Jarvis in the summer of 1851 during a vacation at the glittering resort community of Newport, Rhode Island. A lovely twenty-three-year-old from a distinguished and affluent family, Elizabeth found herself "swept away by the thirty-seven-year-old industrialist"— "fairly awed," as she later confessed, by "the magnetism of his presence . . . More truly than any other, he filled my ideal of a noble manhood, a princely nature, an honest, true, warm-hearted man."[7]

As for Sam, the elegant, well-connected Elizabeth—daughter of a prominent Episcopal minister and descendant of an illustrious "line of religious, military, and political leaders"—was exactly the kind of woman who suited his social ambitions. After several years of courtship, Elizabeth joyfully accepted Sam's offer of marriage, their engagement sealed with a seven-carat diamond ring, a gift originally bestowed on Colt by a grateful king of Sardinia.[8]

Sam, as biographers believe, had been married once before. When he proposed to the estimable Miss Jarvis, however, he was unencumbered, having long since divested himself of his first and far less desirable wife: Caroline Henshaw.

ames Gordon Bennett, who had reported the rumor that Caroline and John were already married "before the murder of Adams took place," had gotten the story half right. Caroline had, in fact, been wed before. But not to John.

The full story would not be made public for many years, when Sam Colt's most authoritative biographer revealed that the beautiful, unschooled sixteen-year-old Sam had so impulsively married during his early trip to Scotland was Caroline Henshaw.[1] Once the heat of youthful passion had subsided, the ambitious young inventor—busily cultivating powerful political connections and ingratiating himself with Washington's social elite—"decided that so humble a bride was no worthy partner for him."[2] In an age that viewed divorce as a shameful, if not immoral, act, he cast about for a way to extricate himself from the inconvenient union. Compounding his predicament was the awkward fact that, by then, Caroline was pregnant with Sam's child.

It was John who, "out of either pity or duty," took the pregnant Caroline in and became her protector and lover. When all the efforts to save John from the gallows failed, "Sam saw a way out." The macabre ceremony in the shadow of the gallows was his doing. By agreeing to the "bigamous and semi-incestuous" marriage with her "condemned brother-in-law on the day of his death," Caroline, already effectively discarded by Sam, was not only spared the stigma of divorce but guaranteed his grateful, lifelong support. John, who had nothing to lose, was able to repay his brother's unwavering devotion during his darkest hours. And Sam had his freedom.[3]

As for the child born to Caroline—later renamed Samuel Caldwell Colt—Sam took an active role in his upbringing, overseeing his education and sending him to the finest private schools. In his correspondence, he consistently referred to the boy as his nephew (or "neffue," as he spelled it), though he always enclosed the word in quotation marks, as if "to maintain a flimsy pretense that the boy was brother John's son, while at the same time letting the world know that the handsome lad sprang from his own manly loins."[4] Sam's will—which bequeathed his namesake a sum totaling more than two million dollars in today's money—was probated in 1862, and it was then that "Samuel Caldwell Colt, Jr., produced a marriage license proving that Colt had married Caroline in Scotland."[5]

63

_W_hat became of Caroline is unknown. There are indications that sometime in the late 1840s, she returned to Europe. A legend arose that she adopted the name Julia Leicester and eloped with a dashing young Prussian nobleman, Count Friedrich August Kunow Waldemar von Oppen, who—having been disinherited because of his unsuitable marriage—became an overseas agent for Colt's arms. Though von Oppen certainly existed and did indeed marry a relation of Sam Colt's, evidence shows that his wife was not Caroline Henshaw.[1]

An equally colorful rumor was said to have originated with one Samuel M. Everett, an acquaintance of John Colt's who supposedly encountered him during a trip to California in 1852. According to this story, John was alive and well and passing himself off as a Spanish grandee named Don Carlos Juan Brewster, complete with "brocaded jacket, silk scarf, silver spurs, sombrero, and trousers slashed to the knees and garnished along the seams with a fringe of little silver bells." Sharing his hacienda were Caroline and two handsome children.[2] Like the sightings of dead celebrities that have become increasingly common in our own time, however, this outlandish tale was a product of folklore, not fact.

. . .

Still, its widespread circulation in 1852—ten years after John's suicide— was significant: a sign of the persistent fascination exerted by the Colt case, which continued to live on in story and song. As early as February 1843, two Colt-related stage melodramas (the era's equivalent of today's "ripped-from-the-headlines" TV crime shows) were mounted in Cincinnati: *John C. Colt, or the Unhappy Suicide*, and *John C. Colt, or the End of a Murderer*, the latter written by and starring the popular actor and dramatist Nathaniel Harrington Bannister.[3]

At roughly the same time, a barroom ballad titled "The Lay of Mr. Colt" began to make the rounds:

> The clock is ticking onward,
>   It nears the hour of doom,
> And no one yet hath entered
>   Into that ghastly room.
> The jailer and the sheriff,
>   They are walking to and fro,
> And the hangman sits upon the steps
>   And smokes his pipe below.
> In grisly expectation
>   The prison all is bound,
> And, save for expectoration,
>   You cannot hear a sound.
> The turnkey stands and ponders,
>   His hand upon the bolt—
> "In twenty minutes more, I guess,
>   'Twill all be up with Colt!"
> But see, the door is opened!
>   Forth comes the weeping bride;
> The courteous sheriff lifts his hat,
>   And saunters to her side.
> "I beg your pardon, Mrs. C.,
>   But is your husband ready?"
> "I guess you'd better ask himself,"
>   Replied the woeful lady.
>
> The clock is ticking onward;
>   Hark! Hark! It striketh one!
> Each felon draws a whistling breath,

"*Time's up with Colt; he's done!*"
The sheriff consults his watch again,
   Then puts it in his fob,
And turning to the hangman, says—
   "*Get ready for the job!*"
The jailer knocketh loudly,
   The turnkey draws the bolt,
And pleasantly the sheriff says—
   "*We're waiting, Mr. Colt!*"

No answer! No—no answer!
   All's still as death within;
The sheriff eyes the jailer,
   The jailer strokes his chin.
"*I shouldn't wonder, Nahum, if*
   It were as you suppose."
The hangman looked unhappy, and
   The turnkey blew his nose.
They entered. On his pallet
   The noble convict lay,—
The bridegroom on his marriage-bed
   But not in trim array.
His red right hand a razor held,
   Fresh sharpened from the hone,
And his ivory neck was severed,
   And gashed into the bone.

And when the lamp is lighted
   In the long November days,
And lads and lasses mingle
   At shucking of the maize;
When pies of smoking pumpkin
   Upon the table stand,
And bowls of black molasses
   Go round from hand to hand;
When flap-jacks, maple-sugared,

Are hissing in the pan,
And cider, with a dash of gin,
   Foams in the social can;
When the goodman wets his whistle,
   And the goodwife scolds the child;
And the girls exclaim convulsively,
   "Have done, or I'll be riled!"
With laughter and with weeping,
   Then shall they tell the tale,
How Colt his foeman quartered
And died within the jail.[4]

· · ·

The following year, the Colt-Adams case inspired a far more enduring piece of American literature, Edgar Allan Poe's classic short story "The Oblong Box." Set aboard a packet ship headed from Charleston, South Carolina, to New York City, the story concerns a passenger named Cornelius Wyatt, a "young artist" with a studio "in Chambers Street," who is traveling with a mysterious pine box "six feet in length by two and a half in breadth." The contents of the box—which Wyatt keeps stored in his own stateroom throughout the trip—remain a mystery until the climax of the tale, when the nameless narrator learns to his amazement that it held the corpse of Wyatt's lovely, recently deceased young wife, packed in salt.[5]

Given his particular obsessions, it is no surprise that Poe latched on to the single most macabre element of the Colt case—the salted remains loaded onto a ship in a wooden crate—and transformed the body of a stout middle-aged male into that of a prematurely dead beautiful young woman. In another great American short story of the period—Herman Melville's masterpiece "Bartleby, the Scrivener"—the Colt-Adams case appears in undisguised form. At one point in this endlessly fascinating parable about (among other things) the limits of Christian charity, the narrator—a mild-mannered, middle-aged lawyer struggling to deal with an increasingly impossible employee—finds himself driven to such heights of exasperation that he fears he might commit violence upon the maddening copyist. It is the sudden recollection of the Colt-Adams case that allows him to keep his temper in check:

I was now in such a state of nervous resentment that I thought it but prudent to check myself at present from further demonstrations. Bartleby and I were alone. I remembered the tragedy of the unfortunate Adams and the still more unfortunate Colt in the solitary office of the latter; and how poor Colt, being dreadfully incensed by Adams, and imprudently permitting himself to get wildly excited, was at unawares hurried into his fatal act—an act which certainly no man could possibly deplore more than the actor himself. Often it had occurred to me in my ponderings upon the subject, that had that altercation taken place in the public street, or at a private residence, it would not have terminated as it did. It was the circumstance of being alone in a solitary office, up stairs, of a building entirely unhallowed by humanizing domestic associations—an uncarpeted office, doubtless, of a dusty, haggard sort of appearance;—this it must have been, which greatly helped to enhance the irritable desperation of the hapless Colt.

But when this old Adam of resentment rose in me and tempted me concerning Bartleby, I grappled him and threw him. How? Why, simply by recalling the divine injunction: "A new commandment give I unto you, that ye love one another." Yes, this it was that saved me. Aside from higher considerations, charity often operates as a vastly wise and prudent principle—a great safeguard to its possessor. Men have committed murder for jealousy's sake, and anger's sake, and hatred's sake, and selfishness' sake, and spiritual pride's sake; but no man that ever I heard of, ever committed a diabolical murder for sweet charity's sake. Mere self-interest, then, if no better motive can be enlisted, should, especially with high-tempered men, prompt all beings to charity and philanthropy.[6]

· · ·

For one woman writer, it was not the killing of Adams, or the boxing-up of his body, or John's iron-nerved resolve to cheat the hangman that made the

Colt case so memorable but the somber wedding ceremony in the Tombs. This author was Theodora De Wolf Colt, wife of Sam and John's brother Christopher, who, in her privately printed volume *Stray Fancies*, included a poem called "The Marriage in a Prison," a sentimental celebration of love's unconquerable might, even in face of imminent death:

> *'Twas not within the sacred aisle,*
> > *Before the altar of our God,*
> *With parents and with sisters near,*
> > *The bridegroom and the fair one stood.*
>
> *'Twas in a dungeon dark and drear,*
> > *With naught to dissipate its gloom,*
> *With nothing genial to efface*
> > *The horrors of that living tomb!*
>
> *The man of God in silence stood,*
> > *His eyes were raised as if in prayer,*
> *And by his side two forms, as still*
> > *As death,—they were the bridal pair!*
>
> *One was a youth of noble mien,*
> > *Ill-fitted for so vile a place,*
> *And on his brow a loftiness*
> > *That prison-walls could not efface.*
>
> *Excepting when he glanced at her,*
> > *That fair young being at his side,*
> *Then agonizing was his gaze,—*
> > *It seemed as if his spirit died.*
>
> *A solemn stillness reigned throughout,*
> > *You might have heard each beating heart,*
> *'Till broken by the preacher's voice:*
> > *"Wilt thou love her 'till death do part?"*

A scaffold near the casement stood!—
*   'Twas there, oh God! That he might see*
That, although innocent of crime,
*   A sufferer he was doomed to be.*

He answered not, nor bowed assent,
*   But pressed that fair girl to his breast,*
As when in days of happiness
*   She knew it as her place of rest.*

The blessing then the priest pronounced,
*   And left them for a last farewell*
They wished to take alone, unseen
*   By any in that gloomy cell!*

Oh, what can woman's love efface?—
*   Not dungeon, scaffold, chains, nor death;*
She clings but with a firmer hold,—
*   She loves until her latest breath.*

She loved him when he was esteemed
*   And honored by his fellow men;*
And now her soul still turns to him,—
*   Though all forsake, she'll not condemn!*[7]

• • •

The contrast between the grim jailhouse nuptials of John Colt and Caroline Henshaw and the wedding, fourteen years later, of Sam Colt and Elizabeth Jarvis couldn't have been more stark. The ceremony, held at the Protestant Episcopal Church at Middletown, Connecticut, on June 5, 1856, was conducted by the Right Reverend T. C. Brownell, bishop of Connecticut. The bride was bedecked in "a dress and jewelry rumored to cost eight thousand dollars"—the equivalent of more than two hundred thousand in today's dollars. The wedding cake, standing six feet tall, was trimmed with confectionery pistols and topped with a spun-sugar colt.

Following the ceremony, the entire bridal party took the evening express to Manhattan, where Sam had rented one of the city's largest hotels, the St. Nicholas, for a gala reception. The next morning, the newlyweds set off by ship on a six-month honeymoon. After an extended stay in London, they traveled to Holland, Bavaria, Vienna, the Tyrolean Alps, and finally Russia, where—along with "princes and princesses and top-ranking diplomats and military officers" from throughout Europe—they were guests at the coronation of Czar Alexander II.[8]

Shortly after their return to Hartford, they moved into the spectacular residence known as Armsmear ("the mansion that 'arms' had built on the 'mere,' or lowlands, of Hartford's South Meadow").[9] Designed by Sam himself, the massive brownstone building, with its five-story tower, its steel and glass conservatories, its exotic minarets and domes, stood as "the perfect model of a Victorian-age mogul's idea of opulence and elegance."[10] Its nearly two dozen rooms—dining room, drawing room, music room, billiard room, ballroom, reception room, library, picture gallery, and various private quarters—were outfitted with imported custom-made furniture, carpets, drapery, and other items of décor costing the equivalent of more than six hundred thousand dollars in today's money. The sweeping grounds of the estate—with its private garden, deer park, artificial lake, terraced lawn, spectacular greenhouses, marble fountains and statuary—was designed by Copeland and Cleveland of Boston, "one of the nation's first and most respected landscape architectural firms."[11]

Between the day that he and Elizabeth moved into Armsmear and Sam's early death of gout and rheumatic fever at the age of forty-seven, only five years elapsed. Still, despite the heart-wrenching loss of his first two children (both memorialized, of course, in the funereal verse of his friend Mrs. Sigourney), those years "were the most stable and prosperous of his life." Some of his most contented hours were spent within his "private room," where Sam "gathered the pictured forms and mementos of those he loved best."[12] Among these precious items were portraits of his long-departed mother and sisters, marble statues of his two tragically short-lived infants, and, it is said, an oil painting of his doomed but indomitable brother, John Caldwell Colt.

ACKNOWLEDGMENTS

I owe my greatest debt of thanks to Professor Richard Vangermeersch, distinguished historian of American accounting, who graciously shared his research material on the Colt case and offered vital assistance throughout the project.

I am also grateful to the following people for their kindness and generosity: Randy Blomquist, Mickey Cartin, Kenneth Cobb, Dale Flesher, Bob Kenworthy, the Hon. Diane Kiesel, Richard Morgan, Karen Nickeson, Richard Pope, Richard Roberts, David Smith, Jamie Stockton, and, as always, Marianne Stein and Evelyn Silverman. The Research Foundation of the City of New York provided generous assistance in the form of a PSC-CUNY Research Award.

I can't adequately convey my appreciation for the love and support of my wife and partner, Kimiko Hahn. To describe my feelings about our life together, I must turn to the words of John Colt's contemporary, Ralph Waldo Emerson: "I am glad to the brink of fear."

NOTES

PROLOGUE: NEW YORK CITY, FRIDAY AFTERNOON, SEPTEMBER 17, 1841

1. We know these details of Samuel Adams's dress and gait from the trial testimony of his acquaintance John Johnson. See Thomas Dunphy and Thomas J. Cummins, *Remarkable Trials of All Countries* (New York: Dossy & Company, 1870), pp. 247–48.

2. Besides Whitman's "Song of Myself," my evocation of the street scene is drawn from several sources, primarily Edgar Allan Poe's story "The Man of the Crowd," Charles Dickens's *American Notes for General Circulation,* and Nathaniel Parker Willis's *Open-Air Musings in the City.* Excerpts from the last two can be found in Phillip Lopate's anthology *Writing New York: A Literary Anthology* (New York: Library of America, 2008), pp. 51–64, 74–90.

3. For example, see J. Disturnell, *The Classified Mercantile Directory for the Cities of New-York and Brooklyn* (New York: J. Disturnell, 1837), and E. Porter Belden, *New-York: Past, Present, and Future* (New York: G. P. Putnam, 1849), pp. 276–450.

4. On the very day of Samuel Adams's disappearance, the *New York Herald* ran a prominent story, "The Case of Mary Rogers—The Place of the Murder," accompanied by a large woodcut illustration showing "The House Where Mary Rogers Was Last Seen Alive." See *New York Herald,* September 17, 1841, p. 2. For a full account of the McLeod case, see William Renwick Riddell, "An International Murder Trial," *Journal of the American Institute of Criminal Law and Criminology,* vol. 10, no. 2 (August 1919): pp. 176–83.

5. For a description of Scudder's American Museum, see Neil Harris, *Humbug: The Art of P. T. Barnum* (Chicago: University of Chicago Press, 1973), p. 39.

6. Dunphy and Cummins, *Remarkable Trials,* p. 248.

7. See *Holden's Dollar Magazine,* vol. 6 (1851): p. 187.

PART ONE: FRAIL BLOOD

CHAPTER 1

1. The school was later renamed the American Asylum at Hartford for the Education and Instruction of Deaf and Dumb Persons.

According to local historian Mary K. Talcott, Captain Lord (1611–62) "was one of the most energetic and efficient men in the colony; when the first troop of horse was organized, he was chosen commander, March 11, 1658, and distinguished himself in the Indian Wars. He was constable, 1642; townsman, 1645; represented Hartford in the General Court from 1656 until his death." Also see J. Hammond Trumbull, ed., *The Memorial History of Hartford County Connecticut 1633–1884* (Boston: Edward L. Osgood, 1886), p. 249.

2. William Hosley, *Colt: The Making of an American Legend* (Amherst, MA: University of Massachusetts Press, 1996), pp. 14, 228. For more about the complicity of New England merchants in the infamous "Triangle Trade," see Janet Siskind, *Rum and Axes: The Rise of a Connecticut Merchant Family, 1795–1850* (Ithaca, NY: Cornell University Press, 2004).

3. Hosley, *American Legend*, p. 15; Josiah Gilbert Holland, *History of Western Massachusetts* (Springfield, MA: Samuel Bowles and Company, 1855), p. 225.

4. Jack Rohan, *Yankee Arms Maker: The Story of Sam Colt and His Six-Shot Peacemaker* (New York: Harper & Brothers, 1948), p. 3.

5. Miriam Davis Colt, *Went to Kansas* (Watertown, MA: L. Ingalls & Co., 1862), p. 250; William B. Edwards, *The Story of Colt's Revolver: The Biography of Col. Samuel Colt* (New York: Castle Books, 1957), p. 15.

6. Rohan, *Yankee Arms Maker*, p. 2.

CHAPTER 2

1. In addition to his sisters Margaret (b. 1806) and Sarah (b. 1808), Sam Colt grew up with three brothers: John (b. 1810), Christopher, Jr. (b. 1812), and James (b. 1816). Two other children—Mary (b. 1819) and Norman (b. 1821)—did not outlive childhood.

2. *Madison* (WI) *Express*, November 7, 1841, p. 3.

3. See *Life and Letters of John C. Colt, Condemned to Be Hung on the Eighteenth of November, 1842, for the Murder of Samuel Adams* (New York: Extra Tattler, October 21, 1842), p. 3; Charles F. Powell, *An Authentic Life of John C. Colt* (Boston: S. N. Dickinson, 1842), p. 14.

4. Powell, *Authentic Life*, pp. viii–ix.

5. Ibid. Also see Edwards, *Colt's Revolver*, p. 16, and Gertrude Hecker Winders, *Sam Colt and His Gun* (New York: John Day Company, 1959), pp. 13–15.

6. John D. Lawson, *American State Trials*, vol. 7 (St. Louis: F. H. Thomas Law Book Co., 1917), p. 464; Henry Barnard, *Armsmear* (New York: Alvord Printer, 1866), p. 295.

7. Lydia H. Sigourney, *Letters to My Pupils* (New York: Robert Carver & Brothers, 1853), pp. 233, 241.

8. See Jane Benardete's biographical entry in *American Women Writers*, ed. Lina Mainero (New York: Frederick Ungar, 1982), pp. 78–81.

9. Lydia H. Sigourney, *Letters of Life* (New York: D. Appleton and Company, 1868), pp. 186–87.

10. Ibid., pp. 203–18.

11. They are part of the Colt Family Papers, donated to the University of Rhode Island Library Special Collections in 1989.

CHAPTER 3

1. The quote is taken from Daniel Walker Howe's Pulitzer Prize–winning *What Hath God Wrought: The Transformation of America, 1815–1848* (New York: Oxford University Press, 2007), p. 38. Though Howe is not referring specifically to Christopher Colt, his description of the quintessential American male of the era applies perfectly to the patriarch of the Colt clan (as well as to his most famous son): "This was not a relaxed, hedonistic, refined, or indulgent society . . . The man who got ahead in often primitive conditions did so by means of innate ability, hard work, luck, and sheer willpower . . . Impatient of direction, he took pride in his personal accomplishments. An important component of his drive to succeed was a willingness . . . to innovate and take risks, to try new methods and locations."

2. See Hosley, *American Legend*, p. 228, n. 15; "Cattle Show," *Connecticut Courant*, November, 3, 1818, p. 2; "Savings Society in the City of Hartford," *Connecticut Courant*, July 6, 1819, p. 3.

3. Sigourney, *Letters of Life*, pp. 243–48, 266–80.

4. Alice Morehouse Walker, *Historic Hadley: A Story of the Making of a Famous Massachusetts Town* (New York: Grafton Press, 1906), pp. 92–93. Also see *History of the Hopkins Fund, Grammar School and Academy, in Hadley, Mass.* (Amherst, MA: Amherst Record Press, 1890).

5. The bylaws of the academy can be found in *History of the Hopkins Fund*, pp. 80–81.

6. Powell, *Authentic Life*, p. 15.

7. The calculation is based on a yearly tuition fee of $12, plus boarding expenses of $1.50 per week for forty-four weeks. (According to official records, the academic year at Hopkins Academy consisted of four terms commencing on the first Wednesdays of December, March, June, and September, with four vacations of two weeks each. See *History of the Hopkins Fund*, p. 81.)

8. See Samuel Rezneck, "The Depression of 1819–1822, A Social History," *American Historical Review*, vol. 39, no. 1 (October 1933): pp. 28–47; Murray N. Rothbard, *The Panic of 1819: Reactions and Policies* (New York: Columbia University Press, 1962).

9. Barnard, *Armsmear*, p. 296.

10. Powell, *Authentic Life*, p. 18.

11. Ibid., p. 19.

12. See Hosley, *American Legend*, p. 15; Luther S. Cushing, *Reports of Cases Argued and Determined in the Supreme Court of Massachusetts*, vol. 1 (Boston: Little, Brown and Company, 1865), p. 232; Siskind, *Rum and Axes*, pp. 78–89.

13. The poem is appended to Powell's book as "Note A." Another poem on the subject by Mrs. Sigourney is inscribed in Sarah Ann Colt's school notebook:

> *"On the death of an infant son of Mr. Colt's who was buried on the first*
> *anniversary of its birth, Sunday May 5th 1822"*

> Sweet bud that on a fading stem
>   Did faintly bloom,
> Then shed thy pure and snowy gem
>   Upon the tomb.
> That day which mark'd with smile of dread
>   Thy feeble birth
> Returns—and lo thy couch is spread
>   In mouldering earth.
>
> One slumbers there who would have sighed
>   O'er thy crush'd head
> To think how soon grim Death had spy'd
>   Thy cradle bed.
> But she hath escaped the torturing wound,
>   The tearful sigh,
> And ere thy brow was pale hath found
>   A brighter day.
> Say! Did her angel vision trace
>   Thy being given
> And her maternal arms embrace
>   Her babe in Heaven?

CHAPTER 4

1. For different accounts of young Sam and his first firearm, see Edwards, *Colt's Revolver*, p. 16; Winders, *Colt and His Gun*, p. 18; Rohan, *Yankee Arms Maker*, p. 9; Barnard, *Armsmear*, p. 298.

2. As many old-timers saw it, Colonel Colt actually improved on the design of the Creator: "God made men, but Sam Colt made them equal," as the saying goes.

3. The entire poem, which appears in Sigourney's *Letters to My Pupils*, pp. 234–36, reads as follows:

> There was an open grave, and many an eye
> Looked down upon it. Slow the sable hearse
> Moved on, as if reluctantly it bare
> The young, unwearied form to that cold couch
> Which age and sorrow render sweet to man.
> There seemed a sadness in the humid air,

Lifting the young grass from those verdant mounds
Where slumber multitudes.
                        There was a train
Of young fair females, with their brows of bloom,
And shining tresses. Arm in arm they came,
And stood upon the brink of that dark pit
In pensive beauty, waiting the approach
Of their companion. She was wont to fly
And meet them, as the gay bird meets the spring,
Brushing the dew-drop from the morning flowers,
And breathing mirth and gladness. Now, she came
With movements fashioned to the deep-toned bell;
She came with mourning sire and sorrowing friends,
And tears of those who at her side were nursed
By the same mother.
                        Ah! and one was there,
Who, ere the fading of the summer rose,
Had hoped to greet her as his bride. But death
Arose between them. The pale lover watched
So close her journey through the shadowy vale,
That almost to his heart the ice of death
Entered from hers. There was a brilliant flush
Of youth about her, and her kindling eye
Poured such unearthly light, that hope would hang
Even on the archer's arrow, while it dropped
Deep poison. Many a restless night she toiled
For that slight breath that held her from the tomb,
Still wasting like a snow-wreath, which the sun
Marks for his own, on some cool mountain's breast,
Yet spares, and tinges long with rosy light.

Oft o'er the musings of her silent couch
Came visions of that matron form which bent
With nursing tenderness to soothe and bless
Her cradle dream: and her emaciate hand
In trembling prayer she raised, that He who saved
The sainted mother would redeem the child.
Was the orison lost? Whence then that peace
So dove-like, settling o'er a soul that loved
Earth and its pleasures? Whence that angel smile
With which the allurements of a world so dear
Were counted and resigned? That eloquence
So fondly urging those whose hearts were full
Of sublunary happiness, to seek
A better portion? Whence that voice of joy,
Which from the marble lip, in life's last strife
Burst forth to hail her everlasting home?

Cold reasoners! be convinced. And when ye stand

Where that fair brow, and those unfrosted locks
Return to dust, where the young sleeper waits
The resurrection morn, oh! Lift the heart
In praise to Him who gave the victory.

4. These contrasting views of the wicked stepmother can be found in Bruno Bettelheim, *The Uses of Enchantment: The Meaning and Importance of Fairy Tales* (New York: Alfred A. Knopf, 1976), pp. 66–73; and Iona Opie and Peter Opie, *The Classic Fairy Tales* (London: Oxford University Press, 1974), p. 15.

5. William Upson, b. October 24, 1824, d. September 28, 1848; Mary Lucretia, b. July 29, 1826, d. November 23, 1828; Olivia Paine, b. September 26, 1828, d. April 5, 1838.

6. Rohan, *Yankee Arms Maker*, p. 8.

7. Ibid.; Edwards, *Colt's Revolver*, p. 17; Ben Keating, *The Flamboyant Mr. Colt and His Deadly Six-Shooter* (New York: Doubleday & Co., 1978), p. 5.

8. Powell, *Authentic Life*, p. 22. Information on the Union Manufacturing Company of Marlborough, Connecticut, can be found online at the website of the Richmond Memorial Library (www.richmondlibrary.info/blog/historic_buildings/mills). For interesting material on the use of double entry bookkeeping by early nineteenth-century Connecticut merchants, see Siskind, *Rum and Axes*, pp. 50–52.

9. For example, see Edwards, *Colt's Revolver*, p. 17; Rohan, *Yankee Arms Maker*, p. 9; Winders, *Colt and His Gun*, p. 38.

CHAPTER 5

1. It should be said that the meandering course of John's career was more typical of his era than the unswerving trajectory of Sam's. As historian Donald M. Scott explains, "Those who sought professional or intellectual careers in mid-nineteenth-century America faced a chaotic, confusing, and frequently unpredictable occupational life. Few whose adulthoods spanned these decades had careers that followed a course that they could have either planned or predicted. They frequently made their way by moving into and through a series of institutions, places, and activities that had not even existed when they started out and that they themselves often had to invent . . . Indeed, many career seekers shifted around in a manner hard to imagine for either the eighteenth or the twentieth centuries as they tried to get 'a hold' on life." See Donald M. Scott, "The Popular Lecture and the Creation of a Public in Mid-Nineteenth-Century America," *Journal of American History*, vol. 66 (March 1980): p. 795.

2. See Edward K. Spann, *The New Metropolis: New York City, 1840–1857* (New York: Columbia University Press, 1981), pp. 1–7; Edwin Burrows and Mike Wallace, *Gotham: A History of New York City to 1898* (New York: Oxford University Press, 1999), pp. 430–32; Ric Burns and James Sanders, *New York: An Illustrated History* (New York: Alfred A. Knopf, 2005), pp. 56–58.

3. Spann, *New Metropolis*, p. 1. The material in this chapter regarding John Colt's life between 1826 and 1829—including all quoted passages of text—comes from Powell, *Authentic Life*, pp. 22–31.

4. Hosley, *American Legend*, p. 15. Also see Cushing, *Reports of Cases Argued*, vol. 1, p. 232. Christopher Colt remained with the company until 1835; two years later, it went under during the panic of 1837. See Arthur Chase, *History of Ware, Massachusetts* (Cambridge, MA: Harvard University Press, 1911), p. 220.

5. Sigourney, *Letters to My Pupils*, p. 258.

6. *Madison (WI) Express*, November 7, 1841, p. 3.

CHAPTER 6

1. John Phelan, *Readings in Rural Sociology* (New York: Macmillan, 1920), pp. 5–6.

2. Ibid., p. 6.

3. Barnard, *Armsmear*, p. 298.

4. Phelan, *Rural Sociology*, p. 3.

5. Rohan, *Yankee Arms Maker*, pp. 10–11; Edwards, *Colt's Revolver*, p. 17.

6. Rohan, *Yankee Arms Maker*, p. 11.

7. Philip K. Lundeberg, *Samuel Colt's Submarine Battery: The Secret and the Enigma* (Washington, DC: Smithsonian Institution Press, 1974), p. 8. Also see Rohan, *Yankee Arms Maker*, p. 12, and Edwards, *Colt's Revolver*, p. 17.

8. L. P. Brockett, *The Silk Industry in America: A History: Prepared for the Centennial Exposition* (New York: George F. Nesbitt & Co., 1876), p. 110.

9. Edwards, *Colt's Revolver*, p. 17.

10. Ibid., p. 18; Lundeberg, *Submarine Battery*, p. 8; Rohan, *Yankee Arms Maker*, p. 26.

11. Frederick Tuckerman, *Amherst Academy: A New England School of the Past, 1814–1861* (Amherst, MA: printed for and published by the trustees, 1929), pp. 82–83.

12. Ibid., p. 67.

13. Claude Moore Fuess, *Amherst: The Story of a New England College* (Boston: Little, Brown and Company, 1935), p. 27.

14. Rufus Graves, "Account of a Gelatinous Meteor," *American Journal of Science*, vol. 2 (1820), pp. 335–37. Also see Hilary Belcher and Erica Swale, "Catch a Falling Star," *Folklore*, vol. 95 (1984): pp. 210–20.

15. My description of these experiments is taken from a standard text of the time, *Chemical Instructor: Presenting a Familiar Method of Teaching the Chemical Principles and Operations* (Albany, NY: Webster and Skinners, 1822). Designed specifically for the use of chemistry teachers in public schools and academies, this manual was written by Amos Eaton, later a renowned botanist, geologist, and chemist who taught for a short time at Amherst College.

16. John White Webster, *A Manual of Chemistry* (Boston: Marsh, Capen, Lyon, and Webb, 1839), p. 142. For Sam's familiarity with Webster's text, see Martin

Rywell, *Samuel Colt: A Man and an Epoch* (Harriman, TN: Pioneer Press, 1952), p. 18. In later years, Webster, a Harvard professor of chemistry and mineralogy, would become the central figure in a sensational murder case that almost uncannily mirrored that of Sam's own brother, John.

17. All quotes and information relating to this period of John Colt's life are taken from Powell, *Authentic Life*, pp. 29–32. As for his possible real estate ventures, the speculation that he owned property in Baltimore derives from a contract signed several years later by Sam Colt's employee John Pearson, who agreed to rent workspace from John Colt at the rate of four dollars per month. See Edwards, *Colt's Revolver*, p. 32.

18. The definitive work on this subject is Ronald E. Shaw, *Canals for a Nation: The Canal Era in the United States, 1790–1860* (Lexington: University of Kentucky Press, 1990). For more specific information about the project in which John Colt was reportedly involved, see Chester Lloyd Jones, "The Anthracite-Tidewater Canals," *Annals of the American Academy of Political and Social Science*, vol. 31 (January 1908): pp. 102–16.

19. All quotes about the Reverend Mr. Fisk and the Wesleyan Academy are taken from George Prentice, *Wilbur Fisk* (Boston and New York: Houghton, Mifflin and Company, 1890), pp. 78–86.

20. See *Madison* (WI) *Express*, November 17, 1841, p. 3; Powell, *Authentic Life*, p. 32; *Life and Letters*, p. 4. James's remarks about Sarah Ann's "derangement" appear in a letter to Sam, dated October 6, 1841, that is among the Colt archives at the Connecticut State Library. For Lydia Sigourney's tribute to Sarah Ann, see Sigourney, *Letters to My Pupils*, pp. 242–43.

21. *Life and Letters of John C. Colt*, p. 4; Powell, *Authentic Life*, p. 32.

PART TWO: FORTUNE'S TRAIL

CHAPTER 7

1. Barnard, *Armsmear*, p. 296.

2. Ibid., p. 276.

3. The author of the "Battle of the Kegs" (a satirical ballad apparently performed to the tune of "Yankee Doodle") was Francis Hopkinson, judge, author, and one of the signers of the Declaration of Independence. The complete poem consists of twenty-two stanzas. The ones reprinted here are excerpted from the version in Samuel Kettell, *Specimens of American Poetry: With Critical and Biographical Notices* (Boston: B. G. Goodrich and Co., 1829), pp. 202–5. Also see Rywell, *Man and Epoch*, pp. 14–15.

4. See E. Taylor Parks, "Robert Fulton and Submarine Warfare," *Military Affairs*, vol. 25 (Winter 1961–62): pp. 177–82; Robert Fulton, *Torpedo War, and Submarine Explosions* (New York: William Elliot, 1810); Edwards, *Colt's Revolver*, pp. 160–61; Lundeberg, *Submarine Battery*, p. 7.

5. Barnard, *Armsmear*, p. 275; Edwards, *Colt's Revolver*, p. 18; Rohan, *Yankee Arms Maker*, pp. 14–15; Hosley, *American Legend*, p. 25. Also see Paul Uselding, "Elisha K. Root, Forging, and the 'American System,' " *Technology and Culture*, vol. 15, no. 4 (October 1974): pp. 543–68.

6. Herman Melville, *Moby-Dick* (New York: W. W. Norton & Company, 2002), p. 19.

7. Edwards, *Colt's Revolver*, pp. 19–20.

8. Herbert G. Houze, *Samuel Colt: Arms, Art, and Invention* (New Haven, CT, and London: Yale University Press and the Wadsworth Museum of Art, 2006), p. 37. Also see Fuess, *Amherst College*, p. 108; Edward Wilton Carpenter and Charles Frederick Morehouse, *The History of the Town of Amherst, Massachusetts* (Amherst, MA: Carpenter & Morehouse, 1896), pp. 460–61; Margaret Hope Bacon, *But One Race: The Life of Robert Purvis* (Albany, NY: SUNY Press, 2007), p. 22.

9. The Joneses were transporting "two hundred reams of paper, a quantity of printing ink, and other articles to facilitate the printing of the Burman bible, tracts, &c." See James D. Knowles, *Memoir of Mrs. Ann H. Judson, Late Missionary to Burmah; Including a History of the American Baptist Mission in the Burman Empire* (Boston: Lincoln & Edmonds, 1831), p. 389.

10. Colt's official biographer itemizes the expenditures thus (see Barnard, *Armsmear*, p. 300):

Seaman's cap	$ 3.50
Quadrant, almanac, and compass	18.50
Mattress, bedding, &c.	9.00
Slop clothes	38.92
Boots and shoes	8.00
Stockings	2.00
Jackknife &c.	1.00
Custom House	.25
Seaman's Chest	4.62
	85.79
Cash	5.00
Paper &c.	.45
Total	$ 91.24

11. Houze, *Colt: Arms, Art, Invention*, p. 38; Rohan, *Yankee Arms Maker*, pp. 19–20.

CHAPTER 8

1. According to his biographer, Charles Powell, John had come across "a Navy Department Order in a newspaper to prepare the Frigate Constitution for a Mediterranean cruise" (p. 32). While "Old Ironsides" did, in fact, serve as the flagship of the navy's Mediterranean Squadron between 1821 and 1828, she was laid up in

Boston Harbor, undergoing extensive repairs, at the time of John's enlistment and did not return to active service until 1835. If John intended to embark on a Mediterranean cruise, it would have been on a different vessel.

2. Powell, *Authentic Life*, pp. 32–33.

3. Ibid., pp. 35–36; Rohan, *Yankee Arms Maker*, p. 40.

4. Rywell, *Man and Epoch*, p. 74.

CHAPTER 9

1. I am referring here to the 1961 best-seller *African Genesis* (New York: Atheneum, 1961), by Robert Ardrey, a highly successful Hollywood screenwriter turned amateur anthropologist. Though Ardrey's work has not completely stood the test of time, it offers profoundly important insights into the savage springs of human behavior and culture.

2. For the development of repeating handguns, see W. Y. Carman, *A History of Firearms: From Earliest Times to 1914* (London: Routledge & Kegan Paul, 1955), pp. 131–48; Roger Pauly, *Firearms: The Life Story of a Technology* (Westport, CT: Greenwood Press, 2004), pp. 39–58; Charles T. Haven and Frank A. Belden, *A History of the Colt Revolver: And Other Arms Made by Colt's Patent Fire Arms Manufacturing Company from 1836 to 1940* (New York: Bonanza Books, 1940), pp. 3–13; Houze, *Colt: Arms, Art, Invention*, pp. 22–36. Samuel Colt himself provided a useful survey of the subject in a lecture delivered to the Institution of Civil Engineers in London in 1851. It is reprinted in Haven and Belden, pp. 312–26.

3. Quoted in Rywell, *Man and Epoch*, p. 45.

4. For example, see Ellsworth S. Grant, *The Colt Legacy: The Colt Armory in Hartford, 1855–1980* (Providence, RI: Mowbray Company, 1982), pp. 2–4.

5. Houze, *Colt: Arms, Art, Invention*, p. 38. In other versions, Sam derived his inspiration not from watching the *Corvo*'s wheel but from observing either the windlass used to load and unload the hold or the capstan for raising and lowering the anchor. See Edwards, *Colt's Revolver*, p. 23; Harold Evans, *They Made America: From the Steam Engine to the Search Engine: Two Centuries of Innovators* (New York: Little, Brown and Company, 2004), p. 62.

6. *Beecher's Illustrated Magazine*, May 1871, pp. 343–47.

7. The precise date of Sam's return is unknown. However, "based upon Olivia Colt's remark in her letter of 23 June 1830 telling Samuel that the *Corvo* would be at sea for 'about ten months,' " it "most likely occurred either in May or June of 1831." See Houze, *Colt: Arms, Art, Invention*, p. 38; Edwards, *Colt's Revolver*, pp. 23–24.

CHAPTER 10

1. Powell, *Authentic Life*, pp. 36–37.

2. The seal is divided into two halves. The upper portion depicts the sun rising over a mountain behind the university building. The lower half consists of three

emblems: a quadrant, a globe, and an ideogram of two small squares balanced atop a much larger third. This latter is meant to signify "the Pythagorean proposition that, in a right-handed triangle, the square of the hypotenuse equals the sum of the squares of the two other sides." See Julian Ira Lindsay, *Tradition Looks Forward: The University of Vermont: A History, 1791–1904* (Burlington, VT: University of Vermont and State Agricultural College, 1954), p. 88.

3. John's precise movements during these years and the exact locations of his various enterprises are difficult to sort out. This summary is extrapolated from information in Powell, *Authentic Life*, pp. 40–43, as well as from a letter on file at the Connecticut Historical Society, dated 1833, in which James Colt writes to Sam: "John has returned to New York . . . He has got a notion in his head that he thinks will pay him 20 thousand dollars, it is making oil sope [*sic*] and I think it is a foolish one."

4. Ibid., p. 41.

5. John C. Colt, *The Science of Double Entry Book-Keeping: Simplified, Arranged and Methodized*, 10th ed. (New York: Nafis & Cornish, 1844), p. 191.

6. Cary John Previts and Barbara Dubis Merino, *A History of Accounting in the United States: The Cultural Significance of Accounting* (Columbus, OH: Ohio State University Press, 1998), p. 21.

7. Powell, *Authentic Life*, p. 43.

8. Ibid., p. 44.

9. Daniel Aaron, *Cincinnati, Queen City of the West: 1819–1938* (Columbus, OH: Ohio State University Press, 1992), pp. 7, 17.

10. Scott, "Popular Lecture," p. 792.

11. Four of Colt's talks—three given to "public meeting[s]" in Cincinnati, Dayton, and Boston and one prepared for Cincinnati's College of Professional Teachers but never delivered—are appended to the tenth edition of his textbook, *The Science of Double Entry Book-Keeping*. All quotes come from pp. 191–253 of that volume.

CHAPTER 11

1. According to his own account, Sam Colt's original conception was a gun with multiple barrels that rotated when the hammer was cocked. He soon abandoned this pepperbox design, however, for the far less unwieldy one of a single-barrel firearm with a revolving six-chambered cylinder. See Houze, *Colt: Arms, Art, Invention*, pp. 38–39, and Barnard, *Armsmear*, p. 162.

2. Edwards, *Colt's Revolver*, p. 24. Edwards describes Bassett as the captain of a whaler but a congressional document identifies him as "a merchantman, principally in the European trade." See *Executive Documents of the House of Representatives at the Second Session of the Twenty-first Congress, Begun and Held at the City of Washington, December 6, 1830*, vol. 3 (Washington, DC: Duff Green, 1831), document No. 104, p. 123.

3. Edwards, *Colt's Revolver*, p. 24; Rohan, *Yankee Arms Maker*, p. 25; Houze, *Colt: Arms, Art, Invention*, p. 45.

4. Evans, *They Made America*, pp. 62–63.

5. Ibid., p. 63.

6. Houze, *Colt: Arms, Art, Invention*, p. 41.

7. See Ellen Hickey Grayson, "Social Order and Psychological Disorder: Laughing Gas Demonstrations, 1800–1850," in *Freakery: Cultural Spectacles of the Extraordinary Body,* ed. Rosemarie Garland Thomson (New York: New York University Press, 1996), pp. 108–20.

8. William Hosley, "Guns, Gun Culture, and the Peddling of Dreams," in *Guns in America: A Reader*, ed. Jan E. Dizard, Robert Merrill Muth, and Stephen P. Andrews, Jr. (New York: New York University Press, 1999), p. 54.

9. Edwards, *Colt's Revolver*, p. 18.

10. Rohan, *Yankee Arms Maker*, pp. 36–37. Colt's standard introductory speech at his performances was much the same as his newspaper advertisements. Sometime in 1832 or 1833, he committed this speech to paper. This document (reprinted in Houze, *Colt: Arms, Art, Invention*, p. 40) conveys not only the learned tone of "Dr. Coult's" spiel but the inimitably wretched spelling of its author:

> Ladies & Gentlemen
> If you will give me your attention for a few minuits, I wil commence the evenings entertainment with a few intraductary remarks.
> Nitrous Oxide, or the Prot Oxide of Azot. which is more generally known by the name Exhilarating Gas, was discovered by Dr. Priestley in 1772 but it was first acurateley investigated by Sir Humphrey Davy in 1799 . . .
> Sir Humphrey Davy first shode that by breathing a few quarts of it contain in a Silk bag for too or three minuets effects analagus to those occasioned by drinking formented liquors were produced. Individuals who differ in temperament, are however, as one might expect differantly effected.
> It effects uppon some people are truly ludicrus, producing involuntary muscular motion, & a propensity for leaping & Running. In others involuntary fits of laughter & in all high spirrits & the most exquisately pleashourable sensations, without any subsequent feelings of debility . . .
> Agreable to my usual custum, I wil enhale the first dose of Gas myself, in order to show you that it is purfectly pure & that there need be no fear of enhaling it—I would observe to all pursuns who inten taking the Gas, this evening, to dispose of their nives, or other weppins, preaveous to there taking it, in order to gard against an accident, altho I do not apprehend any danger for I have never had an accident hapin.

11. Haven and Belden, *History of Colt*, pp. 17–18.

12. Rohan, *Yankee Arms Maker*, p. 38; Rywell, *Man and Epoch*, p. 27.

CHAPTER 12

1. Theophilus E. Padnos, "Here Is a Cabinet of Curiosities: Collecting the Past on the American Frontier" (PhD diss., University of Massachusetts, 2000), pp. 23–27; Louis Leonard Tucker, " 'Ohio Show-Shop': The Western Museum of Cincinnati, 1820–1867," in *A Cabinet of Curiosities: Five Episodes in the Evolution of American Museums,* eds. Whitfield J. Bell, Jr., et al., (Charlottesville, VA: University Press of Virginia, 1967): pp. 73–105.

2. Aaron, *Cincinnati,* p. 276.

3. Edward P. Hingston, *The Genial Showman, vol. 1, Being Reminiscences of the Life of Artemus Ward and Pictures of a Showman's Career in the Western World* (London: John Camden Hotten, 1870), pp. 11–12, quoted by Tucker, " 'Ohio Show-Stop,' " p. 74.

4. Padnos, "Cabinet of Curiosities," pp. 61–64, 117; Tucker, " 'Ohio Show-Stop,' " p. 85.

5. Richard P. Wunder, *Hiram Powers: Vermont Sculptor* (Taftsville, VT: Country Press, 1974), p. 11.

6. Frances Trollope, *Domestic Manners of the Americans* (London: Whitaker, Treacher & Co., 1832), p. 53.

7. Padnos, "Cabinet of Curiosities," p. 48.

8. Houze, *Colt: Arms, Art, Invention,* p. 40; Rywell, *Man and Epoch,* p. 28.

9. Rywell, *Man and Epoch,* p. 27; Rohan, *Yankee Arms Maker,* pp. 38–50.

10. See John Colt, *Double Entry Book-Keeping,* pp. 29, 30, 34, 40; Powell, *Authentic Life,* p. 8.

11. Colt, *Double Entry Book-Keeping,* p. 40.

12. For example, see Edwards, *Colt's Revolver,* p. 61.

13. Charles Theodore Greve, *Centennial History of Cincinnati and Representative Citizens,* vol. 1 (Chicago: Biographical Publishing Company, 1904), pp. 643–44. Also see the Cincinnati *Public Ledger,* February 20, 1841, p. 3.

14. Aaron, *Cincinnati,* p. 278.

15. All information about Frances Anne Frank and her tragic relationship with John Colt comes from Powell, *Authentic Life,* pp. 44–52.

16. Powell—whose biography was clearly composed with John's cooperation and represents him in the best possible light—insists that his subject nobly resisted Frances Anne's seductive advances: "deep as was his interest in her, he saw that it would be ruinous to give way to it" (p. 46). His repeated assertions of Colt's purity and restraint, however, have a distinct air of protesting too much. Everything that Powell reports about the relationship suggests that John and Frances were lovers.

17. Claudia D. Johnson, "Enter the Harlot," in *Women in American Theatre,* ed. Helen Krich Chinoy and Linda Walsh Jenkins (New York: Crown Publishing, 1980), pp. 57–66.

18. The account of Frances Anne Frank's final twenty-four hours is based on a letter from Joseph Adams to John Colt, printed verbatim in the appendix to Powell, *Authentic Life*, pp. 69–70.

CHAPTER 13

1. Charles Varle, *A Complete View of Baltimore* (Baltimore: Samuel Young, 1833), p. 41.

2. Hosley, *American Legend*, p. 16; Evans, *They Made America*, p. 63; Edwards, *Colt's Revolver*, p. 35.

3. Edwards, *Colt's Revolver*, p. 32; Keating, *Flamboyant Mr. Colt*, p. 13.

4. Edwards, *Colt's Revolver*, p. 42.

5. Ibid., p. 182. Also see Andie Tucher, *Froth & Scum: Truth, Beauty, Goodness, and the Ax Murder in America's First Mass Medium* (Chapel Hill, NC: University of North Carolina Press, 1994), pp. 173–75.

CHAPTER 14

1. The story of the Patent Arms Manufacturing Company is told most fully in Edwards, *Colt's Revolver*, pp. 43ff., and Haven and Belden, *History of Colt*, pp. 20–43. Also see Rohan, *Yankee Arms Maker*, pp. 72–116, and Keating, *Flamboyant Mr. Colt*, pp. 1–49.

2. Nathaniel C. Fowler, *Getting a Start: First Aids to Success* (New York: Sully and Kleintech, 1915), p. 43.

3. Edwards, *Colt's Revolver*, p. 44.

4. Keating, *Flamboyant Mr. Colt*, p. 19.

5. Edwards, *Colt's Revolver*, p. 50; Evans, *They Made America*, p. 65.

6. Edwards, *Colt's Revolver*, p. 56; Houze, *Colt: Arms, Art, Invention*, p. 54; Rohan, *Yankee Arms Maker*, p. 91.

7. Edwards, *Colt's Revolver*, p. 62.

8. Evans, *They Made America*, p. 65; Keating, *Flamboyant Mr. Colt*, p. 32; Hosley, "Guns, Gun Culture," p. 62.

9. Edwards, *Colt's Revolver*, p. 70. Though it took some doing, Sam was ultimately able to wrest a replacement payment from the army.

10. Ibid., p. 80.

11. Keating, *Flamboyant Mr. Colt*, pp. 41–42.

12. Ibid., p. 35; Edwards, *Colt's Revolver*, p. 89.

CHAPTER 15

1. Edwards, *Colt's Revolver*, pp. 60–61.

2. Powell, *Authentic Life*, p. 52.

3. Aaron, *Cincinnati*, p. 232. Also see Walter Sutton, *The Western Book Trade: Cincinnati as a Nineteenth-Century Publishing and Book-Trade Center* (Columbus: Ohio State University Press, 1961), pp. 5–18, 67ff.

4. Sutton, *Western Book Trade*, pp. 41, 175.

5. Jay Ruby, *Secure the Shadow: Death and Photography in America* (Cambridge, MA: MIT Press, 1996), p. 44.

6. Sutton, *Western Book Trade*, pp. 315, 341.

7. Powell, *Authentic Life*, p. 53. In accordance with the then prevalent view that the double entry method originated with the fifteenth-century monk Luca Pacioli, author of the first published treatise on the subject, the first edition of Colt's textbook bore the title *The Italian System of Double Entry Book-Keeping*. The word *Italian* was dropped in subsequent editions. Also see Grant I. Butterbaugh, "Dr. Stands for Debt," *Accounting Review*, vol. 20, no. 3 (July 1945): pp. 341–42.

8. *Merchants' Magazine and Commercial Review*, vol. 1 (July 1839): pp. 462–63.

9. Jan R. Heier, "A Critical Look at the Thoughts and Theories of the Early Accounting Educator John C. Colt," *Accounting, Business and Financial History*, vol. 3, no. 1 (1993): pp. 21–22.

10. For an example of the first, see Previts and Merino, *History of Accountancy*, pp. 75–77.

CHAPTER 16

1. Located, according to contemporary city directories, at no. 15 Pearl Street, Cincinnati.

2. Besides being close friends with Washington Irving, Delafield was the first president of the New York Philharmonic Society and a founder of New York University. His interest in the artifacts at the Western Museum is mentioned by M. H. Dunlop, "Curiosities Too Numerous to Mention: Early Regionalism and Cincinnati's Western Museum," *American Quarterly*, vol. 36, no 4 (Autumn 1984): p. 540.

3. See the long, unsigned review-essay on Delafield's book in the *New York Review*, vol. 5 (July 1839), pp. 200–222.

4. See Burgess's testimony at John Colt's trial in Dunphy and Cummins, *Remarkable Trials*, p. 261.

5. Powell, *Authentic Life*, p. 55.

6. Ibid., p. 56.

7. See the *Philadelphia North American*, January 1, 1842, p. 3; *Madison (WI) Express*, November 13, 1841, p. 3.

8. See Lydia Maria Child, *Selected Letters, 1817–1880*, ed. Milton Meltzer and Patricia G. Holland (Amherst, MA: University of Massachusetts Press, 1982), p. 183.

9. Powell, *Authentic Life*, p. 57; Dunphy and Cummins, *Remarkable Trials*, pp. 262–63.

CHAPTER 17

1. Rywell, *Man and Epoch*, p. 66; Edwards, *Colt's Revolver*, pp. 126, 133; Hosley, *American Legend*, pp. 18–19.

2. McLeod turned out to be nothing more than a "blustering braggart." At his trial in October 1841, "it was conclusively shown that he was not even a member of the attacking party. The jury, after thirty minutes' consultation, returned with a verdict of acquittal" and the threat of war with Great Britain instantly evaporated. See Frederic Bancroft, *The Life of William H. Seward*, vol. 1 (New York: Harper and Brothers, 1900), pp. 111–13; John Charles Dent, *The Last Forty Years: Canada Since the Union of 1841*, vol. 1 (Toronto: George Virtue, 1881), p. 175; William Renwick Riddell, "An International Murder Trial," *Journal of the American Institute of Criminal Law and Criminology*, vol. 10, no. 2 (August 1919): pp. 176–83.

3. Houze, *Colt: Arms, Art, Invention*, p. 66. The definitive study of Colt's harbor defense system is Lundeberg, *Submarine Battery*.

4. Edwards, *Colt's Revolver*, pp. 160–61; Lundeberg, *Submarine Battery*, pp. 17–18.

5. Rosa Pendleton Chiles, *John Howard Payne: American Poet, Actor, Playwright, Consul and the Author of "Home, Sweet Home"* (Washington, DC: Columbia Historical Society, 1930), p. 44. Chiles's book draws heavily on what remains the most comprehensive biography of Payne: Gabriel Harrison's *John Howard Payne, Dramatist, Poet, Actor, and Author of Home, Sweet Home!* (Boston: Lippincott, 1885).

6. See the news item "A Great Day for Paterson," *New York Times*, July 5, 1892, p. 8.

7. Edwards, *Colt's Revolver*, p. 162; Lundeberg, *Submarine Battery*, p. 19.

PART THREE: THE SUBLIME OF HORROR

CHAPTER 18

1. Michael Schudson, *Discovering the News: A Social History of American Newspapers* (New York: Basic Books, 1978), p. 15.

2. John D. Stevens, *Sensationalism and the New York Press* (New York: Columbia University Press, 1991), p. 15.

3. James L. Crouthamel, *Bennett's New York Herald and the Rise of the Popular Press* (Syracuse, NY: Syracuse University Press, 1989), p. 25.

4. Stevens, *Sensationalism*, p. 43.

5. *New York Herald*, April 11, 1836.

6. See Daniel Stashower, *The Beautiful Cigar Girl: Mary Rogers, Edgar Allan Poe and the Invention of Murder* (New York: Columbia University Press, 1981), p. 94; Amy Gilman Srebnick, *The Mysterious Death of Mary Rogers: Sex and Culture in Nineteenth-Century New York* (New York: Oxford University Press, 1995), p. 66.

7. Despite overwhelming circumstantial evidence of his guilt, Robinson was ultimately acquitted. The definitive account of the case is Patricia Cline Cohen's *The Murder of Helen Jewett: The Life and Death of a Prostitute in Nineteenth-Century New York* (New York: Alfred A. Knopf, 1998).

8. Tucher, *Froth & Scum*, p. 149.

9. Srebnick, *Mary Rogers*, pp. 4, 17.

10. Stashower, *Beautiful Cigar Girl*, pp. 77–78.

11. Ibid., pp. 15–17.

12. Ibid., pp. 80–82; *New York Herald*, August 17, 1841, p. 2; Srebnick, *Mary Rogers*, pp. 18–19.

13. Stashower, *Beautiful Cigar Girl*, pp. 89–90.

14. Edgar Allan Poe, "The Mystery of Marie Roget," reprinted in John Walsh, *Poe the Detective: The Curious Circumstances Behind "The Mystery of Marie Roget"* (New Brunswick, NJ: Rutgers University Press, 1968), p. 100.

15. Walsh, *Poe the Detective*, p. 26.

16. Stashower, *Beautiful Cigar Girl*, p. 96.

17. Ibid., p. 192.

18. Ibid., p. 16; Walsh, *Poe the Detective*, p. 10.

19. Walsh, *Poe the Detective*, p. 98.

20. See Stashower, *Beautiful Cigar Girl*, pp. 91–92, 132–54.

21. See Walsh, *Poe the Detective*, p. 34.

22. Ibid., p. 33. Though the case was never definitively solved, the most likely explanation was provided by Frederica Loss. In a deathbed confession made in the fall of 1842, the innkeeper claimed that on Sunday, July 25, 1841, Mary Rogers had come to her roadhouse from the city in the company of a young physician and had died at his hands during a botched abortion. Her body—with a strip of cloth wound around the neck to make it appear as if she had been assaulted and murdered—was then dumped in the river. Also see Srebnick, *Mary Rogers*, pp. 29–30.

CHAPTER 19

1. Copies of the *Literary Cadet and Rhode-Island Statesman* (which began life as a weekly called the *Literary Cadet, and Saturday Evening Bulletin*) are on file at the

Rhode Island Historical Society Library in Providence. Information on the firm of Smith & Parmenter can be found in Glenn H. Brown and Maude O. Brown, *A Directory of Printing, Publishing, Bookselling and Allied Trades in Rhode Island to 1865* (New York: New York Public Library, 1958), p. 156; Frederic Hudson, *Journalism in the United States, from 1690 to 1872* (New York: Harper & Brothers, 1873), p. 337; *Printers and Printing in Providence 1762–1907* (Providence, RI: Providence Printing Company, 1907), pp. 27–28. For the scant facts about Samuel Adams's early life, see the *New England Historical and Genealogical Register*, vol. 33 (Boston: New-England Historic, Genealogical Society, 1879), p. 104; Brown and Brown, *Directory*, p. 15.

2. See Hudson, *Journalism in the United States*, p. 337. Also see Grant James Wilson and John Fiske, *Appleton's Cyclopedia of American Biographies*, vol. 5 (New York: D. Appleton & Co., 1900), p. 588. Interestingly, John Howard Payne worked as an editor for Smith's *Sunday News*, which suggests the possibility that the famed author of "Home, Sweet Home" was not only a friend of both Colt brothers but an acquaintance of Samuel Adams.

3. Unsigned notice in "Monthly Commentary" section, *American Monthly Magazine*, vol. 10 (December 1837): p. 596.

4. See the testimony of Samuel Adams's foreman, James Monahan, in Lawson, *American State Trials*, vol. 7, pp. 468–69. The panic of 1837 precipitated an economic depression that lasted seven years. Also see Howe, *What Hath God Wrought*, pp. 502–4.

5. Ransom's testimony appears in a handwritten deposition before District Attorney J. R. Whiting, dated November 17, 1841, in the file of the New York City Municipal Archives. Nicholas Conklin's testimony is part of the trial transcript, reprinted in Dunphy and Cummins, *Remarkable Trials*, p. 253.

6. *New York Herald*, September 25, 1841, p. 2.

7. Founded by a group of culture-minded business and professional men, the Apollo Association—which evolved after a few years into the American Art-Union—mounted public exhibitions of paintings and sculptures by the country's leading artists. For an annual subscription of five dollars, members received free family admissions to the shows, an engraving published by the association from a painting by a contemporary American artist, and a lottery ticket for an original artwork from its collection. The definitive history of the organization is Mary Bartlett Cowdry, *American Academy of Fine Arts and American Art-Union: Introduction 1816–1852* (New York: New York Historical Society, 1953).

8. Trial testimony indicates that Adams and Colt had known each other for three years at the time of the murder. See Lawson, *American State Trials*, p. 467.

CHAPTER 20

1. For information on the Granite Building and its tenants, see *Transactions of the Apollo Association for the Promotion of Fine Arts in the United States, for the Year 1841*, p. 3; *The Knickerbocker, or New-York Monthly Magazine*, vol. 17, no. 5 (May 1841): p. 445; Beaumont Newhall, *The Daguerreotype in America* (New York: Dover, 1975),

p. 25; John Flavel Mines, *A Tour Around New York and My Summer Acre: Being the Recreations of Mr. Felix Oldboy* (New York: Harper & Brothers, 1893), pp. 60–61; Hugh Macatamney, *Cradle Days of New York: 1609–1825* (New York: Drew & Lewis, 1909), p. 191; *New York Times*, February 12, 1876, p. 8.

2. As late as 1856, Wheeler's blurb was still being used in ads for Colt's textbook. For example, see the promotional appendix in P. A. Fitzgerald, *The Exhibition Speaker: Containing Farces, Dialogues, and Tableaux, with Exercises for Declamation in Prose and Verse* (New York: Sheldon, Lamport & Blakeman, 1856).

3. Dunphy and Cummins, *Remarkable Trials*, p. 253.

4. In his classic story "Bartleby, the Scrivener."

5. Colt's threats to George Spencer and Mr. Howard are described in two letters— one anonymous, the other signed "H. W. Robinson"—sent to District Attorney J. R. Whiting, on file in the New York City Municipal Archives. For information on the Broadway bookseller Homer Franklin, see Ronald J. Zboray, *A Fictive People: Antebellum Economic Development and the American Reading Public* (New York: Oxford University Press, 1993), pp. 137–38.

6. Dunphy and Cummins, *Remarkable Trials*, p. 230.

7. See Zboray, *Fictive People*, p. 24; Michael Winship, *American Literary Publishing in the Mid-Nineteenth Century: The Business of Ticknor and Fields* (Cambridge, UK: Cambridge University Press, 2003), p. 138.

8. *Life and Letters of John C. Colt*, p. 8.

9. Dunphy and Cummins, *Remarkable Trials*, p. 252.

CHAPTER 21

1. Dunphy and Cummins, *Remarkable Trials*, p. 249.

2. Ibid., p. 246.

3. Ibid., p. 248.

4. Ibid., p. 250. Also see Wells's deposition before Police Magistrate Robert Taylor on September 24, 1841, in the John C. Colt file, New York City Municipal Archives.

5. Kenneth Holcomb Dunshee, *As You Pass By* (New York: Hastings House, 1952), p. 184; Stephen Jenkins, *The Greatest Street in the World: The Story of Broadway, Old and New, from the Bowling Green to Albany* (New York: G. P. Putnam's Sons, 1911), p. 129.

6. Dunphy and Cummins, *Remarkable Trials*, p. 249.

CHAPTER 22

1. See Dunphy and Cummins, *Remarkable Trials*, pp. 230–31; Asa Wheeler's deposition on September 24, in the John C. Colt file of the New York City Municipal Archives.

2. Ibid.

3. Reverend Enoch Hutchinson and Reverend Stephen Remington, eds., *The Baptist Memorial and Monthly Record: Devoted to the History, Biography, Literature & Statistics of the Denomination*, vol. 8 (New York: Z. P. Hatch, 1849), p. 299.

4. Dunphy and Cummins, *Remarkable Trials*, pp. 233–34.

5. George J. Lankevich, *American Metropolis: A History of New York City* (New York: NYU Press, 1998), p. 84; Stashower, *Beautiful Cigar Girl*, p. 88; Augustine Costello, *Our Police Protectors: History of the New York Police* (New York: Augustine Costello, 1885), pp. 158–59; George W. Walling, *Recollections of a New York Chief of Police: An Official Record of Thirty-eight Years as Patrolman, Detective, Captain, Inspector, and Chief of the New York Police* (New York: Caxton Book Concern, 1887), p. 32.

6. Dunphy and Cummins, *Remarkable Trials*, pp. 234–35.

7. Ibid., pp. 262–63, 277.

8. Ibid., p. 234.

CHAPTER 23

1. Dunphy and Cummins, *Remarkable Trials*, p. 235; Deposition of Law Octon before Police Magistrate Robert Taylor, December 24, 1841, in the John C. Colt folder, New York City Municipal Archives.

2. Affidavit of John B. Hasty, February 4, 1842, on file in the John C. Colt folder, New York City Municipal Archives.

3. Dunphy and Cummins, *Remarkable Trials*, p. 235; Deposition of Law Octon before Police Magistrate Robert Taylor, December 24, 1841, in the John C. Colt folder, New York City Municipal Archives.

4. The definitive work on this subject is Graham Russell Hodges, *New York City Cartmen, 1667–1850* (New York: New York University Press, 1986). Hodges also supplies the illuminating introduction to the facsimile edition of Isaac S. Lyon, *Recollections of an Old Cartman* (New York: New York Bound, 1984).

5. For the detail of the green umbrella, see *New York Times*, December 4, 1887, p. 12.

6. Howard Clark, *The Mill on Mad River* (Boston: Little, Brown & Company, 1948), p. 252.

7. This account of Barstow's activities comes from his trial testimony (Dunphy and Cummins, *Remarkable Trials*, pp. 235–36), as well as from two separate depositions he made before Police Magistrate Robert Taylor, the first on September 25, the second on September 26, 1841, both in the John C. Colt file, New York City Municipal Archives. Thomas Russell (whose trial testimony appears in Dunphy and Cummins, *Remarkable Trials*, p. 236) made depositions on the same dates.

8. Dunphy and Cummins, *Remarkable Trials*, p. 232.

9. Ibid.

10. Ibid., p. 262.

CHAPTER 24

1. Dunphy and Cummins, *Remarkable Trials*, p. 232.

2. New York *Sun*, September 22, 1841, p. 2. For information on the changes Beach made to Day's original format, see Frank M. O'Brien, *The Story of the Sun: New York, 1833–1918* (New York: George H. Doran, 1928), pp. 89ff.

3. Dunphy and Cummins, *Remarkable Trials*, p. 250; *New-York Commercial Advertiser*, September 28, 1841, p. 2; Mabel Abbott, "A Mystery of the Tombs," *Detective Fiction Weekly*, February 1, 1930, p. 687.

4. New York *Sun*, September 23, 1841, p. 2.

5. *Morning Courier and New-York Enquirer*, September 23, 1841, p. 3; *New York Tribune*, September 23, 1841, p. 2; *New York Herald*, September 23, 1841, p. 2.

6. Dunphy and Cummins, *Remarkable Trials*, pp. 239–40.

CHAPTER 25

1. Dunphy and Cummins, *Remarkable Trials*, pp. 240, 260.

2. Like John Colt's onetime business partner Nathan Burgess, Chilton would go on to become a pioneering practitioner of the new art of photography. See Newhall, *Daguerreotype*, p. 22.

3. Dunphy and Cummins, *Remarkable Trials*, p. 242; New York *Sun*, September 27, 1841, p. 2. Also see Chilton's deposition before Robert Taylor, September 26, 1841, on file at the New York City Municipal Archives. Precisely what chemical analysis Chilton employed is unclear, since the first reliable test for bloodstains was not devised until the latter half of the nineteenth century. Also see Tal Golan, *The Laws of Men and the Laws of Nature: The History of Scientific Expert Testimony in England and America* (Cambridge, MA: Harvard University Press, 2004), pp. 144–51; W. D. Sutherland, *Blood-stains: Their Detection, and the Determination of Their Source* (New York: William Wood & Company, 1907), pp. 11–37.

4. *Morning Courier and New-York Enquirer*, September 25, 1841, p. 2.

5. Dunphy and Cummins, *Remarkable Trials*, pp. 240–41, 266; *New York Herald*, September 27, 1841, p. 2.

CHAPTER 26

1. Hodges, *Cartmen*, pp. 139–40.

2. Dunphy and Cummins, *Remarkable Trials*, p. 237. See also depositions of Thomas Russell and Richard Barstow, John C. Colt file, New York City Municipal Archives.

3. Dunphy and Cummins, *Remarkable Trials*, p. 237.

4. *New York Times*, December 4, 1887, p. 12.

5. *New York American*, September 27, 1841, p. 2.

6. See Emeline Adams's deposition, John C. Colt file, New York City Municipal Archives.

7. *New York American*, September 27, 1841, p. 2.

CHAPTER 27

1. All of these accounts are taken from page 2 of the *New York Herald* on the following dates: September 11, 12, 16, 19, 22, 1841.

2. Though the banner headline was first used as early as 1851, it didn't become a regular feature of American newspapers until the advent of the yellow press in the 1890s. See Helen MacGill Hughes, *News and the Human Interest Story* (Somerset, NJ: Transaction Publishers, 1980), p. 33, n. 2.

3. All of these headlines appeared on the second pages of the newspapers on Monday, September 27, 1841.

4. *New-York Commercial Advertiser*, September 28, 1841, p. 2.

5. *Transactions of the Apollo Association*, p. 5.

6. *New York American*, September 27, 1841, p. 2.

7. *New York Herald*, September 28, 1841, p. 2.

8. *New-York Commercial Advertiser*, September 28, 1841, p. 2.

9. Ibid.

10. Ibid.

11. *New York Herald*, September 28, 1841, p. 2.

12. *New-York Commercial Advertiser*, September 28, 1841, p. 2.

13. *New York Herald*, September 28, 1841, p. 2.

14. Ibid., September 29, 1841, p. 2.

15. *New-York Commercial Advertiser*, September 28, 1841, p. 2.

CHAPTER 28

1. Edwards, *Colt's Revolver*, pp. 162–63.

2. Maurice G. Baxter, *One and Inseparable: Daniel Webster and the Union* (Cambridge, MA: Harvard University Press, 1984), p. 308; Lundeberg, *Submarine Battery*, p. 20.

3. Rohan, *Yankee Arms Maker*, pp. 140–41.

4. See the unsigned article "Repeating Fire-Arms. A Day at the Armory of 'Colt's Patent Fire-arms Manufacturing Company,' " *United States Magazine and Democratic Review* (March 1857): p. 248.

5. Edwards, *Colt's Revolver*, p. 169.

6. Ibid., p. 170.

7. See the *Southport (WI) Telegraph*, November 2, 1841, p. 3.

8. *Brooklyn Daily Eagle*, November 8, 1841, p. 2.

9. John Livingston, ed., *Biographical Sketches of Eminent American Lawyers, Now Living* (New York: United States Monthly Magazine, 1852): pp. 96–97.

10. From a letter to Samuel in the Connecticut State Library. From remarks made by James in subsequent letters to Sam, it appears that Christopher Colt, Jr., distanced himself entirely from John's case and had no contact with his doomed brother throughout the crisis.

11. This and the following letter are in the collection of the Connecticut State Library.

12. Smethport (PA) *Settler and Pennon*, November 4, 1841, p. 3.

CHAPTER 29

1. *Brooklyn Daily Eagle*, November 8, 1841, p. 2.

2. For example, see the *Maine Farmer and Journal of the Useful Arts*, October 30, 1841, p. 9.

3. Tucher, *Froth & Scum*, p. 143.

4. *New York Herald*, September 30, 1841, p. 2. The text that Colt had allegedly plagiarized was James Arlington Bennett's *The American System of Practical Book-Keeping*, originally published in 1831.

5. *Brooklyn Daily Eagle*, November 8, 1841, p. 2.

6. *Life and Letters of John C. Colt*, p. 7.

7. *New York Herald*, October 18, 1841, p. 2.

8. According to an item on page 3 of the October 16, 1841, issue of the *New York Evangelist*, Colt's trial was originally scheduled for Monday, October 4, but "postponed on application of the prisoner's counsel to Monday the 1st of November."

9. *New York Herald*, November 2, 1851, p. 2.

10. Ibid., October 25, 1841, p. 2, November 2, 1841, p. 2; *Morning Courier and New-York Enquirer*, November 3, 1841, p. 2.

11. *Morning Courier and New-York Enquirer*, November 3, 1841, p. 2; *New York Herald*, November 2, 1841, p. 2.

12. *New York Herald*, November 2, 1841, p. 2.

13. Ibid.

14. *Brooklyn Daily Eagle*, November 3, 1841, p. 2.

PART FOUR: THE GARB OF JUSTICE

CHAPTER 30

1. Letters dated December 18, 1841, and January 10, 1842, in the Samuel Colt archives, Connecticut State Library.

2. See Edwards, *Colt's Revolver*, pp. 170–71, and Lundeberg, *Submarine Battery*, p. 21.

3. Lundeberg, *Submarine Battery*, pp. 20, 22.

4. See Rywell, *Man and Epoch*, p. 80; Evans, *They Made America*, pp. 74–84; Lundeberg, *Submarine Battery*, pp. 34–35.

5. Lundeberg, *Submarine Battery*, p. 21.

6. Edwards, *Colt's Revolver*, p. 170.

CHAPTER 31

1. *New York Herald*, January 18, 1842, p. 1.

2. Herbert Bergman, ed., *The Collected Writings of Walt Whitman: The Journalism: Volume 2: 1846–1848* (New York: Peter Lang, 2003), p. 205.

3. *New York Herald*, January 18, 1842, p. 1.

4. Rossiter Johnson, *The Twentieth Century Biographical Dictionary of Notable Americans*, vol. 3 (Boston: Biographical Society, 1904), p. 471; Tucher, *Froth & Scum*, p. 101; Srebnick, *Mary Rogers*, pp. 31–32; Clifford Browder, *The Wickedest Woman in New York: Madame Restell, the Abortionist* (Hamden, CT: Archon Books, 1988), pp. 35ff. In one of those six-degrees-of-separation instances, Madame Restell first came under attack in the pages of the *Morning Courier and New-York Enquirer*, whose editor, Samuel Jenks Smith, was the original employer of Samuel Adams in Providence, Rhode Island. In an editorial published in July 1839, Smith denounced Restell's newspaper advertisements for her contraceptive "Preventive Powder" as "monstrous and destructive"—"subversive of all family peace and quiet." Also see Browder, pp. 17–18.

5. Browder, *Wickedest Woman*, p. 40. Three years later, the conviction was overturned on appeal, and Restell won a new trial. By then, however, the "chief witness had died and her depositions had been invalidated." The prosecution dropped the indictment, and Madame Restell went back to work peddling her birth control nostrums and procuring abortions. After relentless persecution by the moral reformer Anthony Comstock, Restell (who was suspected of having performed the procedure that killed the "beautiful cigar girl," Mary Rogers) would commit suicide in 1878 by slitting her throat.

6. Geoffrey O'Brien, *The Fall of the House of Walworth: A Tale of Murder and Madness in Saratoga's Gilded Age* (New York: Henry Holt, 2010), p. 60.

7. *New York Herald*, October 6, 1841, p. 2.

8. Her second husband was a New York City educator named William H. Vanderhoof. See Charles Adams, Jr., *A Genealogical Register of North Brookfield Families, Including the Records of Many Early Settlers of Brookfield* (published by the Town of North Brookfield, 1887), p. 487, and *The New York Supplement, Vol. 17, Containing the Decisions of the Supreme, Superior, and Lower Courts of Record of New York State. February 11–March 24, 1892* (St. Paul, MN: West Publishing Co., 1892), p. 712.

9. *New York Herald*, January 18, 1842, p. 2.

10. Ibid., January 20, 1842, p. 1.

11. Ibid.

CHAPTER 32

1. New York *Sun*, January 21, 1842, p. 2; *Morning Courier and New-York Enquirer*, January 21, 1842, p. 2; *New York Herald*, January 21, 1842, p. 2.

2. *New York Herald*, January 20, 1842, p. 1.

3. New York *Sun*, January 21, 1842, p. 2; *New York Herald*, January 20, 1842, p. 1.

4. Ibid.

5. *New York Herald*, January 21, 1842, p. 1.

6. Ibid.

7. Ibid.

8. Tucher, *Froth & Scum*, p. 152.

9. *New York Herald*, January 21, 1842, p. 1.

CHAPTER 33

1. *New York Herald*, January 23, 1842, p. 2.

2. New York *Sun*, January 23, 1842, p. 2.

3. *New York Herald*, January 22, 1842, pp. 1–2.

4. Ibid.

5. Ibid., January 22, 1842, p. 1; Meyer Berger, "That Was New York: The Tombs—I," *New Yorker*, August 30, 1941, p. 24.

6. *New York Herald*, p. 2.

CHAPTER 34

1. New York *Sun*, January 22, 1842, p. 1.

2. Tucher, *Froth & Scum*, p. 103.

3. *New York Herald*, January 23, 1842, p. 1.

4. Ibid.; Lawson, *American State Trials*, p. 464.

5. Dunphy and Cummins, *Remarkable Trials*, p. 246; New York *Sun*, January 23, 1842, p. 1; *New York Herald*, January 23, 1842, p. 2.

6. Lawson, *American State Trials*, pp. 465–66.

7. Ibid., pp. 465, 468.

8. New York *Sun*, January 23, 1842, p. 1.

9. Ibid.

CHAPTER 35

1. *New York Herald*, January 24, 1842, p. 2.

2. Ibid.

CHAPTER 36

1. Tucher, *Froth & Scum*, p. 103.

2. L. J. Bigelow, *Bench and Bar: A Complete Digest of the Wit, Humor, Asperities, and Amenities of the Law* (New York: Harper & Brothers, 1871), p. 214.

3. *Morning Courier and New-York Enquirer*, January 26, 1842, p. 2; New York *Sun*, January 26, 1842, p. 2; *New York Herald*, January 26, 1842, p. 1.

4. Ibid.

5. *New York Herald*, January 26, 1842, p. 1.

6. Ibid., p. 2.

CHAPTER 37

1. Bigelow, *Bench and Bar*, p. 214.

2. New York *Sun*, January 26, 1842, p. 2; *New York Herald*, January 26, 1842, p. 1.

3. Dunphy and Cummins, *Remarkable Trials*, p. 256.

4. Bigelow, *Bench and Bar*, p. 215.

5. New York *Sun*, January 26, 1842, p. 2.

6. *Morning Courier and New-York Enquirer*, January 26, 1842, p. 1.

7. *New York Herald*, January 26, 1841, p. 1.

8. Tucher, *Froth & Scum*, p. 104; New York *Sun*, January 26, 1842, p. 2.

9. New York *Sun*, January 26, 1842, p. 2.

10. Dunphy and Cummins, *Remarkable Trials*, p. 260.

11. Bigelow, *Bench and Bar*, p. 215.

12. New York *Sun*, January 26, 1842, p. 2.

13. Ibid.

14. *New York Herald*, January 26, 1842, p. 2.

15. Bigelow, *Bench and Bar*, p. 215.

CHAPTER 38

1. *Philadelphia North American*, January 26, 1842, p. 3. The story was widely reprinted in newspapers throughout the Northeast.

2. *New-York Commercial Advertiser*, January 27, 1842, p. 1; New York *Sun*, January 27, 1842, p. 2.

3. *New York Herald*, January 27, 1842, p. 1.

4. New York *Sun*, January 27, 1842, p. 2.

5. Ibid.

6. Dunphy and Cummins, *Remarkable Trials*, pp. 262–67.

7. Ibid., p. 267.

CHAPTER 39

1. *New York Herald*, January 28, 1842, p. 1; New York *Sun*, January 28, 1842, p. 2.

2. *New York Herald*, January 28, 1842, p. 1.

3. Ibid.; New York *Sun*, January 28, 1842, p. 2.

4. New York *Sun*, January 28, 1842, p. 2.

CHAPTER 40

1. Colt's confession was widely reprinted in its entirety in the penny papers. This transcription is taken from Dunphy and Cummins, *Remarkable Trials*, pp. 272–78.

Though Emmett was permitted to read the statement aloud, it was ruled inadmissible as evidence, and the jury was told to disregard it during its deliberations. Once having heard it, of course, the jurors could not possibly banish it from their minds. As the *Brooklyn Daily Eagle* put it, "its effect [could] scarcely be less as a 'statement' than as testimony" (January 28, 1842, p. 2).

CHAPTER 41

1. New York *Sun*, January 28, 1842, p. 2.

2. *New York Herald*, January 29, 1842, p. 1.

3. Ibid.; New York *Sun*, January 28, 1842, p. 2.

CHAPTER 42

1. Lawson, *American State Trials*, p. 279.

2. *New York Herald*, January 29, 1842, p. 1.

3. On August 4, 1806, Federalist attorney Thomas O. Selfridge shot and killed Charles Austin, the eighteen-year-old son of the "venomous" Republican newspaper editor Benjamin Austin. The murder stemmed from a dispute between Selfridge and the elder Austin, who had excoriated Selfridge in print. The latter demanded a retraction, which the editor refused to supply. Soon afterward, Austin's teenaged son, Charles, encountered Selfridge on State Street in Boston. Words passed between them. When Austin struck Selfridge on the forehead with his hickory cane, Selfridge drew a pistol and shot the boy dead. Charged with manslaughter, Selfridge was tried in December and eventually acquitted. This highly controversial and unpopular verdict "affected the lives and reputations of several individuals involved in the case," including the jury foreman, Paul Revere, whose "honor came under fire." See Jane E. Triber, *A True Republican: The Life of Paul Revere* (Amherst, MA: University of Massachusetts Press, 2001), pp. 189–90.

4. Lawson, *American State Trials*, pp. 279–83.

5. New York *Sun*, January 29, 1842, p. 2.

CHAPTER 43

1. Alexander Marjoribanks, *Travels in South and North America* (New York: D. Appleton & Co., 1854), p. 184; Thomas M. McDade, *Annals of Murder: A Bibliography of Books and Pamphlets on American Murders from Colonial Times to 1900* (Norman, OK: University of Oklahoma Press, 1961), p. 240. Also see *The Trial of Peter Robinson or the Murder of Abraham Suydam, Esq., President of the Farmers' and Mechanics' Bank of New Brunswick* (New York: S. G. Deeth Bookseller, 1841).

2. *New York Herald*, January 29, 1842, p. 2.

3. New York *Sun*, January 29, 1842, p. 3. Also see Tucher, *Froth & Scum*, p. 166.

4. New York *Sun*, January 29, 1842, p. 1.

5. Ibid., p. 2; Dunphy and Cummins, *Remarkable Trials*, pp. 287–95.

6. See Berger, "The Tombs," pp. 23–24.

7. Dunphy and Cummins, *Remarkable Trials*, pp. 296–301; New York *Sun*, January 29, 1842, pp. 2–3; *Dollar Weekly Herald*, February 1, 1842, pp. 1–2.

CHAPTER 44

1. Hubert Howe Bancroft, *The Works of Hubert Howe Bancroft*, vol. 36 (San Francisco: History Company, 1887), p. 425.

2. *New York Herald*, January 31, 1842, p. 2.

3. Ibid.; *Morning Courier and New-York Enquirer*, January 31, 1842, p. 2.

4. *Morning Courier and New-York Enquirer*, January 31, 1842, p. 2.

5. See Michael Kaplan, "New York City Tavern Violence and the Creation of a Working-Class Male Identity," *Journal of the Early Republic*, vol. 15, no. 4 (Winter 1995): pp. 603–5.

6. *New York Herald*, January 31, 1842, p. 2.

PART FIVE: THE NEW YORK TRAGEDY

CHAPTER 45

1. Tucher, *Froth & Scum*, pp. 105, 224. Held on Valentine's Day at the Park Theatre, the gala event in Dickens's honor, known as the "Boz Ball," was, in the amused estimation of diarist Philip Hone, "the greatest affair in modern times, the tallest compliment ever paid to a little man, the fullest libation ever poured upon the altar of the muses."

2. For example, see *Maine Farmer and Journal of the Useful Arts*, October 30, 1841; *Ohio Repository*, February 10, 1842; *Norwalk (OH) Experiment*, February 16, 1842; *Portland (ME) Tribune*, May 24, 1842, p. 3; *Milwaukee Sentinel & Farmer*, April 2, 1842), *Madison (WI) Express*, March 5, 1842; *Boston Recorder*, November 24, 1842. The story was also covered, among other publications, in the *New York Evangelist*, the *Catholic Telegraph*, the *Trumpet and Universalist Magazine*, the *Christian Reflector*, the *Christian Secretary*, the *Christian Register and Boston Observer*, the *Biblical Reporter and Princeton Review*, *Brother Jonathan: A Weekly Compendium of Belle Lettres and the Fine Arts*, the *Weekly Messenger*, *Youth's Companion*, and *Yankee Doodle*.

3. *Episcopal Recorder*, February 19, 1842, p. 192.

4. *Youth's Companion*, March 16, 1842, p. 126.

5. *American Phrenological Journal* (April 1842): vol. 4, no. 2, p. 312.

6. Offered for sale just days after John's conviction, this cheaply printed sheet of doggerel did not stint on gruesome details, catering to the public's prurient appetite for gore even while affecting an ostentatiously pious tone. (A parenthetical note at the top of the sheet suggests that the verses be sung to the "solemn tune of *Come Christian People*.") The surviving stanzas of the ballad read as follows:

> *Good people all, I pray give ear;*
>   *My words concern ye much;*
> *I will repeat a Tragedy:*
>   *You never heard of such.*

There was a man, an Author good
    For making a BOOK you'll own;
And for the KEEPING of the same
    No better than was known.

Besides all this, I can you tell,
    That he was well endow'd
With many graces of the mind
    Had they been well bestow'd.

To print the book and have it bound,
    Colt, by agreement say,
The printer should, the work when done,
    Be first to have his pay.

Upon the books, when they were sent,
    Cash would advanced be;
Adams was to have his money,
    For so they did agree.

Wicked man, for the sake of gold;
    Which he would never pay,
He murder did commit, and then
    The body put away!

In New York City, Adams liv'd
    A chaste and pious life.
And there he might have lived still
    Had Debt not caused a strife.

'Twas in the year Eighteen Hundred
    and Forty One, they say.
The Seventeenth of September,
    It was the fatal day.

To see about the books, being
    Four hundred vols. Or more:
On Friday afternoon, it was
    About the hour of four.

To Colt's room, Samuel Adams
    Went, you will remember:
In the Granite Building, corner
    Of Broadway and Chamber.

This vex'd the man unto the heart;
    He was of wrath so fell,
That finding no hole in his bill,
    He pick'd two in his skull.

Behind him with a Burkite rope,
    Round his neck did bundle,

For quickly then the slip knot flew,
　So the printer struggl'd.

Oh savage man! For blood did thirst,
　And with blows so violent
Out of his head the brains did gush;
　Down fell he all silent.

But then his heart 'gan to relent,
　And griev'd he was full sore;
The bloody Axe to scrape with glass,
　Then wash and scrub the floor.

For blood will always leave a stain,
　Whatever we may think,
And to completely hide the same,
　He'd cover all with ink.

All in the darkness of the night,
　A large box then he made,
When he'd wrapped the body round,
　Within this box 'twas laid.

On board the ship Ka-la-ma-zoo,
　A Cartman did convey,
In the hold of the ship,
　'Twas snugly stowed away.

But heav'n whose pow'r no mortal knows,
　On earth or on the main,
Soon caus'd the body to be found,
　And brought it back again.

The box, when open'd, what a sight,
　Was never seen before,
A rope made fast to neck and knee,
　And maggots crawling oe'r.

And that it no self-murder was,
　The case itself explains,
No man could his head knock holes,
　To let out his own brains.

Ere many days were gone and past,
　The deed it was made known,
And John C. Colt confess'd at last,
　The fact to be his own.

The trial came on for murder,
　In Court it must appear,
The Doctors they did examine,
　The head of Adams there.

The skull was brought into court,
  For all to witness it,
The Jury saw the holes and hatchet,
  Did well each other fit.

The district attorney, he did
  His duty well discharge,
Twelve upright men then heard, the Judge
  Deliver his law charge.

The dreadful case being ended,
  The Jury did agree,
Of willful MURDER, guilty found,
  John Caldwell Colt to be.

God prosper long the jury, who
  Protect the lives of all.
And grant that we may a warning take,
  By John C. Colt's fall.

I have related all that's past,
  Let Justice have its due.
Many years hence, this may be read
  Because it all is true.

An image of the original, albeit damaged, ballad sheet (two verses are missing between stanzas seven and eight) can be found online at the site American Time Capsule: Three Centuries of Broadsides and Other Printed Ephemera (http://memory.loc.gov/ammem/rbpehtml).

7. The image of Barnum published in the *Albany Evening Atlas* is reprinted in Philip B. Kunhardt, Jr., et al., *P. T. Barnum: America's Greatest Showman* (New York: Alfred A. Knopf, 1995), p. 54. It does indeed bear a remarkable similarity to the portrait of Samuel Adams in the *Sun* pamphlet.

8. P. T. Barnum, *The Life of P. T. Barnum, Written by Himself* (New York: Redfield, 1855), pp. 356–57.

CHAPTER 46

1. See *New York Herald*, February 1, February 15, February 22, March 1, and March 2, 1842, p. 2.

2. Charles Sutton, *The New York Tombs: Its Secrets and Its Mysteries* (New York: United States Publishing Company, 1874), p. 44. According to Sutton, the name evolved from *Kalchook* to the abbreviated *Kalch*, and then to *Callech, Colleck,* and, finally, *Collect*.

3. Sutton, *New York Tombs*, p. 47; Berger, "The Tombs," p. 23.

4. Charles Dickens, *American Notes for General Circulation* (New York: D. Appleton & Company, 1863), p. 37.

5. Berger, "The Tombs," p. 22; Edward H. Smith, "New Scene Added to the Drama of the Tombs," *New York Times*, November 14, 1926, p. 23.

6. Berger, "The Tombs," p. 23; Timothy Gilfoyle, " 'America's Greatest Criminal Barracks': The Tombs and the Experience of Criminal Justice in New York City, 1838–1897," *Journal of Urban History*, vol. 29, no. 5 (July 2003): p. 528.

7. Gilfoyle, "Tombs and Criminal Justice," p. 530.

8. Berger, "The Tombs," p. 28.

9. Ibid., pp. 24, 27; Gilfoyle, "Tombs and Criminal Justice," p. 532.

10. *Life and Letters of John C. Colt*, letter 5, November 10, 1841.

11. Quoted in Alfred Henry Lewis, *Nation-Famous New York Murders* (New York: G. W. Dillingham Company, 1914), pp. 232–34.

12. John's letters first appeared in the daily press (see the *Morning Courier and New-York Enquirer*, February 24, 1842, where they occupy all of pp. 1–2). In October 1842, they were published in pamphlet form as an *Extra Tattler* under the title *Life and Letters of John C. Colt, Condemned to Be Hung on the Eighteenth of November, 1842, for the Murder of Samuel Adams*. A selection of them was also printed as an appendix to later editions of the *Sun* pamphlet (see Tucher, *Froth & Scum*, p. 230, n. 4). The quoted passages in this chapter are taken from the letters dated November 10, 1841; February 6, 8, 10, 11, 15, and 22, 1842; March 15, 1842.

CHAPTER 47

1. Rogers's handwritten report can be found on the microfilm edition of the William Henry Seward Papers, University of Rochester, River Campus Libraries, Department of Rare Books, Special Collections, and Preservation, reel 165, items 5894–5901.

CHAPTER 48

1. Edwards, *Colt's Revolver*, p. 173.

2. Lundeberg, *Submarine Battery*, p. 23.

3. Leonard F. Guttridge, *Our Country, Right or Wrong: The Life of Stephen Decatur, the U.S. Navy's Most Illustrious Commander* (New York: Forge Books, 2007), pp. 154–55.

4. Lundeberg, *Submarine Battery*, p. 74; Edwards, *Colt's Revolver*, p. 173. Sam's notebook sketch of Halsey's submersible—the only surviving image of the boat—can be found on Captain Brayton Harris's website World Submarine History Timeline: 1580–2000 (www.submarine-history.com/NOVAone.htm).

5. Edwards, *Colt's Revolver*, pp. 173–74.

6. Ibid., p. 174.

7. Ibid.

8. Ibid.; Lundeberg, *Submarine Battery*, p. 26; Rohan, *Yankee Arms Maker*, pp. 148–49; Keating, *Flamboyant Mr. Colt*, p. 59.

9. Rohan, *Yankee Arms Maker*, p. 149.

CHAPTER 49

1. *New York Herald*, May 7, 1842, p. 1.

2. Ibid., May 13, 1842, p. 1.

3. Edwin Burritt Smith and Ernest Hitchcock, *Reports of Cases Adjudged and Determined in the Supreme Court of Judicature and Court for the Trial of Impeachments and Correction of Errors of the State of New York*, book 15 (Newark, NY: The Lawyers' Co-Operative Publishing Company, 1885), pp. 431–37.

CHAPTER 50

1. *New York Herald*, September 28, 1842, p. 1; New York *Sun*, September 28, 1842, p. 2; *Hagerstown* (MD) *Mail*, October 7, 1842, p. 3.

2. As John himself described it. See *Life and Letters of John C. Colt*, letter 19.

3. Ibid.

4. *New York Herald*, September 28, 1842, p. 1.

CHAPTER 51

1. New York *Sun*, September 28, 1842, p. 2; *Morning Courier and New-York Enquirer*, October 28, 1842, p. 2; *Brooklyn Daily Eagle*, September 28, 1842, p. 2.

2. Bennett ranked the murder of Adams with three other violent incidents that had riveted the city in recent years. In March 1838, U.S. Representative Jonathan Cilley of Maine was shot to death in a duel with a fellow congressman, William Graves of Kentucky, who had taken offense at a remark Cilley had made about Graves's friend James Watson Webb, editor of the *Morning Courier and New-York Enquirer*. Four years later, Webb himself was badly wounded in a pistol duel with Kentucky congressman Thomas Marshall. Most savage of all was the September 1842 grudge match between prizefighters Thomas McCoy and Christopher Lilly that did not end until—after nearly three hours and 120 rounds—McCoy was beaten to death, "his face literally knocked to pieces." For accounts of the Graves-Cilley and Marshall-Webb duels, see Don C. Seitz, *Famous American Duels* (New York: Thomas Y. Crowell, 1929), pp. 251–82, 283–309. The McCoy-Lilly fight is described in George N. Thomson, *Confessions, Trials and Biographical Sketches of the Most Cold-Blooded Murderers, Who Have Been Executed in the Country from Its First Settlement Down to the Present Time* (Hartford, CT: S. Andrus and Son, 1887), pp. 411–12.

3. *New York Herald*, September 28, 1842, p. 2.

CHAPTER 52

1. Tucher, *Froth & Scum*, p. 168.

2. Powell, *Authentic Life*, pp. 6, 14, 23, 31, 49, 61.

3. *Life and Letters of John C. Colt*, p. 5.

4. Ibid., p. 16.

CHAPTER 53

1. *New York Times*, June 4, 1873, p. 8. The best and most complete account of the scandal is Geoffrey O'Brien, *The Fall of the House of Walworth*.

2. For example, see Charles Edwards, *Pleasantries About Courts and Lawyers of the State of New York* (New York: Richardson & Company, 1867), p. 317.

3. In his autobiography, Governor William Seward notes that John's "counsel applied to me thirteen days only before the day of his execution." See Frederick W. Seward, *William H. Seward: An Autobiography from 1801 to 1834: With a Memoir of His Life, and Selections from His Letters, 1831–1846* (New York: D. Appleton and Company, 1877), p. 629.

CHAPTER 54

1. Bancroft, *Life of William H. Seward*, p. 120.

2. Ibid., pp. 122–23; Earl Conrad, *The Governor and His Lady: The Story of William Henry Seward and His Wife Frances* (New York: G. P. Putnam's, 1960), p. 238.

3. Conrad, *Governor*, p. 247.

4. Seward, *William H. Seward*, p. 629.

5. Ibid.

6. All quotes are taken from letters found on the microfilm edition of the William Henry Seward Papers, University of Rochester, River Campus Libraries, Department of Rare Books, Special Collections, and Preservation, reel 165, items 5894–5901.

7. Seward, *William H. Seward*, p. 633. Seward would, in fact, become the victim of an assassination attempt—not, however, as a result of his decision in the Colt case. On the night of April 15, 1865—at the same time that Abraham Lincoln was shot by John Wilkes Booth—Seward, then Lincoln's secretary of state, was savagely attacked at home by Lewis Powell, one of Booth's coconspirators in a plot to decapitate the Union government. Stabbed in the face with a bowie knife, Seward survived, though he bore disfiguring scars for the rest of his life.

8. George Baker, ed., *The Works of William H. Seward*, vol. 2 (New York: Redfield, 1853), pp. 648–61.

9. New York *Sun*, November 14, 1842, p. 2.

CHAPTER 55

1. New York *Sun*, November 16, 1842, p. 2; *New-York Commercial Advertiser*, November 17, 1842, p. 2; Seward, *William H. Seward*, pp. 632–33; Lydia Maria Child, *Letters from New-York*, ed. Bruce Mills (Athens, GA: University of Georgia Press, 1998), p. 242, n. 4.

2. Child, *Letters from New-York*, p. 241, n. 4; p. 137.

3. Allan Nevins and Milton Halsey Thomas, *The Diary of George Templeton Strong: Young Man in New York 1835–1848* (New York: Macmillan, 1952), p. 189.

4. Child, *Letters from New-York*, p. 137.

5. Ibid. Also see "Everything Is Changed: The Old Salt Still Brooding Over Early New-York," *New York Times*, May 16, 1886, p. 5.

6. Nevins and Thomas, *George Templeton Strong*, pp. 188–90.

7. Ibid., pp. 190–91; *Brooklyn Daily Eagle*, November 17, 1842, p. 2.

8. *New York Times*, May 16, 1886, p. 5.

9. Nevins and Thomas, *George Templeton Strong*, p. 190.

CHAPTER 56

1. New York *Sun*, November 19, 1842, p. 2.

2. Nevins and Thomas, *George Templeton Strong*, p. 190; *New York Herald*, November 18, 1842, p. 1.

3. Child, *Letters from New-York*, pp. 137–38; *New York Times*, May 16, 1886, p. 5.

4. *New York Herald*, November 18, 1842, p. 1; *New-York Commercial Advertiser*, November 19, 1842, p. 2; *Morning Courier and New-York Enquirer*, November 19, 1842, p. 2.

5. *Morning Courier and New-York Enquirer*, November 19, 1842, p. 2.

6. *New-York Commercial Advertiser*, November 19, 1842, p. 2.

7. Ibid.

8. Child, *Letters from New-York*, p. 139.

9. *New York Herald*, November 18, 1842, p. 1; *New-York Commercial Advertiser*, November 19, 1842, p. 2.

10. Sutton, *New York Tombs*, p. 76.

11. *New-York Commercial Advertiser*, November 19, 1842, p. 2.

12. *New York Herald*, November 18, 1842, p. 1.

13. *Morning Courier and New-York Enquirer*, November 22, 1842, p. 2.

14. Sutton, *New York Tombs*, p. 77; *New York Herald*, November 18, 1842, p. 1.

15. *New York Herald*, November 18, 1842, p. 1.

16. Ibid.; *New-York Commercial Advertiser*, November 19, 1842, p. 2.

17. Nevins and Thomas, *George Templeton Strong*, p. 191.

18. *New York Herald*, November 18, 1842, p. 1.

19. *New-York Commercial Advertiser*, November 19, 1842, p. 2.

20. Ibid.

21. *Morning Courier and New-York Enquirer*, November 19, 1842, p. 2.

22. *New York Herald*, November 18, 1842, p. 1; *New-York Commercial Advertiser*, November 19, 1842, p. 2.

23. *New York Times*, May 16, 1886, p. 5.

24. *New-York Commercial Advertiser*, November 19, 1842, p. 2.

25. Nevins and Thomas, *George Templeton Strong*, p. 192.

26. Abbott, "Mystery of the Tombs," p. 690; Jan Seidler Ramirez, *Painting the Town: Cityscapes of New York* (New York: Museum of the City of New York, 2000), pp. 96–97.

27. Child, *Letters from New-York*, pp. 242, 138.

CHAPTER 57

1. *New York Herald*, November 17, 1842, p. 2.

2. "A Crime of Forty Years Ago," *New York Times*, December 18, 1880, p. 12.

3. *New-York Commercial Advertiser*, November 19, 1842, p. 2.

4. Seward, *William H. Seward*, p. 635; *Morning Courier and New-York Enquirer*, November 19, 1842, p. 2.

5. Abbott, "Mystery of the Tombs," p. 690; *New York Herald*, November 18, 1842, p. 2.

6. *Morning Courier and New-York Enquirer*, November 22, 1842.

7. New York Sun, November 19, 1842, p. 2; *New York Tribune*, November 19, 1842, p. 2; *New-York Commercial Advertiser*, November 19, 1842, p. 2.

8. Seward, *William H. Seward*, p. 634.

CONCLUSION: LEGENDS

CHAPTER 58

1. *New York Herald*, November 23, 1842, p. 2.

2. *Christian Reflector*, November 23, 1842, p. 5.

3. *Ohio Repository*, December 1, 1842, p. 3.

4. *Life and Letters of John C. Colt*, letter 18, June 10, 1842.

5. For a thorough discussion of Universalism, see Ann Lee Bressler, *The Universalist Movement in America 1770–1880* (New York: Oxford University Press, 2001).

6. Bressler, *Universalist Movement*, p. 39.

7. Review of *Universalism Examined, Renounced, Exposed* by Matthew Hale Smith, *Princeton Review*, no. 4 (October 1843): pp. 527–28.

8. *Christian Watchman*, December 10, 1842, p. 12.

9. *Trumpet and Universalist Magazine*, December 31, 1842, p. 15.

10. *New York Evening Journal*, December 27, 1842, p. 3.

11. See Louis P. Masur, *Rites of Execution: Capital Punishment and the Transformation of American Culture, 1776–1865* (New York: Oxford University Press, 1989).

12. Child, *Letters from New-York*, p. 139.

13. *New York Tribune*, November 19, 1842, p. 2.

14. New York *Sun*, November 24, 1842, p. 2.

15. Bergman, *Collected Writings of Walt Whitman*, pp. 162–63.

CHAPTER 59

1. New York *Sun*, November 21, 1842, p. 2.

2. Macatamney, *Cradle Days*, p. 191.

3. "Everything Is Changed," p. 5.

4. Nevins and Thomas, *George Templeton Strong*, p. 193; *Hartford Daily Courant*, December 12, 1842, p. 2.

5. *New-York Commercial Advertiser*, November 19, 1842.

6. New York *Sun*, November 19, 1842.

7. *New York Herald*, November 20, 1842, p. 2.

CHAPTER 60

1. Carolyn L. Karcher, *The First Woman in the Republic: A Cultural Biography of Lydia Maria Child* (Durham, NC: Duke University Press, 1998), p. 303. Despite the prominent literary and intellectual status she enjoyed in her own time, Child is best known today (to the extent that she is remembered at all) as the author of the holiday chestnut "Over the river and through the woods / To grandfather's house we go," originally published in the second volume of her collection *Flowers for Children* (1844).

2. These remarks were excised from the later, edited version published in Child's book *Letters from New-York*. See p. 243, n. 16.

3. Mrs. Sigourney was a regular contributor to the *Juvenile Miscellany*, the popular bimonthly magazine that Mrs. Child founded in 1826. See Carolyn L. Karcher, "Lydia Maria Child and the *Juvenile Miscellany*: The Creation of an American Children's Literature," in *Periodical Literature in Nineteenth-Century America*, ed. Kenneth M. Price and Susan Belasco Smith (Charlottesville, VA: University of Virginia Press, 1995), pp. 93–109.

4. For more on this famously unsuccessful experiment in cooperative living, see Sterling F. Delano, *Brook Farm: The Dark Side of Utopia* (Cambridge, MA: Harvard University Press, 2004).

5. Child, *Selected Letters*, pp. 183–84.

6. See Lundeberg, *Submarine Battery*, pp. 31–34.

7. Ibid., p. 31.

8. A summary of James's career can be found in Livingston, *Biographical Sketches*, pp. 93ff. For an account of the duel, see Dick Steward, *Duels and the Roots of Violence in Missouri* (Columbia, MO: University of Missouri Press, 2000), pp. 126–27.

9. This and the other letters from James are on file at the Connecticut Historical Society.

10. Keating, *Flamboyant Mr. Colt*, p. 69; Rywell, *Man and Epoch*, p. 72; Hosley, *American Legend*, pp. 22–23.

11. Lundeberg, *Submarine Battery*, p. 46.

12. Ibid., p. 55; Hosley, *American Legend*, p. 22.

CHAPTER 61

1. See Edwards, *Colt's Revolver*, pp. 195–204; Houze, *Colt: Arms, Art, Invention*, p. 68.

2. Evans, *They Made America*, pp. 60–61; Edwards, *Colt's Revolver*, p. 99.

3. Houze, *Colt: Arms, Art, Invention*, p. 73; Evans, *They Made America*, p. 66.

4. Evans, *They Made America*, p. 68.

5. Hosley, *American Legend*, p. 23.

6. Ibid., p. 26.

7. Ibid., p. 28.

8. Rywell, *Man and Epoch*, p. 130.

CHAPTER 62

1. Edwards, *Colt's Revolver*, p. 42.

2. Tucher, *Froth & Scum*, p. 173.

3. Ibid., pp. 173–74.

4. Keating, *Flamboyant Mr. Colt*, p. 145.

5. Ibid., p. 65.

CHAPTER 63

1. The source of the Julia Leicester legend appears to be Colt biographer William Edwards (see *Colt's Revolver*, pp. 309, 340–42). Contrary to the claims by Edwards and subsequent writers who have unquestioningly accepted his statements, Colt historian Herbert G. Houze has conclusively shown that the woman who married Friedrich von Oppen was *not* Caroline Henshaw but rather the much younger Julia Colt, a distant cousin of Sam's. Also see Houze, *Colt: Arms, Art, Invention*, p. 69, n. 14; p. 247.

2. See Lewis, *Nation-Famous New York Murders*, pp. 240–41.

3. *Christian Reflector*, February 1, 1843, p. 19; *Brother Jonathan: A weekly Compendium of Belle Lettres and the Fine Arts*, vol. 4 (February 4, 1843), p. 137. For a concise account of Bannister's career, see Martin Banham, ed., *The Cambridge Guide to Theatre* (Cambridge, MA: Cambridge University Press, 1995), p. 76.

Ninety-five year later, a dramatization of the Colt affair was broadcast on the airwaves. Scripted by George J. Throp, "The Case of John C. Colt" was the debut episode of *Out of the Hall of Records*, a weekly radio series of "dramatized programs based on the annals of notorious court cases preserved in the Hall of Records of New York City." The episode was broadcast on WNYC, Monday, December 5, 1938, 4:00–4:30 EST. The original script can be found in the WPA Radio Scripts collection at the Lincoln Center Library for the Performing Arts, box 40, file 1, "The Case of John C. Colt" (Collection ID# T-MSS 2000–005).

4. See Bon Gaultier, "A Night at Peleg Longfellow's," *The New World: A Weekly Family Journal of Popular Literature, Science, and the Arts*, vol. 7 (August 26, 1843): p. 227.

5. *The Complete Stories and Poems of Edgar Allan Poe* (Garden City, NY: Doubleday & Company, 1966), pp. 237–45.

6. Warner Berthoff, ed., *Great Short Works of Herman Melville* (Harper & Row/Perennial Library, 1969), pp. 63–64.

7. Theodora De Wolf Colt, *Stray Fancies* (Boston: published for private circulation, 1872), pp. 118–22.

8. Hosley, *American Legend*, pp. 30–31.

9. Ibid., p. 138.

10. Keating, *Flamboyant Mr. Colt*, p. 187.

11. Hosley, *American Legend*, p. 145.

12. Barnard, *Armsmear*, p. 295.

BIBLIOGRAPHY

Aaron, Daniel. *Cincinnati, Queen City of the West: 1819–1838*. Columbus, OH: Ohio State University Press, 1992.

Abbott, Mabel. "A Mystery of the Tombs." *Detective Fiction Weekly*, February 1, 1930, pp. 683–91.

Adams, Charles, Jr. *A Genealogical Register of North Brookfield Families, Including the Records of Many Early Settlers of Brookfield*. Published by the Town of North Brookfield, 1887.

Bacon, Margaret Hope. *But One Race: The Life of Robert Purvis*. Albany, NY: SUNY Press, 2007.

Baker, George, ed. *The Works of William H. Seward*. Vol. 2. New York: Redfield, 1853.

Bancroft, Frederic. *The Life of William H. Seward*. Vol. 1. New York: Harper and Brothers, 1900.

Bancroft, Hubert Howe. *The Works of Hubert Howe Bancroft*. Vol. 36. San Francisco: History Company, 1887.

Barnard, Henry. *Armsmear: The Home, the Arm, and the Armory of Samuel Colt: A Memorial*. New York: Alvord Printer, 1866.

Barnum, P. T. *The Life of P. T. Barnum, Written by Himself*. New York: Redfield, 1855.

Baxter, Maurice G. *One and Inseparable: Daniel Webster and the Union*. Cambridge, MA: Harvard University Press, 1984.

Beeghley, Leonard. *Homicide: A Sociological Explanation*. Lanham, MD: Rowman & Littlefield, 2003.

Belcher, Hilary, and Erica Swale. "Catch a Falling Star." *Folklore*, vol. 95 (1984): pp. 210–20.

Belden, E. Porter. *New-York: Past, Present, and Future: Comprising a History of the City of New York*. New York: G. P. Putnam, 1849.

Bell, Whitfield J., Jr., et al. *A Cabinet of Curiosities: Five Episodes in the Evolution of American Museums*. Charlottesville, VA: University Press of Virginia, 1967.

Berger, Meyer. "That Was New York: The Tombs—I." *New Yorker*, August 30, 1941, pp. 22–29.

Bergman, Herbert, ed. *The Collected Writings of Walt Whitman: The Journalism: Volume 2: 1846–1848*. New York: Peter Lang, 2003.

Bettelheim, Bruno. *The Uses of Enchantment: The Meaning and Importance of Fairy Tales*. New York: Alfred A. Knopf, 1976.

Bigelow, L. J. *Bench and Bar: A Complete Digest of the Wit, Humor, Asperities, and Amenities of the Law*. New York: Harper & Brothers, 1871.

Bressler, Ann Lee. *The Universalist Movement in America 1770–1880*. New York: Oxford University Press, 2001.

Brockett, L. P. *The Silk Industry in America. A History: Prepared for the Centennial Exposition*. New York: George F. Nesbitt & Co., 1876.

Browder, Clifford. *The Wickedest Woman in New York: Madame Restell, the Abortionist*. Hamden, CT: Archon Books, 1988.

Brown, H. Glenn, and Maude O. Brown. *A Directory of Printing, Publishing, Bookselling and Allied Trades in Rhode Island to 1865*. New York: New York Public Library, 1958.

Burlingame, Roger. *March of the Iron Men: A Social History of Union Through Invention*. New York: Grosset & Dunlap, 1938.

Burns, Ric, and James Sanders. *New York: An Illustrated History*. New York: Alfred A. Knopf, 2005.

Burrows, Edwin, and Mike Wallace. *Gotham: A History of New York City to 1898*. New York: Oxford University Press, 1999.

Butterbaugh, Grant I. "Dr. Stands for Debt." *Accounting Review*, vol. 20, no. 3 (July 1945): pp. 340–44.

Caldwell, Mark. *New York Night: The Mystique and Its History*. New York: Scribner, 2005.

Carman, W. Y. *A History of Firearms: From Earliest Times to 1914*. London: Routledge & Kegan Paul, 1955.

Carpenter, Edward Wilton, and Charles Frederick Morehouse. *The History of the Town of Amherst, Massachusetts*. Amherst, MA: Carpenter & Morehouse, 1896.

Chase, Arthur. *History of Ware, Massachusetts*. Cambridge, MA: Harvard University Press, 1911.

Child, Lydia Maria. *Letters from New-York*. Edited by Bruce Mills. Athens, GA: University of Georgia Press, 1998.

———. *Selected Letters, 1817–1880*. Edited by Milton Meltzer and Patricia G. Holland. Amherst, MA: University of Massachusetts Press, 1982.

Chiles, Rosa Pendleton. *John Howard Payne: American Poet, Actor, Playwright, Consul and the Author of "Home, Sweet Home."* Washington, DC: Columbia Historical Society, 1930.

Chinoy, Helen Krich, and Linda Walsh Jenkins, eds. *Women in American Theatre.* New York: Crown Publishing, 1980.

Cist, Charles. *Cincinnati in 1841: Its Early Annals and Future Prospects.* Cincinnati, OH: E. Morgan & Co., 1841.

Clark, Howard. *The Mill on Mad River.* Boston: Little, Brown & Company, 1948.

Cohen, Patricia Cline. *The Murder of Helen Jewett: The Life and Death of a Prostitute in Nineteenth-Century New York.* New York: Alfred A. Knopf, 1998.

Colt, John C. *The Science of Double Entry Book-Keeping: Simplified, Arranged, and Methodized, After the Forms of Grammar and Arithmetic; Explained by Definite Rules, and Illustrated by Entries Classed, in a Manner Materially Different from Any Work Ever Before Offered to the Public. Containing Also, a Key, Explaining the Manner of Journalizing, and the Nature of the Business Transaction of Each of the Day-Book Entries, Together with Practical Forms for Keeping Books, as Circumstances May Require in Different Commercial Houses.* 10th ed. New York: Nafis & Cornish, 1844.

Colt, Miriam Davis. *Went to Kansas; Being a Thrilling Account of an Ill-Fated Expedition to That Fairy Land, and Its Sad Results; Together with a Sketch of the Life of the Author, and How the World Goes with Her.* Watertown, MA: L. Ingalls & Co., 1862.

Conrad, Earl. *The Governor and His Lady: The Story of William Henry Seward and His Wife Frances.* New York: G. P. Putnam's Sons, 1960.

Cooke, D. B. "My Memories of the Book Trade." *Publisher's Weekly,* no. 217 (March 11, 1876): pp. 321–22.

Costello, Augustine. *Our Police Protectors: History of the New York Police.* New York: Augustine Costello, 1885.

Cowdry, Mary Bartlett. *American Academy of Fine Arts and American Art-Union: Introduction 1816–1852.* New York: New York Historical Society, 1953.

Crouthamel, James L. *Bennett's New York Herald and the Rise of the Popular Press.* Syracuse, NY: Syracuse University Press, 1989.

Cushing, Luther S. *Reports of Cases Argued and Determined in the Supreme Court of Massachusetts.* Vol. 1. Boston: Little, Brown and Company, 1865.

Delano, Sterling F. *Brook Farm: The Dark Side of Utopia.* Cambridge, MA: Harvard University Press, 2004.

Dennett, Andrea Stulman. *Weird and Wonderful: The Dime Museum in America.* New York: New York University Press, 1997.

Dent, John Charles. *The Last Forty Years: Canada Since the Union of 1841.* Vol. 1. Toronto: George Virtue, 1881.

Dickens, Charles. *American Notes for General Circulation*. New York: D. Appleton & Company, 1863.

Disturnell, J. *The Classified Mercantile Directory for the Cities of New-York and Brooklyn*. New York: J. Disturnell, 1837.

———. *New-York as It Is in 1837*. New York: J. Disturnell, 1837.

Dizard, Jan E., Robert Merrill Muth, and Stephen P. Andrews, Jr. *Guns in America: A Reader*. New York: New York University Press, 1999.

Dormandy, Thomas. *The White Death: A History of Tuberculosis*. New York: New York University Press, 1999.

Duke, Thomas S. *Celebrated Criminal Cases of America*. San Francisco: James H. Barry Company, 1910. Reprint, Montclair, NJ: Patterson Smith, 1991.

Dunlop. M. H. "Curiosities Too Numerous to Mention: Early Regionalism and Cincinnati's Western Museum." *American Quarterly*, vol. 36, no. 4 (Autumn 1984): pp. 524–48.

Dunphy, Thomas, and Thomas J. Cummins. *Remarkable Trials of All Countries*. New York: Dossy & Company, 1870.

Dunshee, Kenneth Holcomb. *As You Pass By*. New York: Hastings House, 1952.

Eaton, Amos. *Chemical Instructor: Presenting a Familiar Method of Teaching the Chemical Principles and Operations of the Most Practical Utility to Farmers, Mechanics, Housekeepers and Physicians; and Most Interesting to Clergymen and Lawyers. Intended for Academies and for the Popular Class-Room*. Albany, NY: Websters and Skinners, 1822.

Edgerly, James H. *The Revolving-Cylinder Colt Pistol Story from 1839 to 1847*. Topeka, KS: F. Theodore Dexter, 1937.

Edwards, Charles. *Pleasantries About Courts and Lawyers of the State of New York*. New York: Richardson & Company, 1867.

Edwards, William B. *The Story of Colt's Revolver: The Biography of Col. Samuel Colt*. New York: Castle Books, 1957.

Elbert, Monika. *Enterprising Youth: Social Values and Acculturation in Nineteenth-Century American Children's Literature*. London: Routledge, 2008.

Evans, Harold. *They Made America: From the Steam Engine to the Search Engine: Two Centuries of Innovators*. New York: Little, Brown and Company, 2004.

Fitzgerald, P. A. *The Exhibition Speaker: Containing Farces, Dialogues, and Tableaux, with Exercises for Declamation in Prose and Verse. Also a Treatise on Oratory and Elocution, Hints on Dramatic Characters, Costumes, Position on the Stage, Making Up, Etc., Etc*. New York: Sheldon, Lamport & Blakeman, 1856.

Fowler, Nathaniel C. *Getting a Start: First Aids to Success*. New York: Sully and Kleintech, 1915.

Fuess, Claude Moore. *Amherst: The Story of a New England College*. Boston: Little, Brown, and Company, 1935.

Fulton, Robert. *Torpedo War, and Submarine Explosions*. New York: William Elliot, 1810.

Gilfoyle, Timothy. " 'America's Greatest Criminal Barracks': The Tombs and the Experience of Criminal Justice in New York City, 1838–1897." *Journal of Urban History*, vol. 29, no. 5 (July 2003): pp. 525–54.

Golan, Tal. *The Laws of Men and the Laws of Nature: The History of Scientific Expert Testimony in England and America*. Cambridge, MA: Harvard University Press, 2004.

Goodman, Matthew. *The Sun and the Moon: The Remarkable True Account of Hoaxers, Showmen, Dueling Journalists, and Lunar Man-Bats in Nineteenth-Century New York*. New York: Basic Books, 2008.

Goss, Charles Frederic. *Cincinnati the Queen City: 1788–1912*. Chicago: S. J. Clarke Publishing Company, 1912.

Grant, Ellsworth S. *The Colt Legacy: The Colt Armory in Hartford, 1855–1980*. Providence, RI: Mowbray Company, 1982.

Greve, Charles Theodore. *Centennial History of Cincinnati and Representative Citizens*. Vol. 1. Chicago: Biographical Publishing Company, 1904.

Guttridge, Leonard F. *Our Country, Right or Wrong: The Life of Stephen Decatur, the U.S. Navy's Most Illustrious Commander*. New York: Forge Books, 2007.

Hall, Mary. *Report of the Celebration of the Incorporation of the Town of Marlborough*. Hartford, CT: Hartford Press, 1904.

Harris, Neil. *Humbug: The Art of P. T. Barnum*. Chicago: University of Chicago Press, 1973.

Harrison, Gabriel. *John Howard Payne, Dramatist, Poet, Actor, and Author of Home Sweet Home!* Boston: Lippincott, 1885.

Haswell, Charles H. *Reminiscences of an Octogenarian of the City of New York (1816 to 1860)*. New York: Harper & Brothers, 1897.

Haven, Charles T., and Frank A. Belden. *A History of the Colt Revolver: And Other Arms Made by Colt's Patent Fire Arms Manufacturing Company from 1836 to 1940*. New York: Bonanza Books, 1940.

Heier, Jan R. "A Critical Look at the Thoughts and Theories of the Early Accounting Educator John C. Colt." *Accounting, Business and Financial History*, vol. 3, no. 1 (1993): pp. 21–36.

History of the Hopkins Fund, Grammar School and Academy, in Hadley, Mass.: Prepared and Published Under the Direction and Authority of the Trustees of Hopkins Academy. Amherst, MA: Amherst Record Press, 1890.

Hodges, Graham Russell. *New York City Cartmen, 1667–1850*. New York: New York University Press, 1986.

Holland, Josiah Gilbert. *History of Western Massachusetts*. Springfield, MA: Samuel Bowles and Company, 1855.

Homans and Ellis. *A Picture of New York in 1846; with a Short Account of Places in Its Vicinity*. New York: C. S. Francis & Co., 1846.

Hosley, William. *Colt: The Making of an American Legend*. Amherst, MA: University of Massachusetts Press, 1996.

Houze, Herbert G. *Samuel Colt: Arms, Art, and Invention*. New Haven, CT, and London: Yale University Press and the Wadsworth Museum of Art, 2006.

Howe, Daniel Walker. *What Hath God Wrought: The Transformation of America, 1815–1848*. New York: Oxford University Press, 2007.

Hudson, Frederic. *Journalism in the United States, from 1690 to 1872*. New York: Harper & Brothers, 1873.

Hughes, Helen McGill. *News and the Human Interest Story*. Somerset, NJ: Transaction Publishers, 1980.

Hutchinson, Reverend Enoch, and Reverend Stephen Remington, eds. *The Baptist Memorial and Monthly Record: Devoted to the History, Biography, Literature & Statistics of the Denomination*. Vol. 8. New York: Z. P. Hatch, 1849.

Isenberg, Nancy. *Sex and Citizenship in Antebellum America*. Chapel Hill, NC: University of North Carolina Press, 1998.

Jeffers, H. Paul. *With an Axe*. New York: Kensington/Pinnacle Books, 2000.

Jenkins, Stephen. *The Greatest Street in the World: The Story of Broadway, Old and New, from the Bowling Green to Albany*. New York: G. P. Putnam's Sons, 1911.

Johnson, Rossiter. *The Twentieth Century Biographical Dictionary of Notable Americans: Brief Biographies of Authors, Administrators, Clergymen, Commanders, Editors, Engineers, Jurists, Merchants, Officials, Philanthropists, Scientists, Statesmen, and Others Who Are Making American History*. Vol. 3. Boston: Biographical Society, 1904.

Jones, Chester Lloyd. "The Anthracite-Tidewater Canals." *Annals of the American Academy of Political and Social Science*, vol. 31 (January 1908): pp. 102–16.

Kaplan, Michael. "New York City Tavern Violence and the Creation of a Working-Class Male Identity." *Journal of the Early Republic*, vol. 15, no. 4 (Winter 1995): pp. 591–617.

Karcher, Carolyn L. *The First Woman in the Republic: A Cultural Biography of Lydia Maria Child*. Durham, NC: Duke University Press, 1998.

———. "Lydia Maria Child and the *Juvenile Miscellany*: The Creation of an American Children's Literature." In *Periodical Literature in Nineteenth-Century America*, edited by Kenneth M. Price and Susan Belasco Smith. Charlottesville, VA: University of Virginia Press, 1995.

Keating, Ben. *The Flamboyant Mr. Colt and His Deadly Six-Shooter*. New York: Doubleday & Co., 1978.

Kettell, Samuel. *Specimens of American Poetry: With Critical and Biographical Notices*. Boston: B. G. Goodrich and Co., 1829.

Knowles, James D. *Memoir of Mrs. Ann H. Judson, Late Missionary to Burmah; Including a History of the American Baptist Mission in the Burman Empire*. Boston: Lincoln & Edmonds, 1831.

Kunhardt, Jr., Philip B., et al. *P. T. Barnum: America's Greatest Showman*. New York: Alfred A. Knopf, 1995.

Lankevich, George J. *American Metropolis: A History of New York City*. New York: NYU Press, 1998.

Lawrence, Robert Means. *The Descendants of Major Samuel Lawrence of Groton, Massachusetts: With Some Mention on Allied Families*. Cambridge, MA: Riverside Press, 1904, pp. 68–72.

Lawson, John D. *American State Trials: A Collection of the Important and Interesting Criminal Trials Which Have Taken Place in the United States, from the Beginning of Our Government to the Present Day*. Vol. 7. St. Louis: F. H. Thomas Law Book Co., 1917.

Lewis, Alfred Henry. *Nation-Famous New York Murders*. New York: G. W. Dillingham Company, 1914.

Life and Letters of John C. Colt, Condemned to Be Hung on the Eighteenth of November, 1842, for the Murder of Samuel Adams. New York: *Extra Tattler*, October 21, 1842.

Lindsay, Julian Ira. *Tradition Looks Forward: The University of Vermont: A History, 1791–1904*. Burlington, VT: University of Vermont and State Agricultural College, 1954.

Livingston, John, ed. *Biographical Sketches of Eminent American Lawyers, Now Living*. New York: *United States Monthly Law Magazine*, 1852.

Lopate, Phillip, ed. *Writing New York: A Literary Anthology*. New York: Library of America, 2008.

Lundeberg, Philip K. *Samuel Colt's Submarine Battery: The Secret and the Enigma*. Washington, DC: Smithsonian Institution Press, 1974.

Lyon, Isaac S. *Recollections of an Old Cartman*. New York: New York Bound, 1984.

Macatamney, Hugh. *Cradle Days of New York: 1609–1825*. New York: Drew & Lewis, 1909.

Mainero, Lina. *American Women Writers*. New York: Frederick Ungar, 1982.

Marjoribanks, Alexander. *Travels in South and North America*. New York: D. Appleton & Co., 1854.

Masur, Louis P. *Rites of Execution: Capital Punishment and the Transformation of American Culture, 1776–1865*. New York: Oxford University Press, 1989.

Maverick, Augustus. *Henry J. Raymond and the New York Press*. Hartford, CT: A. S. Hale and Company, 1870.

McDade, Thomas M. *Annals of Murder: A Bibliography of Books and Pamphlets on American Murders from Colonial Times to 1900*. Norman, OK: University of Oklahoma Press, 1961.

Mines, John Flavel. *A Tour Around New York and My Summer Acre: Being the Recreations of Mr. Felix Oldboy*. New York: Harper & Brothers, 1893.

Minutes of the Common Council of the City of New York, 1675–1776. Vol. 4. New York: Dodd, Mead, and Company, 1905.

Monkkonen, Eric H. *Murder in New York City*. Berkeley, CA: University of California Press, 2001.

Nevins, Allan, and Milton Halsey Thomas. *The Diary of George Templeton Strong: Young Man in New York 1835–1848*. New York: Macmillan, 1952.

Newhall, Beaumont. *The Daguerreotype in America*. New York: Dover, 1975.

The New York Supplement, Vol. 17, Containing the Decisions of the Supreme, Superior, and Lower Courts of Record of New York State. February 11–March 24, 1892. St. Paul, MN: West Publishing Co., 1892.

O'Brien, Frank M. *The Story of the Sun: New York, 1833–1918*. New York: George H. Doran, 1918.

O'Brien, Geoffrey. *The Fall of the House of Walworth: A Tale of Murder and Madness in Saratoga's Gilded Age*. New York: Henry Holt, 2010.

Opie, Iona, and Peter Opie. *The Classic Fairy Tales*. London: Oxford University Press, 1974.

Padnos, Theophilus E. "Here Is a Cabinet of Curiosities: Collecting the Past on the American Frontier." PhD diss., University of Massachusetts Amherst, 2000.

Parks, E. Taylor. "Robert Fulton and Submarine Warfare." *Military Affairs*, vol. 25 (Winter 1961–62): pp. 177–82.

Pauly, Roger. *Firearms: The Life Story of a Technology*. Westport, CT: Greenwood Press, 2004.

Pearson, Edmund. *Instigation of the Devil*. New York: Charles Scribner's Sons, 1930.

Phelan, John. *Readings in Rural Sociology*. New York: Macmillan, 1920.

Powell, Charles F. *An Authentic Life of John C. Colt, Now Imprisoned for Killing Samuel Adams, in New York, on the Seventeenth of September, 1841*. Boston: S. N. Dickinson, 1842.

Pray, Isaac Clarke. *Memoirs of James Gordon Bennett and His Times*. New York: Stringer & Townsend, 1855.

Prentice, George. *Wilbur Fisk*. Boston and New York: Houghton, Mifflin and Company, 1890.

Previts, Cary John, and Barbara Dubis Merino. *A History of Accountancy in the United States: The Cultural Significance of Accounting*. Columbus, OH: Ohio State University Press, 1998.

Printers and Printing in Providence 1762–1907: Prepared by a Committee of Providence Typographical Union Number Thirty-three as a Souvenir of the Fiftieth Anniversary of Its Institution. Providence, RI: Providence Printing Company, 1907.

Ramirez, Jan Seidler. *Painting the Town: Cityscapes of New York*. New York: Museum of the City of New York, 2000.

"Repeating Fire-Arms. A Day at the Armory of 'Colt's Patent Fire-Arms Manufacturing Company.' " *United States Magazine* (March 1857): pp. 221–49.

Reynolds, David. *Waking Giant: America in the Age of Jackson*. New York: HarperCollins, 2008.

Rezneck, Samuel. "The Depression of 1819–1822, A Social History." *American Historical Review*, vol. 39, no. 1 (October 1933): pp. 28–47.

Riddell, William Renwick. "An International Murder Trial." *Journal of the American Institute of Criminal Law and Criminology*, vol. 10, no. 2 (August 1919): pp. 176–83.

Rohan, Jack. *Yankee Arms Maker: The Story of Sam Colt and His Six-Shot Peacemaker*. New York: Harper & Brothers, 1948.

Rose, Joel. *The Blackest Bird*. New York: W. W. Norton, 2007.

Rothbard, Murray N. *The Panic of 1819: Reactions and Policies*. New York: Columbia University Press, 1962.

Rubin, Joseph Jay, and Charles H. Brown. *Walt Whitman of the New York Aurora: Editor at Twenty-two. A Collection of Recently Discovered Writings*. State College, PA: Bald Eagle Press, 1950.

Ruby, Jay. *Secure the Shadow: Death and Photography in America*. Cambridge, MA: MIT Press, 1996.

Rywell, Martin. *Samuel Colt: A Man and an Epoch*. Harriman, TN: Pioneer Press, 1952.

Schudson, Michael. *Discovering the News: A Social History of American Newspapers*. New York: Basic Books, 1978.

Scott, Donald M. "The Popular Lecture and the Creation of a Public in Mid-Nineteenth-Century America." *Journal of American History*, vol. 66 (March 1980): p. 795.

Seitz, Don C. *Famous American Duels*. New York: Thomas Y. Crowell, 1929.

Seward, Frederick W. *William H. Seward: An Autobiography from 1801 to 1834: With a Memoir of His Life, and Selections from His Letters, 1831–1846*. New York: D. Appleton and Company, 1877.

Shaw, Ronald E. *Canals for a Nation: The Canal Era in the United States, 1790–1860*. Lexington, KY: University of Kentucky Press, 1990.

Sigourney, Lydia H. *Letters of Life*. New York: D. Appleton and Company, 1868.

———. *Letters to My Pupils: With Narrative and Biographical Sketches*. New York: Robert Carter & Brothers, 1853.

Siskind, Janet. *Rum and Axes: The Rise of a Connecticut Merchant Family, 1795–1850*. Ithaca, NY: Cornell University Press, 2004.

Smith, Edwin Burritt, and Ernest Hitchcock. *Reports of Cases Adjudged and Determined in the Supreme Court of Judicature and Court for the Trial of Impeachments and Correction of Errors of the State of New York: With Copious Notes and References, Tables of Citations, &c.* Book 15. Newark, NY: Lawyers' Co-Operative Publishing Company, 1885.

Spann, Edward K. *The New Metropolis: New York City, 1840–1857.* New York: Columbia University Press, 1981.

Srebnick, Amy Gilman. *The Mysterious Death of Mary Rogers: Sex and Culture in Nineteenth-Century New York.* New York: Oxford University Press, 1995.

Stashower, Daniel. *The Beautiful Cigar Girl: Mary Rogers, Edgar Allan Poe and the Invention of Murder.* New York: Dutton, 2006.

Stevens, John D. *Sensationalism and the New York Press.* New York: Columbia University Press, 1991.

Steward, Dick. *Duels and the Roots of Violence in Missouri.* Columbia, MO: University of Missouri Press, 2000.

Still, Charles E. *Styles in Crime.* Philadelphia: J. B. Lippincott, 1938.

Sutherland, W. D. *Blood-Stains: Their Detection, and the Determination of Their Source.* New York: William Wood & Company, 1907.

Sutton, Charles. *The New York Tombs: Its Secrets and Its Mysteries.* New York: United States Publishing Company, 1874. Reprint, Montclair, NJ: Patterson Smith, 1973.

Sutton, Walter. *The Western Book Trade: Cincinnati as a Nineteenth-Century Publishing and Book-Trade Center.* Columbus, OH: Ohio State University Press, 1961.

Thomas, Lately. *Delmonico's: A Century of Splendor.* Boston: Houghton Mifflin, 1967.

Thomson, George N. *Confessions, Trials and Biographical Sketches of the Most Cold-Blooded Murderers, Who Have Been Executed in the Country from Its First Settlement Down to the Present Time—Compiled Entirely from the Most Authentic Sources; Containing Also, Accounts of Various Other Daring Outrages Committed in This and Other Countries.* Hartford, CT: S. Andrus and Son, 1887.

Thomson, Rosemarie Garland, ed. *Freakery: Cultural Spectacles of the Extraordinary Body.* New York: New York University Press, 1996.

Triber, Jane E. *A True Republican: The Life of Paul Revere.* Amherst, MA: University of Massachusetts Press, 2001.

Triplett, Frank. *History, Romance, and Philosophy of Great American Crimes and Criminals.* Hartford, CT: Park Publishing Company, 1885.

Trollope, Frances. *Domestic Manners of the Americans.* London: Whitaker, Treacher & Co., 1832.

Trumbull, J. Hammond, ed. *The Memorial History of Hartford County Connecticut 1633–1884.* Boston: Edward L. Osgood, 1886.

Tucher, Andie. *Froth & Scum: Truth, Beauty, Goodness, and the Ax Murder in America's First Mass Medium*. Chapel Hill, NC: University of North Carolina Press, 1994.

Tuckerman, Frederick. *Amherst Academy: A New England School of the Past, 1814–1861*. Amherst, MA: Printed for and published by the trustees, 1929.

Uselding, Paul. "Elisha K. Root, Forging, and the 'American System.' " *Technology and Culture*, vol. 15 (October 1974): pp. 543–68.

Varle, Charles. *A Complete View of Baltimore, with a Statistical Sketch, of All the Commercial, Mercantile, Manufacturing, Literary, Scientific, and Religious Institutions and Establishments, in the Same, and in Its Vicinity for Fifteen Miles Round, Derived from Personal Observation and Research into the Most Authentic Sources of Information*. Baltimore: Samuel Young, 1833.

Walker, Alice Morehouse. *Historic Hadley: A Story of the Making of a Famous Massachusetts Town*. New York: Grafton Press, 1906.

Wallach, Glenn. *Obedient Sons: The Discourse of Youth and Generations in American Culture, 1630–1860*. Amherst, MA: University of Massachusetts, 1997.

Walling, George W. *Recollections of a New York Chief of Police: An Official Record of Thirty-eight Years as Patrolman, Detective, Captain, Inspector, and Chief of the New York Police*. New York: Caxton Book Concern, 1888.

Walsh, John. *Poe the Detective: The Curious Circumstances Behind "The Mystery of Marie Roget."* New Brunswick, NJ: Rutgers University Press, 1968.

Webster, John White. *A Manual of Chemistry; Containing the Principal Facts of the Science: Arranged in the Order in Which They Are Discussed and Illustrated in the Lectures at Harvard University, N.E. and Several Other Colleges and Medical Schools in the United States. Compiled and Arranged as a Text Book for the Use of Students, and Persons Attending Lectures on Chemistry*. Boston: Marsh, Capen, Lyon, and Webb, 1839.

Wilson, Grant James, and John Fiske. *Appleton's Cyclopedia of American Biographies*. New York: D. Appleton & Co., 1900.

Winders, Gertrude Hecker. *Sam Colt and His Gun: The Life of the Inventor of the Revolver*. New York: John Day Company, 1959.

Winship, Michael. *American Literary Publishing in the Mid-Nineteenth Century: The Business of Ticknor and Fields*. Cambridge, UK: Cambridge University Press, 2003.

Wolf, Marvin, and Katherine Mader. *Rotten Apples: True Stories of New York Crime and Mystery 1689 to the Present*. New York: Ballantine Books, 1991.

Wunder, Richard P. *Hiram Powers: Vermont Sculptor*. Taftsville, VT: Country Press, 1974.

Zboray, Ronald J. *A Fictive People: Antebellum Economic Development and the American Reading Public*. New York: Oxford University Press, 1993.

INDEX

ABOUT THE AUTHOR

HAROLD SCHECHTER is a professor of American literature, and culture at Queens College, the City University of New York. He is widely celebrated for both fiction and true-crime writing, including *The Serial Killer Files*. He lives in Brooklyn and Mattituck, Long Island, with his wife, the poet Kimiko Hahn.

ABOUT THE TYPE

This book was set in Goudy, a typeface designed by Frederic William Goudy (1865–1947). Goudy began his career as a bookkeeper, but devoted the rest of his life to the pursuit of "recognized quality" in a printing type.

Goudy was produced in 1914 and was an instant bestseller for the foundry. It has generous curves and smooth, even color. It is regarded as one of Goudy's finest achievements.